TEXAS FORTS

A gift from TOMFRA

Please visit and encourage your students to visit our historic sites, a few are preserved or reconstructed. These sites will give them an opportunity to appreciate the people that helped to created Texas.

Texas Old Missions and Forts Restoration Association.

www.TOMFRA.org.

LONE STAR

GUIDE:

WAYNE LEASE

Lone Star Guide: Texas Forts

On the front cover is a photograph of Mission "Concepcion", which was built by the Spanish in 1755. Like other early missions, it became a target of frequent Indian raids. Later it was a battle scene during the 1835 Siege of Bexar, and in 1846, the United States Army used it as a campsite.

On the back cover are photographs of Independence Hall at Washington-on-the-Brazos, where in 1836, Texans signed their Declaration of Independence from Mexico. In the bottom photograph, a ray of sunlight captured the monument which has the inscription, "Here, a nation was born."

Published by Texas Forts Distributors LLC,
Garland, Texas, USA.

Printed by Henington Industries, Wolfe City, Texas, USA.

ISBN 0-9709328-0-4
Library of Congress Number: 2001116834

$18.45 US

Lone Star Guide: Texas Forts

The pre 1900s Forts and Camps, and the 1500s - 1800s Missions and Presidios instrumental in the development of Texas

Compiled by driving to the extremities of Texas and stopping at almost every historical marker in route.

By Wayne Lease

Introduction

Gold ... legends of the Seven Cities of Gold, which had intrigued Spain since Cortez, brought Spanish explorers across the Rio Grande. On galleons and schooners they sailed to the Gulf of Mexico searching for gold. With the Spanish also came their missions. More than just churches, missions were to be a way of life for the Indians. It is difficult to image the hardships endured by early missionaries as they marched from the Rio Grande River. Hardships included stopping to cut trees to build rafts for crossing the many rivers, the Nueces, the San Antonio, the Guadalupe, the Colorado, the Brazos, the Angelina, and Trinity (not counting creeks that became raging walls of water during heavy rains), to reach the territory where they built their missions. With the missions came guardhouses for their defenses and presidios (forts) staffed by soldiers.

News that the French explorer LaSalle had built a fort on the Texas Gulf coast caused the Spanish to attempt to colonize the area called New Philippines (the early name that Spain gave to Texas). Not all of the natives welcomed these intruders, but in some areas the Indians asked to be converted and have missions built. At San Francisco de Los Julimes (now vanished) Indians built that mission as a gift to the church. At San Elizario near El Paso, their Thanksgiving was celebrated 100 years before the Pilgrims; later U. S. soldiers used the Presidio San Elizario when Fort Bliss was established. The San Elizario presidio's beautiful chapel is still used as a church.

New territory and a search for riches brought the French from Louisiana territory into the eastern part of Texas and on to the beaches along the Gulf. Frenchmen built Fort Saint Louis and "Spanish Fort" (the location was a fort with moats and a home for 6,000 Indians; the name is in error). Spanish troops, marching in revenge for an earlier Indian attack, must have been in near shock when they saw this fortress as their meager 600 troops faced such far greater odds. Another French fort, Champ d'Asile, built by exiles from Napoleon's France in 1818 (with possibly the support of the United States) was part of a plot for invading Mexico (or taking control of Texas) so Napoleon Bonaparte could become the King of Mexico (or Texas).

Most of the skirmishes involving government forts were fights away from the physical fortification since Indians did not have cannons and respected the firepower a fort could produce. The family forts, the missions, and many presidios were different stories. They were frequently attacked, ravaged, and destroyed. Though the presidios were truly forts, the Spanish usually placed less than 100 soldiers at each. Spain's failure in Texas may have been because it did not have settlers to tax, and Spain's refusal to spend the money necessary to support its missions.

Anglos, as the Americans were called, came to Texas from Tennessee and from North Carolina, and Illinois and other states hoping for a better life or searching for riches or adventure. Spain (and later Mexico) offered land (4,428 acres for $30 to be paid in six years) to the settlers through a "developer" who received 67,000 acres for every 200 colonists they enticed to come to Texas. Mexico then became alarmed at the great number of arriving Anglos and changed their laws by requiring a Catholic oath, suspended many land grants, and required new arrivals to have passports. Resentments escalated until the Texans fought, and won, their independence.

Early Texans built forts and blockhouses. Many flourished and became towns, while other sites have simply vanished. When Indians from the west created problems, government forts were built. After Texas became a Republic, additional forts were built for attachments of Texas Rangers. The Civil War brought new forts and camps (mostly tents or a place to lay a bedroll). The United States built forts to protect the settlers moving westward to the territories opened by the rush for gold and new opportunities in California. Soldiers under the six flags that flew over Texas, and Texas Rangers, rode from their forts and camps under a burning sun or in rains that could quickly turn to ice as they pursed hostile Indians, bandits, and renegades on the run. They would sleep out in the open under the stars in bedrolls wondering that if they would awaken with a scorpion or rattlesnake in their bedroll, or if they would awaken again at all.

This book is a guide to the locations, the legends, and the histories of the forts, missions, presidios, and camps built before 1900. Pictures were taken while gathering information as we drove south to Brownsville, then west along the Rio Grande River to El Paso. Then southeast to Sabine Pass and San Augustine, and north to the Panhandle then along the Red River, stopping at almost every historical marker, county library and many museums, while compiling this book.

We found history being rediscovered in Nacogdoches. An archeological dig was begun to uncover what may be the ruins of the Mission Nuestra Senora de Guadalupe de Nacogdoches. More digs began in 1999 and 2000 to unearth old Fort Saint Louis and reconstruction continues at Fort Inge and Fort Martin Scott, and it is hoped, at Hacienda Dolores and several other sites.

Many of the forts have vanished; some are now ghost towns. Nashville, Texas, was once a town of 20 stores and 1,000 people but now the town and its fort have vanished. The remains of its neighbor, Fort Sullivan, are large pieces of concrete where settlers attempted to make the town into a river port on the Brazos. Not all ghost towns are old, though. One Saturday night, about 6:00 PM we stopped in a small town to eat and ask questions. We found neither a soul to be seen nor an establishment open — it was ghostlike. I could almost hear and see them, ghosts, waiting for this town to become theirs.

As you drive Texas highways, imagine what it must have been like to travel on foot or wagon across creeks and rivers without any bridge. Imagine a journey through a land where there were trees and vines with thorns as sharp and as long as on any rose. Imagine a country where you find every poisonous snake on the continent, where hurricanes blow in from the sea, or where even stronger winds and devastating rains come with a sudden tornado. Imagine land where temperatures soar over 100°F or where the "blue norther" may blow winds from Canada bringing rain that turns to ice as it falls, and imagine places where wildflowers blanket a hillside with colors as beautiful as any rainbow to be found anywhere.

This book would never have been completed if it included <u>all</u> of the legends of the old forts and <u>all</u> of the history supplied by the many contributors of information; many were passing on their family's history of early days in Texas. For example, at Fortin El Cibolo the walls are covered with stories from early newspapers about the ranch, the family, and their fortunes. This is a very interesting place to visit. A Zane Grey or Louis L'Amour could write a short story, a novel, and a movie script without leaving the fortins of El Cibolo, El Cienega, and La Moritas.

As you travel, get off the Interstate and stop at the next historical marker. The marker's plaque may commemorate a fort, tell of a family whose name is the name of the county or town, describe a history of those villages no longer with us, or tell of a massacre destroying an entire family. Markers include stories of Texas seldom included in textbooks, and they create a feeling of being there. You may hear a crack of an old musket being shot, war cries of intruders, or even smell the inviting aroma of warm cornbread from a chuck wagon. Or you may smell the smoke of a burning house and imagine a musket lying on the ground. Listen closely as you may hear the sounds of ghosts from days gone by, or the firing of a rifle actually fired years earlier.

References are included if you want to learn more about any of the forts, camps, missions or presidios. Masters thesis may be found in university libraries as well as books and historical society papers have been written that includes almost every fort. These references will provide the details of a battle; expedition, massacre, war, and the political maneuvering that may have been behind the story. County libraries will have books or manuscripts of their own history.

Dates important in the history of Texas include the late 1500s when Spaniards arrived in the vicinity of present-day El Paso, and it was 1685 when La Salle's expedition washed ashore and built Fort St. Louis. It was in 1821 that Mexico obtained its independence from Spain. The Battle of the Alamo and Texas' independence came in 1836 followed by the annexation of Texas into the United States in 1845. Civil War disrupted the State and created conflicts in the 1860s.

Use <u>Lone Star Guide: Texas Forts</u> to plan a trip, place it on the coffee table to start or to guide a conversation of stories of the past or tidbits of history, and carry it while touring Texas. The book is divided into six regions with a map and a complete listing at the beginning of each. Regions appear in the order that Texas was developed and the forts appear in an order to allow you to travel without jumping all around. Numbers on the map relate to the listing reference for that location and there you will find a ruin, reconstructions and/or an interesting museum. Many of the museums will only be open on certain days or certain hours. In the text portion there is a telephone number for those museums where you may want to confirm their hours. Most of the museums will also open for groups with advance notice of your arrival. If there is a wedding or any other form of service in a mission chapel while you visit, please give respect with silence.

Dedicated to my wife Goldie, who didn't complain as I stopped, turned around and went back to learn from one more marker, read one more book in a library, or went to other museums.

Region One

After an expedition carrying Cabeza de Vaca was shipwrecked on the Texas Gulf coast, he spent eight years as a refugee and Indian captive in Texas. Cabeza was a Spaniard who, with three other survivors, escaped from captivity by running (at times naked) across half of Texas in 1540. These survivors arrived in Mexico with tales of cities of gold they had heard about from Indians. Vasquez de Coronado then began a search for the seven cities of gold to claim them for Spain. Coronado, and other gold searching expeditions, crossed the Rio Grande to explore areas of Texas, New Mexico and on north into present-day Kansas before returning to Mexico empty handed. He had marched across many silver deposits, but Coronado and the others all returned disappointed because they had not found the fabulous cities of gold.

Years later, Spanish explorers again came to Texas accompanied by missionaries who came to Christianize the Indians that Coronado had reported seeing. While the Spanish marched north to Texas, another culture was moving south to the same area. Apaches who had moved into central Texas were now being pushed south by Comanches. Spanish expeditions would have both the Apaches and Comanches to fight as all three cultures moved into Texas.

A need for forts started with the earliest Spanish explorations and lasted through the nineteenth century. The missions, and their presidios, performed their tasks as long as Spain supported them. Later, governments built forts and camps from the Texas Gulf coast to El Paso. Soldiers and Texas Rangers patrolled while settlers withstood the hardships and multiplied, and stage coaches, wagon trains and cattle drives crossed the area.

This first region covers the forts built along the Rio Grande, starting with the mouth of the river at the Gulf of Mexico and meandering along the river to El Paso and far west Texas. It then includes the forts encountered as you drive east along Interstate 10 towards San Antonio.

This is an area of Texas that suffered from the frequent struggles that contributed to its future development, including the ambitions within Mexicans (with the support of many Texans) for independence from Spain. Later these political fights in Mexico crossed the Rio Grande. The 1834 rise of General Antonio Lopez de Santa Anna to the Presidency of Mexico resulted in a struggle of Texans for their independence from Mexico, and later the Mexican–American War.

After fighting for the Mexicans in 1835, Texans in 1835-36 took up arms for their own independence with both of the countries claiming the area along the Rio Grande for many years. Fighting continued on both sides of the river, as politics in Mexico remained unsettled. Battles of the Mexican-American War, the United States' Civil War, and with Indians were fought here.

Region One Map
(Numbers are as the sites are listed for the text for this region)

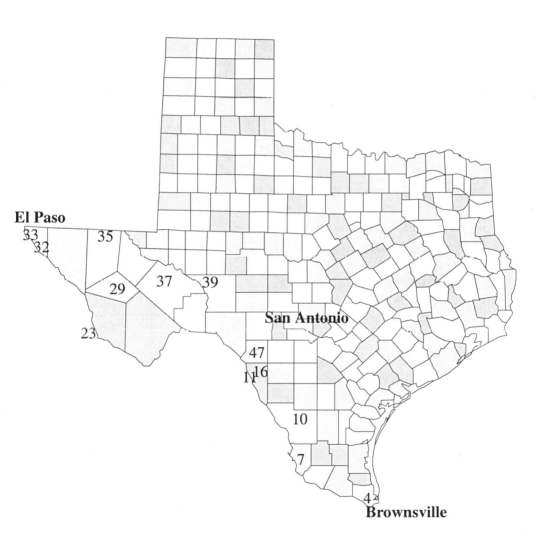

Location   Region One

1   Fort Harney – on Brazos Island
2   Camp Belknap – in Cameron County
3   Fort Polk – in Port Isabel
4   Fort Brown – in Brownsville
5   Camp Edinburg – in Edinburg
6   Fort Ringgold – in Rio Grande City
7   Fort Trevino – in San Ygnacio
8   Mier Expedition – in Zapata County
9   Hacienda Dolores – in Zapata County
10   Fort McIntosh – in Laredo
11   Fort Duncan – in Eagle Pass
12   Camp Rabb – in Maverick County
13   Camp Shafter – in Maverick County
14   Mission San Juan Bautista – near Eagle Pass
15   Presidio de San Juan Bautista de Rio Grande – near Eagle Pass
16   Fort Clark – in Fort Clark Springs
17   Camp Del Rio – in Del Rio
18   Camp Blake – in Val Verde County
19   Fort Hudson – in Val Verde County
20   Fort Meyers – in Terrell County
21   Camp Neville Springs – Brewster County
22   Camp Pena Colorado – in Brewster County
23   Fort Leaton – near Presidio
24   Mission Santa María de la Redonda – in Presidio
25   Presidio del Norte – near Presidio
26   Fortin El Cibolo – in Presidio County
27   Fortin El Cienega – in Presidio County
28   Fortin La Moritas – in Presidio County
29   Fort Davis (Jeff Davis County) – in Fort Davis
30   Fort Quitman – in Hudspeth County
31   Fort Hancock – in Fort Hancock
32   Presidio San Elizario – in San Elizario
33   Fort Bliss – in El Paso
34   Mission San Antonio de la Ysleta del Sur – near El Paso
35   Butterfield Overland Stage Line Station – near Guadalupe

National Park

1. Fort Harney

In 1846, the United States declared war on Mexico, and 50,000 American men and boys volunteered. Overwhelmed by this number of raw recruits, the U. S. government immediately shipped them to Texas. Little thought must have been given for the needs of the troops. When the Sixth Regiment of Persifor F. Smith's Brigade of Louisiana Volunteers was sent to Brazos Island at the southern tip of Texas in the Gulf of Mexico, a camp was hastily established and this fort assembled. Rumors of an imminent attack spurred the soldiers to use barrels of hard bread, of pork, and of beans as materials to build a defensive fortification. It was named Fort Harney.

This camp was necessary. Ships bringing supplies to Fort Polk (built across the bay on the mainland) could not navigate the shallow waters in the pass between Brazos Island and Port Isabel. Deep-draw ships unloaded in the Gulf of Mexico and their cargo was taken to Brazos Island for re-shipment to Fort Polk.

Later, when the Civil War broke out, the depot was surrendered to forces of the State of Texas under Colonel John S. Ford who had fought as a Texas Ranger during the Mexican War. Ford had the responsibility during the Mexican War of writing condolence letters to the relatives of those lost in battle. He always put the initials R.I.P. (for Rest in Peace) at the end of each letter thus earning him the nickname he carried with him for life, "Rip." In November of 1863, when six thousand Union troops landed on Brazos Island to take command of this depot, Ford had abandoned it months earlier to concentrate his forces at Fort Brown.

This depot outlasted Fort Polk as civilian commerce annually brought merchandise valued at more than a million dollars across the island enroute to the King and Kenedy ranches. The end for the depot and Fort Harney came in 1867, however, when a hurricane destroyed the buildings. Luxury hotels and condominiums now stand along a beautiful beach at this location.

One of the soldiers who landed on Brazos Island in 1846 would go on to fame of another sort. His name was Abner Doubleday, who is credited with inventing the game of baseball.

2. Camp Belknap

East of Brownsville on Highway 4 about 20 miles towards the Gulf is a piece of high ground called Loma de la Estrella. This is the site of Camp Belknap, the largest Federal camp during the Mexican War. Five miles up the beach, now identifiable only by remains of cypress pilings, was the camp's depot. These are the only visible remains of the camp.

After the U. S. declared war on Mexico in 1846, General Taylor found he had more troops than he knew what to do with. Men and boys who enlisted for adventure, to escape bankruptcy from the financial depression in the U. S., or for patriotism, found themselves bored, underfed, and living in conditions worst than any ghetto. This was raw country with few settlements, no conveniences, and an inadequate food supply. For many, this was their first encounter with mosquitoes, poisonous snakes (especially rattlesnakes), spiders and other varmints found in the camp.

The fighting these troops discovered was a fight for survival. Dysentery was common, as the water was brackish and the food (when they received any) was bad, as storage facilities were poor. The ground was subject to frequent flooding that brought varmints into the tents and bedrolls. There was fighting among the troops to relieve boredom. They also wrote letters home. Some of the following excerpts describe the conditions of the time with phrases such as:

"I've been sick. Thought I was dying when the Devil came to see me, but he told me to get well, or to behave myself, because he didn't want me bringing my sickness to Hell."

"The expression so common with us, all bushes have thorns, all insects have horns, is almost true without exception. Even the frogs and grasshoppers are in possession of the latter."

"The place abounds in rattlesnakes (we once cooked and ate a seven footer), scorpions, and lizards; also a reptile called Santa Fe that has a sting which produces death in a short time, red ants whose bite is horrible, poisonous spiders, and most bothersome of all, mosquitoes. Though at night the sound of the mosquitoes, joined by the howl of wolfs, and the cry of jackals followed by the croaking of frogs provides us music, of a sort."

Other camps had to be built as the number of volunteers continued to grow. Belknap was estimated to hold up to 6,000 troops camping there at one time. A soldier wrote home that he had to walk two miles from his tent to the river on the other side of the campgrounds. Later, Camp Patterson (the name is all of its history that has survived) was located midway between the village of Burita, site of another camp without a name, and Matamoros. It was to the good of all of the soldiers when the men were able to move up the Rio Grande to new forts and from there to join the Mexican War. It was a fight more in keeping with the battle for which they volunteered.

After the Mexican War, nothing remained of these camps, but any curious sightseers should beware that the descendants of the soldiers' enemies (rattlesnakes, spiders and many mosquitoes) still live nearby. The "Santa Fe" is not a familiar name for any varmint now in the area. It may have been a scorpion, but scorpion stings, though painful, are seldom, a cause of instant death. If bitten by a spider, do not ignore it, as the bite of some species is very serious.

3. Fort Polk

Started by the United States in 1845 in the Republic of Texas, with permission from the Republic, Fort Polk now looks like a lighthouse. In the Mexican War it was an important site. The U. S. was afraid of international reactions if Texas accepted an offer to become part of the United States. General Zachary Taylor was ordered to march an army to the Rio Grande a few months in advance of the official annexation. Because they lacked supplies, Taylor's men stayed in a camp near Corpus Christi until after the annexation of Texas was finalized then moved to Fort Polk in present-day Point Isabel. This lighthouse now stands on the site of the fort.

"Occupation of Point Isabel as a depot will be indispensable," Taylor reported from Fort Polk. Later, Taylor reported he had ordered the advance of an army composed of light artillery, under the command of Colonel Twiggs, to march in the direction of Mexico. The Mexican War had commenced, and Fort Polk was the base for supplying the United States armies at Fort Brown and later the Federal troops as they advanced further up the Rio Grande.

Before the outbreak of the Civil War, in early 1861, Confederate artillery under Colonel Rip Ford seized Fort Polk. The fort was used to expedite the shipment of Southern cotton , which was being sent to Europe on ships flying the flag of Mexico. The Port Isabel lighthouse became a guiding beacon for ships entering the bay to load cotton at Matamoros. The Union warships were also active in the Gulf. Less than 10 miles to the north, Union troops were seizing large Texas cattle herds that were grazing on Padre Island.

When the Civil War was over, the United States kept an eye on this part of Texas because French forces had occupied Mexico under Napoleon's friend, Maximilian, and the Union did not want the Confederates joining the French and starting another war. Many of the Confederate officers, troops and even governors fled across the border into Mexico after the end of the Civil War.

Subsequently, the United States Army Corps of Engineers straightened the channel and later destroyed a Mexican fort near Brazos Santiago. Later they destroyed Fort Polk and built another lighthouse, which stands near the channel in Point Isabel. The commemorative marker by this lighthouse under states the importance of Fort Polk and the role it played in two wars.

4. Fort Brown

In April 1846, troops of the 6th U. S. Infantry, led by General Zachary Taylor built a fort in present-day Brownsville under the eyes of 4,000 Mexican soldiers watching from the south side of the Rio Grande. While Federal troops were building the fort (originally named Fort Texas), Texas Rangers along with Federal troops patrolled the area. Nevertheless, the Mexican troops crossed the river and ambushed Rangers and Federal troops; the Mexican War had began.

The following month, Taylor's troops engaged the Mexicans in the Battle of Palo Alto. On the afternoon of May 8, Mexican cannons opened fire on Taylor's forces at a spot about half- way between Fort Polk and Fort Brown. When the U. S. cannons returned the fire, it was so all encompassing that the U. S. foot soldiers just stood by. Sparks from the barrage ignited the tall grass, creating a smoke screen that allowed the Mexican troops to withdraw. Two days later the two forces met again, this time in a wooded area requiring the use of the infantry, the cavalry and the artillery. This was the Battle of Resaca de la Palma, which ended with Mexican troops retreating back across the river. Many of the Mexican troops drowned while trying to re-cross the river. During both of these battles, the Mexican artillery was bombarding Fort Texas from across the river, shelling the fort for 160 consecutive hours. Fort Brown (still Fort Texas at that time) valiantly withstood the Mexican assaults and answered with its own cannon fire.

After the Battle of Resaca de la Palma, Mexican General Arista withdrew his soldiers deep into Mexico. General Taylor moved his troops further up the Rio Grande in preparation for the invasion of Mexico. The United States declared war on Mexico on March 13, 1846.

Fort Texas was temporarily abandoned in 1859 but was re-occupied during the fight against the border bandit Cortinas. Cheno Cortinas saw himself as a rescuer of the Mexican people. He saved a drunken Mexican from the law by shooting a U. S. marshal in Brownsville, and he proclaimed himself champion of the people when he assembled a small army in Mexico. Cortinas captured Fort Brown while the soldiers were on an Indian fight. He subsequently relinquished control of the fort and moved his operations back into Mexico from where he raided Texas until the Texas Rangers crossed into Mexico to stop him.

Confederate troops took control of Fort Texas in 1863 after Union troops evacuated it in 1861. Several fights between Confederate and Union troops occurred in the area during the Civil War including the Battle of Palmito Ranch on May 12, 1865. After the Confederates won the battle, they learned from their captives that General Lee had already surrendered at Appomatox.

Fort Texas' name was changed to Fort Brown in honor of Major Jacob Brown who had been killed in the Mexican artillery attack on the fort. The fort was built with walls nine and one-half feet tall in an irregular six-point star. That first fort was abandoned and later rebuilt on a new site. Its buildings are now part of the campus of the University of Texas at Brownsville. Around Brownsville are many commemorative markers of the battles that took place in the area.

5. Camp Edinburg

This was a Texas frontier post of the 1850s about which not much is known. Though there are many references to troops or Rangers being at, or coming from Edinburg, the campsite at that location is not usually given a name. The one historical record of the camp where it is named is in the history of the great grand nephew of Napoleon, Lieutenant Jerome Napoleon Bonaparte, who (after he graduated in 1853 from West Point) was stationed at Camp Edinburg.

Throughout the camp's history it appears that troops or Rangers from this camp always arrived in time. Maybe it was from this camp Hollywood learned good guys come to the rescue.

6. Fort Ringgold (Also known as the Post at Davis Landing, Camp Ringgold, Ringgold Barracks. And Mission San Agustin de Laredo a Visita)

Fort Ringgold was the southernmost of the western tier of forts constructed at the end of the Mexican War. It stood guard for nearly a century over the Rio Grande and Rio Grande City. On October 26, 1848, Brevet Major Joseph H. LaMotte led two companies of the First United States Infantry to Davis Landing, near Rio Grande City. The military chose that site to protect the area from both Indian and Mexican attacks. The name given the fort was in honor of Brevet Major Samuel Ringgold, the first United States Army officer to die from wounds received during the Battle of Palo Alto on May 8, 1846.

Fort Ringgold housed the area's first telegraph office, fueled the local economy through Federal appropriations, and waged vigorous warfare on smugglers, rustlers, and the ruthless renegades who ravaged the region. The Cortina War and unrest along the border during the Mexican political uprisings emphasized the importance of the fort. Federal troops under the command of Major Samuel P. Heintzelman ended the threat of Juan Cortina by joining forces with Rip Ford's Rangers illegally crossing the border to bring an end to Cortina's raids.

In 1875, Texas Ranger Captain L.H. McNelly fought the War of Las Cuevas near here. Cattle rustlers from across the Mexican border were a big problem. McNelly, upon learning a buyer of stolen cattle contracted to deliver 18,000 head, had warned the Mexican government and Federal troops at Ringgold. When a band of rustlers stole 250 head and started to take them across the river near Las Cuevas Ranch, McNelly followed with 30 Rangers. Las Cuevas Ranch was the headquarters for Juan Flores, considered to be the chief of the cattle thieves along the Rio Grande. Federal soldiers in the meantime caught up with the bandits before they reached the river and during a brief skirmish killed two rustlers. Without the red tape that slowed the Army (the troops did not have permission to cross the river), the Rangers moved with speed, and crossed the river heading for Las Cuevas. Once there, McNelly found that thieves outnumbered Rangers ten to one, and also had the advantage of the ranch fortification. After a short exchange of fire, McNelly pulled his Rangers back towards the river where they dug into the riverbank. He did not want to return to Texas, his mission having been a failure.

A Ranger sent to find the Federal troops told them of McNelly's predicament, and troops marched to the river, but still did not have authority to cross unless McNelly was under a life threatening attack. An international incident developed when Mexican soldiers joined forces with the cattle rustlers and threatened to march against the Rangers. The Federal troops received revised instructions not to assist McNelly if he was attacked on Mexican soil. Not aware of the troops last order, McNelly pulled a bluff, sending a letter to a Mexican official demanding the return of the cattle to Texas, or Rangers would shoot all of the cattle. Reluctantly the Mexicans drove the cattle across the river, and the Rangers followed. As should be expected, there is more than one version of the War of Las Cuevas, but all tell of the cattle being returned to Texas.

In 1869, construction began at the same location for a new fort made of frame and brick structures along a palm-lined parade ground.

Ringgold was one of the most attractive forts along the border. Some buildings are still used at the site by the Rio Grande City School District.

Nearby was the Mission San Agustin de Laredo a Visita, located west of Rio Grande City opposite Camargo, Mexico. It was used as a route station for a 1750 expedition into Texas. There were over 150 converts and more than 25 Christian marriages in the early days. A resident Father conducted trade in salt to pay off the mission's debt. This mission has since disappeared.

7. Fort Trevino (And Camp Drum also known as Camp Bugle)

This fort is located in San Ygnacio (Ignacio), the oldest town in Zapata County, between the Rio Grande and Highway 83, thirty miles south of Laredo and fourteen miles northwest of Zapata. Fort Trevino still stands where Jesus Trevino built it in the 1830s. The town of San Ygnacio was named for Saint Ignatius Loyola, and was located

in the southwest corner of the original Hacienda de Dolores, a very large land grant made in 1750 to Jose Vazquez Borrego.

Trevino built this sandstone home that became known as Fort Trevino for the protection it offered against Indian raids. The fort was also the scene of border fights throughout the years. A sundial was placed on top of the home in 1851. That timepiece (shown protruding from the top of the building) is still a tourist attraction. A small museum is now located near the fort.

At the beginning of the Civil War the sentiment in the area was mixed between those encouraging secession and those in favor of the Union. Guerrilla raids by the outlaw-politician Juan Cortina crossed the border and attacked ranches of those that were in favor of secession. After one raid, where more than 100 of Cortina's men crossed the river and murdered a rancher, papers were found implicating the United States Consul in Matamoros.

Octaviano Zapata, a highwayman, who once was associated with Juan Cortina, organized a band of men including outlaws, deserters, and political refugees from both sides of the border. They conducted raids in both Texas and Mexico for money, supplies, and munitions. In 1862, Union agents offered rewards of 100 pesos in gold and up to 150 acres of land in Texas to any Tejanos (the name given to Mexicans living in Texas) and to Mexicans who conducted raids into Texas. Zapata and his men were among the first recruited. He was also associated with Edmund J. Davis, a former judge in Texas, who had conducted Union sponsored military activities around Brownsville. For these many reasons, Zapata's cutthroats were locally referred to as the "First Regiment of Union Troops."

In December 1862, Zapata's men attacked a Confederate supply train. Three weeks later a train of three wagons going from Fort Brown toward Fort Barracks (probably a reference to Fort Ringgold) was attacked at Rancho Soledad near Las Cuevas. Five Confederate soldiers escorted the supply train, and all but one was killed. These activities were instrumental in bringing about an extradition agreement whereby Mexican authorities invited Confederate troops to cross the border to assist in the pursuit of outlaws. In late August, after Zapata's men ambushed Mexican troops on the road between Guerrero and Mier, the Mayor of Guerrero requested that Major

Santos Benavides of the Thirty-third Texas Cavalry, a Tejano regiment, intervene. Benavides, on September 1, 1863, crossed the river with men in pursuit of Zapata. The next day Benavides surrounded the outlaws near Mier. After a heavy exchange of fire, Zapata's forces scattered, leaving ten men dead, including Zapata.

Revolutionary opponents of Mexican Porfirio Diaz led raids into Mexico from San Ygnacio, and in 1916, troops of Mexican President Venustiano Carranza raided the border.

Nearby was Camp Drum, also known as Camp Bugle. A United States military post near Zapata on the Rio Grande it was established the same year that it was closed, 1852. The Second U. S. Dragoons under C.H. Tyler had arrived and named the site Camp Bugle. Artillerymen from the Fourth U. S. Artillery already at the camp sought and received permission to use the name, Camp Drum, causing dissension among the troops stationed at the site. The camp was abandoned probably due to the decrease in border disturbances and Indian raids. Little has been written and no ruins remain of the campsite(s) of either name.

8. Mier Expedition

The Mier expedition was the greatest disaster of all of the expeditions by Texans into Mexico. Though not a fort, it was a moving camp and therefore is included in this book. This expedition followed Mexican retaliatory raids into Texas in 1842 and the Texas expedition to Santa Fe the same year. The Mier expedition led to the United States annexation of Texas.

In December 1842, Alexander Somervell headed an expedition that was chasing Mexican troops, who had massacred many Texans at Dawson Creek near San Antonio. Without guidance from Sam Houston, Somervell feared that the expedition would fail and that a longer stay on the Rio Grande might prove disastrous so he ordered his troops to prepare to return home. Many of his men were not satisfied with the expedition and had decided there was little possibility of Somervell successfully fighting the Mexican Army or seizing Mexican towns, so these men established what was to become known as the Mier Expedition.

Separating from Somervell's command, they moved down the

Rio Grande where they camped and selected Ranger William S. Fisher to be the commander. Then they crossed the Rio Grande and in freezing rain attacked Mexican towns to obtain cattle and horses. Many of the Texans wanted revenge, others the adventure, their leaders were all opponents of Sam Houston.

Forty men under Thomas J. Green went further downstream by boats and canoes. A Ranger patrol advanced along the west side of the river, and the remainder of the men under Fisher moved down the river's east side. A total of 308 Texans reached a point opposite Mier on December 22, 1842, and there found a large Mexican force assembling along the river. On Christmas Day, the weather not improved, Texans proceeded to cross the river attacking the town of Mier. Texans were outnumbered almost ten to one. After a prolonged battle, the Texans were hungry and thirsty, their powder was almost exhausted, and their discipline gone. When the Mexicans sent a white flag demanding that they give up the fight, the Texans surrendered.

President Houston announced the men had acted without government authority, thus leaving the Mexicans the impression that the Texans were not entitled to be treated as prisoners of war. So the captured Texans were treated as only criminals and marched through Mexican towns towards Matamoros where they were held captive. However, all except 176 of the Texans managed to escape as they marched. Learning of the escape, General Santa Anna ordered for those that were remaining to be executed. The Mexican governor modified this and ordered that only every tenth man be executed. The condemned men were selected by drawing a bean from a pot. Those that drew a black bean were to be executed by a Mexican firing squad. Seventeen Texans were shot in what became known in Texas history as the Black Bean episode. Years later, those who drew a white bean (surviving the drawing, and life in the Mexican prisons) were released by Mexico at the urging of England and the United States.

9. Hacienda Nuestra Senora de Los Dolores

Twelve men, named the "Flying Squadron", mounted on gray stallions and armed with swords, daggers, pistols and muskets rode constantly on patrol, providing protection to Hacienda Dolores from hostile Indians. It had a fortification, a stone tower ("El Toro" as it was known) as a defense for the more than the 100 people living on the hacienda. It also had a chapel to convert Indians to Christianity. But, it was only a large ranch, a very large ranch.

The Hacienda de Nuestra Senora de Los Dolores was founded in 1750 with a grant of land from Spain to Jose Vazquez Borrego, a rancher from Coahuila. The Hacienda included a 350,000-acre ranching operation, the first of this size in Texas. By the year 1755, Dolores was home to 25 families, it was operating a ferry across the Rio Grande, and it had a chapel for the families and Indians living on the ranch. Ruins are in Zapata County 12 miles north from San Ygnacio. Efforts are being made to have portions of the structure (now on oil leases) restored.

This settlement, at the junction of Dolores Creek and the Rio Grande, is considered to have been the first Spanish colonizing venture north of the Rio Grande. It was part of Spain's plan to populate the area between the Nueces River and the Rio Grande. Dolores was to become a rest stop on a new route to the Spanish presidios at Bexar, La Bahia, and Los Adaes. This was the key crossing on the Rio Grande for travelers, soldiers, and priests going to San Antonio, and other points in Texas. As the population of the surrounding area grew, and as the political forces changed, title to the property became under attack. In 1767, the land that had been granted to Vazquez Borrego was given to settlers of the nearby towns of Revilla and Laredo for villas. Each grant comprised an area of six leagues (26,400-acres) in each direction from that towns' square.

In compensation, Borrego was given land to the east, and in 1792, that land which became known as Jose Vazquez Borrego's land grant, was divided among his heirs. Many early land grants in Texas, including those granted by the Spanish, by the Mexicans, and by the Republic of Texas, were challenged in the courts for years. The original papers showing the grant to Borrego were destroyed in 1811 by forces fighting for control of Mexico. One legal battle over the title to the property was filed in court in 1829. In 1872, the results were reached.

In 1813, Indians repeatedly attacked the ranch headquarters at Dolores, and "El Toro", the stone tower was built for defense. Indian attacks persisted, and the hacienda was abandoned in the ensuing years. The land was the site of two other settlements, Corralitos and San Ygnacio, the latter of which still exists, while the former is no longer listed on Texas maps.

Near the site of Dolores, a marker by the Texas Centennial Commission causes people to believe there was actually a mission at Dolores. However, records show that though priests did regularly visit this ranch, it was not an official mission, although it converted Indians and had regular services for all ranch residents. Recent reports are that ruins of "El Toro" are possibly still visible on private property. Dolores is important as the pioneering ranch that opened vast areas of South Texas to ranching and helped in the settlement of all of Texas.

10. Fort McIntosh (Also known as Camp Crawford)

On the Rio Grande near Laredo, U. S. forces, in November 1846 after the Mexican War, led by Captain Mirabeau B. Lamar (the second President of the Republic of Texas) formed the Laredo Guard of the Texas Volunteers and established a fort on the site of an earlier Spanish presidio. The United States then sent Lieutenant Egbert Ludovicus Viele, subsequent designer of Central Park in New York City, from Fort Ringgold with a company of the First U. S. Infantry. On March 3, 1849, the unit reached the banks of the Rio Grande in Webb County where they set up a camp of tents on a bluff to the west of Laredo. They named the camp "Crawford" in honor of Secretary of War George W. Crawford. In January 1850, the site was renamed Fort McIntosh, after Lieutenant Colonel James S. McIntosh, killed in the Battle of Molino Del Rey.

Fort McIntosh formed a key link in the chain of forts lined along the Rio Grande and the western frontier. The fort was initially a star-shaped earthwork built by army engineers and troop labor. As Comanches and Lipan Apaches harassed settlers in the region the garrison expanded to more than 400 men and included such men as Philip H. Sheridan, Randolph B. Marcy, and Texas Ranger Captain Rip Ford.

The outbreak of the Civil War resulted in the Union abandonment and later a Confederate occupation. During that war, Fort McIntosh repelled several of the Union's assaults including the 1864 incident known as the Battle of Laredo. Union troops had marched up the Rio Grande to burn 5,000 bales of cotton stacked in Laredo. Confederate troops under Refugio Benavides (he became Laredo's mayor) fought Union troops for three hours until Union troops retreated.

The fort was reopened in 1865 after the Civil War because the U. S. feared a possible invasion from Mexico. The French, who after foreclosing on debts of the Mexican government, had installed Archduke Maximilian as Emperor and were reportedly recruiting ex-Confederates to join an army to invade Texas. The U. S. demanded that France withdraw from Mexico and again sent 50,000 soldiers to the border. Napoleon withdrew his troops and Maximilian without military support was captured in Mexico and executed. In December, with U. S. support Benito Juarez was then elected president of Mexico.

In 1878, Mexican renegades and Kickapoo and Apache Indians enmasse crossed the border north of the fort. They moved northeast into Texas raiding ranches, stealing horses, and murdering whites that resisted them. The band of horse thieves then recrossed the border before troops arrived. They had been in Texas for six days and had stolen 250 horses before the Federal troops from the fort receiving permission to follow and capture the bandits.

The name Tin Horn War is given to a series of disturbances along the border that accompanied activities of Catarino Garza against Porfirio Diaz between December 1891 and January 1893. Both United States and Mexican authorities were hunting Garza's raiders when on December 21, 1891, the revolutionists surrounded a scouting party from Laredo near Fort McIntosh and killed one man and wounded another. In the following months, additional guard units under the direction of General Woodford H. Mabry were posted along the border to prevent movement of the bandits back and forth across the Rio Grande. A sheriff's posse and United States troops from the fort ended the disturbances on January 21, 1893, when surviving leaders of Garza's band were captured about 60 miles from Rio Grande City.

Laredo Junior College now occupies a large portion of the fort's original grounds.

11. Fort Duncan (Also once known as Rio Grande Station and as the Camp Eagle Pass)

Fort Duncan, on the Rio Grande above Eagle Pass, was established on March 27, 1849. Captain Sidney Burbank with companies of the First U. S. Infantry occupied the 5,000-acre site. On November 14, 1889, the post was named Fort Duncan after James Duncan, a hero of the Mexican War. The fort was valuable because of its location near the trade crossing into Mexico at Eagle Pass, its location on the road to California, and primarily for its position for scouting against Indians. Men stationed here suffered from exposure so much that Company C, First Artillery, asked permission to construct quarters at their own expense. The troops and hired workers constructed the storehouse, two magazines, four officers' quarters, and a stone hospital, in addition to quarters for the enlisted men. There was ample stone but no timber for building.

Fort Duncan became involved in the Callahan expedition of 1855, when Texas Ranger James H. Callahan led an effort to repel attacks of Lipan Apaches and capture runaway slaves. A runaway Seminole Indian known as Wild Cat had formed a plan to lead Indians into Mexico. He agreed to defend the Mexicans against the wild Indian tribes living in Texas. It appeared that Wild Cat had a different story for each tribe that he met. In his negotiations to enlist Caddo Indians to join his forces, he said that his intentions were to raid in Texas, and any tribe that did not join his forces would be punished. To the Creeks he offered land in Texas, and he was very successful in recruiting the Kickapoos who later received land grants from Mexico.

Wild Cat did not limit his recruits to Indians. He found runaway slaves, from both the whites and from different Indian tribes. In total, Wild Cat assembled a sizable army, including approximately 4,000 slaves. All found a home south of the Rio Grande across from Eagle Pass.

An Indian Agent named Marcus Duval learned of Wild Cat's slaves and informed the Governor of Texas who sought the help of Rangers "in freeing the slaves." Duval, however, was probably interested only in the reward of $50 commonly offered for any slave returned to his master.

In the meantime, a company of Rangers led by J.H. Callahan was following a tribe of raiding Apaches and crossed the river at Eagle Pass. When they met a larger force of Mexicans and Indians, the Rangers moved back to Piedras Negras and captured the town. Callahan then sent a message to the Mexicans that all of Wild Cat's slaves were to be returned to the Rangers or the Mexicans would have to answer to Texas. His message unanswered, Callahan ordered his men to set fire to houses to cover their retreat. Then on the evening of October 6, Major Sidney Burbank, Commander of the U. S. soldiers at Fort Duncan, moved his four cannons to cover the Texans as they recrossed the river. Claims originating with this invasion of Mexico were not officially settled until 1876, after the U. S. Claims Commission finished a study in 1868. The Commission awarded 150 Piedras Negras citizens a total of $50,000 for damages.

The site was listed in the National Register of Historic Places in 1971. Seven of the original buildings are restored and the headquarters building is used as a museum.

At the start of the Mexican War in 1846 a temporary post, named Camp Eagle Pass, had been established at the site. "Rio Grande Station" was the name given to old Fort Duncan in 1862, by Texas Ranger James M. Norris when he selected the site as a station for a Texas' Frontier Regiment manned by members of Captain Thomas Rabb's company. Rio Grande Station remained a Texas Ranger post until March 1864.

12. Camp Rabb (And Camp Sibley)

This camp was built as a Texas Ranger station by James M. Norris in 1862, for the Frontier Regiment at the crossing of the San Antonio-to-Eagle Pass Road and Elm Creek, in Bexar Territory (present-day Maverick County). Under Commander Captain Thomas Rabb, the camp guarded the road and the frontier until the consolidation of the regiment in March 1864.

The Frontier Regiment had been established on December 21, 1861, by the Legislature. Detachments of at least 25 men each were to be stationed 25 miles apart just west of the line of settlements along a line from the Red River to the Rio Grande. Between March 17 and April 7, 1862, Colonel Norris and his officers rode along the line establishing sixteen camps. They were Rio Grande Station and camps Cureton, Belknap, Breckenridge, Salmon, Pecan, Collier, McMillan, San Saba, Llano, Davis, Verde, Montel, Dix, Nueces, and Rabb.

In its first months of duty the regiment, with 1,000 men, established patrols at regular intervals from each camp. Each patrol usually consisted of five privates and one officer. The Indians soon discovered the weakness of a patrol system with its familiar routine and during the winter of 1862-63 they began to make numerous bold raids while the patrols were elsewhere.

Politics between the Confederacy and the State delayed this force in entering the ranks of the Confederacy. Texas wanted to retain control of the troops to ensure that the protection of settlements remained their primary responsibility. Finally, state authorities transferred control of the regiment to the Confederacy after the Legislature approved the establishment of the "Frontier Organization" to ensure protection of the frontier. Transfer took place officially March 1, 1864.

The Frontier Regiment's six companies were joined by two other organizations to cover the northwestern settlement line. Captain Henry S. Fossett's two companies at Fort Colorado patrolled south of that point. Barry's four-company battalion covered the region between Camp Colorado and Fort Belknap, while Colonel James G. Bourland's Border Regiment protected the region from the Red River to Fort Arbuckle in Indian Territory. Companies of the Frontier Organization filled the gaps. However, during the last eighteen months of the war, the Frontier Regiment was more likely to be used to enforce the Confederate conscription laws, arrest any deserters, and track down renegades and outlaws than to meet the threat of the Indian attacks.

A Ranger post by the name of Camp Sibley was also located on Elm Creek. It may have actually been Camp Rabb but was called Camp Sibley, as General Sibley was active in this area.

13. Camp Shafter

Twenty-six miles southeast of Fort Duncan and Eagle Pass this outpost on Comanche Creek was established May 28, 1873, in Maverick County by Company M of the Fourth United States Cavalry. The cavalry was commanded by Captain William O'Connell, and the fort was named for Lieutenant Colonel William R. Shafter, then in command at Fort Duncan.   A few days before the camp was established, six companies of the Fourth Cavalry had returned with Lieutenant John L. Bullis of the Twenty-fourth U. S. Infantry. Bullis had just carried out the raid on the Kickapoo Village near Remolino in Mexico. Camp Shafter was established to guard against Indian or Mexican retaliation for the Remolino raid. (See Fort Clark for more details).

During the eight years following the end of the Civil War, Indians, striking from below the Rio Grande into South Texas, had stolen tens of thousands of head of livestock, had burned countless ranches, and murdered scores of settlers. Most of the raiders (Kickapoos who had migrated to Mexico from the United States during the previous quarter century) had been enticed by the Seminole chief, Wild Cat with a promise of free land grants and money from the Mexican government. In return, the Kickapoos were told they would defend Mexico against Comanches.

The Kickapoo alliance with Mexico worked so well that soon many Kickapoos settled on the Mexican side of the Rio Grande. They soon discovered South Texas contained over 90,000 horses, mules, and cattle, and fewer than 5,000 residents to protect them. Stealing was easy, and local Mexican government officials helped the Indians by refusing to allow U. S. troops to chase the Indians into Mexico. In January 1873, President Grant gave up on diplomacy and ordered the Fourth Cavalry to move to Fort Clark. He also may have given Colonel Ranald Mackenzie the orders to strike from Fort Clark at the camps of the Indians, which meant crossing into Mexico. The response to that raid was immediate and favorable.

Although Mackenzie had technically violated Mexican sovereignty and attacked allies of the Mexican government without official orders, the Texas legislature extended to Mackenzie "the grateful thanks of the people of our State." The Mexican government did not want the raid to become an international issue, and after an exchange of notes, dropped the matter. The Indian raids all but stopped. Fearing more U. S. retaliation the Kickapoo bands divided and moved to the mountains. Many of the Kickapoos, in exchange for the wives and children Mackenzie had taken prisoner, returned to the United States.

When the Indians and Mexicans did not retaliate for Mackenzie's attack, Camp Shafter was used as a base for scouting along the Rio Grande. During May and June 1873, the camp was home for the M and E companies of the Fourth Cavalry. Units from forts Clark and Duncan used the camp throughout 1873. Camp Shafter later became part of the Ewing Halsell ranch.

14. Mission San Juan Bautista (And Mission San Francisco Solano)

Founded in Mexico on St. John's Day, June 24, 1699, this mission was reestablished January 1, 1700, at the site of present-day Guerrero, Coahuila, 35 miles down the Rio Grande from Eagle Pass and Piedras Negras. This site was five miles from the Rio Grande and located strategically near a series of crossings providing access to Texas. San Juan Bautista grew into a complex of three missions and a presidio and served as a way station and gateway to Texas.

From 1700 to 1716 this settlement was the most advanced on New Spain's northeastern frontier. It served as a base for exploration beyond the Rio Grande, serving also as a listening post for news of the French, who after settling at Biloxi Bay, were thought to be exploring west of the Mississippi. Reestablishment of the Spanish East Texas missions in 1716 started here at Mission Bautista. In every respect San Juan Bautista was the mother of the Texas missions.

As Lipan and Mescalero Apaches fled before the Comanches they moved southward into Texas. There, they collided with the Spanish, who were advancing northward. In 1743 Fray Benito Fernández de Santa Anna had urged the establishment of missions for the Apaches in their own lands, arguing that this was the best solution to the most serious Indian problems. On August 19, 1749, four Apache chiefs had buried a hatchet along with other instruments of war in a peace ceremony at San Antonio. Both sides genuinely desired peace. The Apaches, decimated by Comanche raids, appeared willing to accept Christian conversion in exchange for Spanish protection from Comanches, but that was short-lived when Spain stopped sending them gifts. The Apaches became discontented, and revolted, burning the mission buildings they deserted. Missionaries blamed failure of the first Apache mission on the natural inconstancy of the tribe.

Another mission was established in the area when Mission San Francisco Solano was founded five miles from the Rio Grande at the site of present-day Guerrero in 1700. The water supply in the area proved to be insufficient for both missions and Solano was moved to San Antonio, where it was renamed as Mission San Antonio de Valero, now known as the Alamo.

Mission San Juan Bautista has been reduced to a pile of earth and stone, frequently disturbed by treasure hunters. A historical study published in 1968 awakened an interest in Guerrero, and it became the focus of architectural, archeological, and other investigations funded by the Mexican government and the United States National Endowment for Humanities.

15. Presidio de San Juan Bautista de Rio Grande (Also known as Presidio del Rio Grande)

Imagine being with the first Spanish expedition to reach the area we now know as Padre Island. When that expedition arrived, they found beaches littered with masts, spars, and rigging from ships. In Brazos Island Bay was a hulk skeleton of a 20-gun English man-o-war that had been washed ashore. The only inhabitants found living along the beaches were Indians.

The Gulf Coast Expedition of Ortiz Parilla and Captain Blas Maria de la Garza Falcon left San Juan Bautista in 1765 when the Malaguita Indians reported rumors of white invaders exploring this unknown area of Texas. However, the expedition found no verification of the Indians' stories, or any evidence of Englishmen ever settling on the

"Islas Blancas" as Padre Island was once know. Still the expedition of Ortiz Parrilla started investigations that produced reports and maps, which in the estimate of Parrilla "superseded all those that have come to the courts of Spain." To gain more accurate assessments of the Texas coast, later explorers would have to overcome three stumbling blocks for any accurate assessment of the Texas coast: the shallow bays, frequent hurricanes, and the (sometimes called cannibalistic) Karankawas Indians.

Early in 1703, responding to the pleas of missionaries at Mission San Juan Bautista for protection, the Spanish government established the garrison of Presidio de San Juan Bautista Del Rio Grande. It was charged with defending the three missions in the area: San Francisco Solano, Mission San Bernardo, and San Juan Bautista. If Mission San Juan Bautista was the Mother of the Texas Missions, then this Presidio was the Father to the early Spanish expeditions in Texas. From it expeditions went up the Frio River, along the Nueces and Colorado rivers, and to San Antonio on a journey that would start the establishment of many missions and presidios in Texas.

Soldiers of this presidio provided escorts for travelers and supply trains. When Spain, in an attempt to settle Texas, bribed Canary Islanders into coming to Texas, these troops were their escorts to San Antonio. Troops of this presidio were also involved in fights with Apaches north and south of the Rio Grande, taking part in running battles as far away as the Gulf of California.

In the early 1800s, the presidio became the center of the town of Guerrero. It was from Guerrero in 1836, that Mexican General Santa Anna with a force of 6,000 experienced soldiers (exclusive of new recruits, muleteers, teamsters, and other auxiliaries) marched to San Antonio and the Alamo. In 1842, Mexican General Woll assembled men and horses at the old presidio and launched an invasion of Texas when they marched to San Antonio to recapture the Alamo.

One of the many changes in the flow of the Rio Grande put the site of Guerrero on the south side of the river in Mexico. A Laredo-to-Piedras Negras road runs to Guerrero where ruins from this old presidio and mission buildings have been used as a base for new structures.

16. Fort Clark (Originally named Fort Riley)

As the frontier of the West expanded, a string of forts was established in the 1840–1850 era to protect the telegraph lines and settlers going west towards the California goldrush. Fort Clark was founded in 1852. During the Civil War, Fort Clark was held by Confederates to provide protection from Indians, and guard against possible Union invasions from Mexico.

One of the most daring military expeditions ever conducted started from Fort Clark when in 1873 U. S. Colonel Ranald S. Mackenzie in an illegal, and possibly unauthorized act, launched an invasion into Mexico in search of Kickapoo Indian desperadoes and bandits. His troops were to become famous as Mackenzie's Raiders. The purpose of this daring raid was retaliatory as the Indians had been raiding in Texas and had cost settlers close to $48 million in property losses.

Mackenzie had been warned that Indian tribes responsible for a massacre at the nearby stage depot at Howard Wells were now living only 50 miles within the Mexican border. Leaving Fort Clark at nightfall, Mackenzie's troops marched towards the border and arrived at the Rio Grande by dark the next evening. Continuing their march under darkness the troops reached the destination, Rey Molina, at dawn. On command, the troops charged towards the town. Caught

asleep, the Indians were killed or captured and their village burned. This, however, was only the first half of the story. The soldiers had to recross the Rio Grande without being captured by the Mexican army. Riding for three days straight without sleep, without much food and keeping an eye on their captives, the soldiers managed to safely return to Fort Clark.

Abandoned in 1946, Fort Clark remained in service longer than any other fort in Texas. Located in Fort Clark Springs near Brackettville bordering US Highway 90, Fort Clark is now a 2,700-acre resort and leisure living community with a nine-hole golf course. It is still one of the most complete forts, with 80 buildings of which many are used for the original purpose. The old kitchen will prepare meals for tourists and stalls in the barn still house ponies. Visitors enjoy staying in rented rooms on the grounds and eating at the restaurant in the restored Officers' Club.

In Brackettville you can see the historic 1878 St. Mary Magdalene Church. While in the area, visit the Alamo Village built for John Wayne's movie, The Alamo. Legend has it that the film studio was planning on creating the set in Mexico. A Texas rancher, upset at the

possibility, offered his ranch if the movie would be filmed in Texas. When his offer was refused he engaged help from the Daughters of the Republic who started a barrage of telephone calls to John Wayne. The result was the film set being built where you may now see it at the nearby Alamo Village. Its authentic cantina, saddle shop, trading post, and chapel (above) are a photographer's dream.

17. Camp Del Rio (Also known as Camp San Felipe)

Near the San Felipe Springs where Camp Del Rio (meaning camp of the river) was established in 1881 as a subpost of Fork Clark. The site may have also been known as Camp San Felipe built in 1857 along San Felipe Springs in the same area and also a subpost to Fort Clark. It was active until 1896.

Nearby, interesting prehistoric shelters and paintings are found in Seminole Canyon, which flows into the Rio Grande a few miles east of the Pecos River. On the east wall of the canyon are three rock shelters. On the west wall there are five shelters between the river bridges of the Pecos and the Rio Grande. In the shelters are Indian pictographs of prehistoric times painted with red (from iron oxide), yellow (from ocher) and black (from charcoal). Pictures measure as long as 17 feet and are as high as 55 feet. One painting shows a horned creature with an arrow piercing its neck. The creature in the pictograph is 39 inches in height and the arrow is 20 ½ inches long.

18. Camp Blake

Camp Blake was established after the Mexican War as a temporary Federal military installation on Devils River in southeastern Val Verde County. The camp was named for Lieutenant Jacob E. Blake, a topographical engineer who fought in the Battle of Palo Alto. It was located on the road from San Antonio to El Paso, though it is difficult to imagine a stage or wagon route through this country as its only access from north to south was through rugged canyons. The river was, however, well known to early travelers as it offered precious water. East-west expeditions followed its banks as far as possible before striking out into the desert.

The flow of Devils River dissects massive limestone, and deposits of sand, gravel, and mud on flat terrain. In 1590 Gaspar Castano de Sosa, a Spanish explorer, traveled along the river and called it Laxas, meaning "slack" or "feeble." Later travelers and settlers called the river San Pedro, but in the 1840s Captain John Coffee (Jack) Hays of the Texas Ranger asked the name of the river as he stood before one of its deep canyons. Upon hearing its name, he replied that it looked more like the Devil's river than Saint Peter's, and the name Devils River stayed with it.

Devils River now runs southwest for 94 miles to its mouth on the northeastern shore of Amistad Reservoir in southern Val Verde County. The river passes through such interestingly named places such as Dark Canyon, Dead Mans Creek, and Satan Canyon that create a beautiful and interesting area for exploration. In the vicinity of Amistad Reservoir are large and ancient cliff caves and pictographs by an earlier civilization. Access may only be by boat. Obtaining advice from the local authorities about exploring safely is highly recommended.

19. Fort Hudson (Also known as Camp Hudson)

Established in 1857 on a tributary of the Devils River, 21 miles north of Comstock, this camp was one of several built between San Antonio and El Paso to protect travelers along the Chihuahua Trail. The post was built along an elevated but isolated section of the creek, and few travelers or settlers passed through in the early years. A soldier who was stationed at Hudson for two years, reported seeing only four or five people who were not related to the army.

He should have been at the site a few years earlier; for then he would have met a real character. In 1850, a man named Parker H. French organized the French Expedition, a scheme for raising money by promoting a wagon train across Texas to California for gold seekers. He placed a large, fraudulent advertisement in a New York newspaper promising fast and safe travel to the California gold fields. He promised the protection of 60 Texas Rangers while crossing the easy terrain and through the mild weather of Texas (also fraudulent descriptions). Supplies, including food, wagons, mules, tents, cooks, and a physician's care, would be provided for the price of $250 a person. Men agreeing to work for their passage paid $100 each. Sixty men enlisted at the lower price and 120 passengers paying full fare fell for French's scheme.

The group left New York by steamboat on May 13, 1850, stopping in Cuba and New Orleans before landing on the Texas coast at Port Lavaca where they journeyed to San Antonio. There, French replenished supplies by using forged bank drafts and claiming he was an agent of the United States government. In route to El Paso, they crossed the Devils River in the area of Fort Hudson a number of times where one of the travelers reported that they watched a Texas Ranger named Black Warrior shoot an Indian (the reason for the killing was not stated).

After 130 days of travel from New York, the expedition reached El Paso. The travelers, noting that French wrote forged bank drafts in New Orleans, San Antonio, and El Paso finally acknowledged they had been defrauded, and they mutinied. French avoided arrest by crossing into Mexico. His expedition continued to California: two groups by land and others a sea trip.

French later traveled to California, where claiming to be a lawyer replacing his imaginary law partner (who had suddenly died), he took a seat in the 1854 California legislature. Then he traveled to Nicaragua where he represented himself to be a U. S. envoy. During the Civil War, he was arrested in Connecticut outfitting a pirate ship supposedly for the Confederacy. He later worked for the Knights of the Golden Circle (Confederacy) and also the Knights of the Golden Square (Union). In the 1893 list of California legislators, the comment beside the name of Parker H. French is simply, "Dead." Thus ended the strange career of Mr. Parker H. French.

In 1859, when the U. S. Army experimented with using camels in Texas, caravans of camels from Camp Verde passed through Camp Hudson. The troops from Fort Hudson then abandoned the camp on March 17, 1861, to volunteer for service in the Civil War. In October 1867, Indians ambushed a stage traveling from Fort Hudson to Fort Stockton, and two military escorts were killed. In November, immediately after the attack, companies D and G of the Ninth Cavalry were moved to Camp Hudson. By April 1868, other troops were returned to the area.

In March 1876, Lieutenant Colonel George Pearson Buell came with two companies of cavalry to Fort Hudson when the Devils Canyon was called the "Den of the Apaches." Under his leadership, the post was used as a camp to protect settlers. The troops at Camp Hudson fought Indians on several occasions and sometimes followed them into Mexico. Later, Lieutenant Louis Henry Orleman commanded Company B of the Tenth Cavalry at the fort, but Fort Hudson was soon closed when the Indian attacks had temporarily stopped.

Camp Hudson's buildings were constructed of a mixture of gravel and lime, which made the buildings cool in summer and warm in winter. Today no buildings are standing. In 1936, the Texas Historical Commission placed a marker at the site (now on private property).

20. Fort Meyers

Meyers Canyon begins just west of State Highway 349 in central Terrell County at the juncture of Downie and Eight-Mile draws, and runs southeast for 20 miles to its mouth on Lozier Canyon in the southeastern part of Terrell County. Prehistoric people lived here in the limestone caves and rockshelters in Meyers Canyon and took water from Meyers Spring. They left fire-blackened cave walls, and broken tools. Sixteenth-century Comanches left cave art on the overhanging ledges at Meyers Spring; the cave art proves their early contact with the Spanish.

Meyers Canyon and Meyers Spring were named for one of the Black Seminole soldiers who served under Lieutenant John L. Bullis and who lived at Fort Meyers. In the late 1870s and early 1880s Black Seminole scouts, who were known as the Black Watch, occupied the small outpost called Fort Meyers. It consisted of fifteen one-room adobe huts and two stone houses, all roofed with branches from the ocotillo, a Mexican pine. The fort was located on the canyon near Meyers Spring. Scouts patrolled the area to protect settlers from Indian attack. In 1882, troops went to Mexico on a raid against the

Kickapoo and Lipan Indians who had been raiding the settlers, stealing cattle and horses, and often taking lives. They attacked the Indian's village, killing most. On the return trip the troops met Mexican troops who stopped them. But when Bullis told the Mexicans what he had accomplished, the Mexican troops decided they did not want trouble and let them pass.

When Lieutenant Bullis retired from the army, he lived for a time at the old fort. He built a rock reservoir at the spring, which he signed with his name and the year, 1896. In the early 1990s ruins of the fort remained on private property where trespassers are not welcomed.

Further south in Terrell County is the site of the "Lost Gold Mine" which J. Frank Dobie wrote of in his Coronado's Children. The mine was on the Mexican side of the Rio Grande.

21. Camp Neville Springs (And Camp Nowlin and Presidio and Mission San Vicente)

One and one-half miles from the east boundary marker in Big Bend National Park is the site of Camp Nowlin. This temporary camp was established to protect settlers from Apache Indian raids and the bandits of Mexico who frequently crossed the Rio Grande. A patrol of 20 troops scouted the area under Lieutenant Woodbridge Geary of the Nineteenth Infantry and J. W. King of the Eighth Cavalry. The troops were on 60-day rotations of duty from Fort Clark.

While at the camp, the troops lived in a barracks 60 feet long and 20 feet wide. It was 600 yards from the officers quarters, a one-room stone house. Some walls may still be standing. A trip to Big Bend National Park is worth a trip to find out even if there are no ruins.

Also near Big Bend Park was the Presidio and Mission San Vicente that were established near Lajitas around 1760. They were located on the Comanche War Trail and were protected by a Spanish Flying Company sent to stop Indian raids into Mexico. The community of Lajitas, with its old western town appearance, has been the site of the filming of many famous movies.

22. Camp Pena Colorado

Rainbow Cliffs are unique geological formations located four miles south of Marathon in central Brewster County. Indians had occupied the area around the springs here for thousands of years and the area had once been a major stopping place on the Comanche Trail to Mexico. The outcroppings of the cliffs served as protection against Indian attacks and harsh winter winds for nearby Camp Pena Colorado, a United States Army post dating from 1879. First known as Cantonment Pena Colorado, the camp was built on Pena Colorado Creek near a large spring and beneath a high bluff called Pena Colorado (Spanish for "red rock," and known also in English as Rainbow Cliffs). Later the creek, spring, and the army post itself were named for the formations.

In late August 1879, United States soldiers first occupied the camp when Companies F and G, Twenty-fifth Infantry Regiment moved there from Fort Stockton. The post consisted of several crude huts made of stone and mud. It also included two long and narrow buildings, one of which served as the enlisted men's barracks and the other as a storehouse. Other buildings included two smaller huts for officers' quarters and a stone granary. Its location lay on the road connecting Fort Clark and Fort Davis, which was also the prospective southern route of the new transcontinental railroad. The cavalry was needed for scouting missions and inspection for any raiding Apaches and bandits crossing the Mexican border

The establishment of Camp Pena Colorado was most likely part of a larger army strategy to increase pressure on the Apaches living in the Pecos region, who were still forcefully resisting Anglo settlement. It is probably not coincidence that the outpost was founded the same month that Victorio and his Warm Springs Apaches escaped from confinement on the Mescalero reservation in New Mexico and began their flight across the Southwest towards Mexico.

In 1882, the coming of the Southern Pacific Railroad to the north brought refined living conditions to the post with the increased availability of commodities from the East. After July 1884, the garrison was principally composed of units of the Tenth U. S. Cavalry. Among the Tenth's famous "Buffalo Soldiers" who served at Camp

Pena Colorado was Lieutenant Henry O. Flipper, the army's only African-American officer at the time. The Third Cavalry replaced the Tenth in the summer of 1885, when a band of Apaches under Chief Geronimo were causing trouble in Arizona and New Mexico. Camp Pena Colorado was finally abandoned in 1893. By that time the settling of the country around the post was well along, and the need for troops in the Big Bend area had shifted closer to the border.

The site of the camp is located on Post Ranch, part of the Combs Cattle Company. The company's founder, David St. Clair Combs, was an early trail driver as well as prominent Texas rancher. He donated the land around Pena Colorado Springs for a park in 1935. A historical marker was erected the next year on the location of the former outpost. The Pena Colorado Park is still enjoyed by residents and visitors to the area. Nearby is the town of Marathon located at the intersection of US Highways 90 and 385. The Gage Hotel, established by an early rancher, located there has an interesting museum, an old-style hotel and serves excellent food.

23. Fort Leaton
(See colored pictures in center section)

Fort Leaton is five miles southeast of Presidio and sits on a bluff overlooking the Rio Grande and the Chihuahua Trail. It was the private fort of a Chihuahua Trail freighter, Ben Leaton, who was called a "noble desperado" by some who knew him. He built the fort on the ruins of a Spanish fort, the original Presidio Del Norte that was founded in 1773. Leaton later established Fort Leaton as his home, trading post, and his private fort. Because of its isolated location and the constant threat of Indian attack, Fort Leaton offered a much-needed frontier defense. Military maps of the 1850s listed Fort Leaton along with the official army posts.

The fort was built in an L shape with the long side along the river for about 200 feet. Its 18-inch walls were made from adobe bricks laid crossways, which provided protection from rifle fire. Large doors allowed for freight wagons to drive into the structure to safety.

There is no record of Indian attacks on Fort Leaton. The reason for this may be deducted from an accusation made by the Mexican inspector for the military colonies at El Paso. He accused Leaton of trading guns to Indians for horses they had stolen in Mexico. Such illegal trading with the Indians might have gained him their favor and protected his fort from attack.

There is a legend that Leaton once invited Indian chiefs, whom he was having some difficulties with, to attend a feast in the fort. When everyone was seated, Leaton opened a door. Over-looking the dining table was a cannon pointing at the table where the chiefs sat. When Leaton fired, his problems with the chiefs disappeared in a puff of smoke, so to speak. Leaton died before any official charges were made against him.

In 1967, the state acquired a five-acre tract around the old fort, and the restored structure became the Fort Leaton State Historic Site. The restored fort (open daily 8 a.m. to 4:30 p.m. except Christmas) is very impressive. It has a very good museum and educational presentation of the history of the area. A Christmas celebration is held at the fort in early December each year with colorful lights and good foods. Visitors and Presidio area families are invited

24. Mission Santa María de la Redonda de Los Cibolos

Shipwreck survivor Alvar Nunez Cabeza de Vaca was one of the first Spaniards to reach La Junta near Presidio as he made his way across Texas. In December 1535, he erected a cross on the mountainside and named the place La Junta de Las Cruces. After Cabeza de Vaca, three other Spanish expeditions came to La Junta. In 1581, Fray Agustin Rodriguez accompanied by two other friars and soldiers arrived in the area and celebrated the first recorded mass at La Junta.

Then in 1582, an expedition of Antonio de Espejo passed through, and in 1683-84 Juan Dominguez de Mendoza explored, mapping trails and water sources. He named this area La Navidad en Las Cruces. The Mendoza expedition may have established five missions at La Junta: La Navidad en Las Cruces, San Antonio de Los Puliques, San Francisco de Los Julimes, Santa María de la Redonda, and Apostol Santiago. These were probably located on both sides of the Rio Grande. There are no visible ruins.

Chief of the Jumano and Cibola Indians at La Junta, Juan Sabeata, once led a delegation asking the Spaniards to establish missions in their pueblos. When the Spanish hesitated, the Indians told of the miraculous appearance of a cross above their village. (Later the Spaniards were to learn that the story was a fabrication of a Tejas Indian accompanying Sabeata.) At the time, however, the custodian of religion agreed to send missionaries on the condition that the Indians build a church and living quarters to accommodate them. The Indians sent messengers to the village with orders to build religious establishments at La Junta. Within only days the messengers returned, reporting all available Indians were employed in building two churches.

Mission Apostol Santiago, named on January 1, 1684, was the Spanish name the Dominguez de Mendoza expedition conferred on the village of Puliques, and the Mission San Antonio de Los Puliques (or El Senor San Jose) was located south of the Rio Grande. The river has changed it course over the years since that date. Mission San Francisco de Los Julimes was possibly built in Mexico near where the Rio Conchos meets the Rio Grande. The Mission Santa Maria de la Redonda de Los Cibolos may have been located near the silver mining community of Shafter. Mission Pueblo of Santa Cruz de Tapaculmcs was probably on the Texas side near Redford. Another, Mission Pueblo San Cristobal, was located across the Rio Grande from Redford. None of these missions survived, so precise locations remain unknown.

Although the Spanish clergy worked to convert Indians to Christianity, other Spaniards wanted to enslave them in the silver mines. Spanish slavers raided La Junta from 1563 until 1760, leading to Indian protests that periodically closed the missions and led to the building of the Presidio de la Junta de Los Rios Norte y Conchos (Del Norte) in 1760. Then new missions were established: they were Mission San Francisco de Los Conchos, San Cristobal, San Pedro Alcantara, San Lorenzo, and a second El Senor San Jose. None of these missions survived. A larger mission established in this area during this era was Mission Nuestra Senora de Guadalupe located at a Polacme Indian village where the Rio Grande and Rio Conchos meet. Each of these missions may have at one time been referred to as the Mission La Junta de Los Rios.

Why were so many missions established in the vicinity of Presidio? Besides the fact that this was an excellent place for raising animals and crops, the Spanish were interested in this area for another reason. There was silver mining to the north in the vicinity of Shafter and to the northwest beyond Candelaria, and there are legends of gold mines on the south side of the Rio Grande further down the river. For almost 200 years there was mining activity. Mine owners frequently supplied the financial support for these missions as they provided some protection.

25. Presidio Del Norte (Presidio de la Junta de Los Rios Norte y Conchos and Presidio Pilares)

In 1874, within a mile of Presidio Del Norte, Mescalero Apaches raided a ranch stealing a dozen cows and kidnapping two children. When the eldest child, who was unable to run as fast as the Indians' horses, fell behind, the Indians killed him. Shortly thereafter they raided another ranch, killed the owner, and burned his house. Three years later, ranchers from both sides of the river combined in an attack against Indians camping near Eagle Springs, north of the river.

An Indian woman in the town knew her son was with the Indians and warned him of the coming attack. When the vigilantes reached their destination, the Indians were gone, but they had left tracks, which the vigilantes followed. From Eagle Springs the pursuers went west, following the El Paso road towards the Guadalupe Mountains and the Pecos River. They traveled at night due to the heat and to keep dust, raised by the horses, from being seen.

Almost two weeks later, the Indians saw one of the vigilantes' scouting party. Indians attacked, but the main force of pursuers was behind the Indians and saw the attack. This main force then raced to catch the Indians in crossfire. Six braves were killed and 13 Indian women were captured along with 69 horses and mules. The vigilantes, mostly Mexicans, also recovered the plunder the Indians had stolen. Not wanting trouble with the U. S. soldiers, before leaving Presidio Del Norte, the vigilantes had sent word to Fort Davis of their intended actions. When they returned to Presidio Del Norte, the official approval of their actions had been received.

Located three miles south of Presidio at present-day Ojinaga was the Presidio Del Norte. The Presidio de la Junta de Los Rios Norte y Conchos (Presidio Del Norte) was completed on July 22, 1760, for the protection of the missionaries. A presidio was needed to stabilize the area, and allow for peaceful settlement, and guard missionary activities. It was located on the north side of the Rio Grande, below the Rio Conchos, and was commanded by the Spanish Captain, Manuel Munoz. In July 1760, a fiesta was held to celebrate the presidio's completion. Apache and other Indians camped nearby, supposedly to join the celebration, but instead they attacked at sunrise. Fortunately for the Spanish, the Indians were driven back, but this was not the last time the presidio was attacked. It was abandoned in 1767 when the soldiers moved from La Junta to Julimes. It was reopened in 1773 and remained open until 1835, then it was permanently closed.

La Junta de Los Rios resumed its old role as a trade and cultural junction in 1839, when Dr. Henry Cannily opened what is sometimes called the Chihuahua Trail. Traders hauled goods in carts between Independence, Missouri, and Chihuahua, Mexico, by way of La Junta.

In 1830, the name of the area was changed from La Junta de Los Rios to Presidio del Norte, and white settlers came to Presidio in 1848 after the Mexican War. Among them was John Spencer, who operated a horse ranch on the United States side of the Rio Grande near Presidio. Then Ben Leaton and Milton Faver built private forts in the area for their trading, farming, and ranching. In 1849, a Comanche raid almost destroyed Presidio, and in 1850 Indians drove off most of the cattle in town.

The La Junta area is considered the oldest continuously cultivated farmland in Texas. Corn farmers settled here for its water, fertile farmland, and bountiful game. Mountains on the north and south and hot springs offer winter protection. The drive from Lajitas is beautiful, but not recommended when driving west, looking into a bright setting sun.

Nearby was a relatively unknown presidio. It was on the Rio Grande a mile from Quinn Creek and eight miles southwest of Gettysburg Peak and San Carlos in southwestern Presidio County near the Sierra Viega Mountains. Located at that site were the presidio, a penal colony, and a silver ore smelter. The source of the silver ore, as well as the time when the extensive smelting at Pilares took place, are unknown but the mission near Candelaria, in rugged land, was reported to have had a silver mining operation with Indians from a mission used like slave labor.

26. Fortin El Cibolo

(See colored pictures in center section)

Fortin El Cibolo is north of Presidio off of Highway 67 and is an oasis of beauty. It is one of three private forts built by pioneer rancher Milton Faver in the 1850s in an area where the Apaches had destroyed a dozen missions. El Cibolo has now been reconstructed as a fort on the outside. Inside it is a luxurious and very interesting resort. It is easy to imagine the double door entrance, still in place, protecting a family. The first door would stop an arrow or repel a bullet. The second door had a hole to fire your rifle through. Another protective feature is that all of the outside walls are without windows so no one could force entry or fire shots or arrows into the buildings. In the center, a beautiful garden provides an area to relax (then and even now).

Rooms at the fort are decorated with prints of early newspapers with old tales of Faver who was a little eccentric about money. It is said that when he sold cattle, he demanded coins for each animal as it passed. After returning from cattle sales he would take the coins in the hills with a hired hand accompanying him. Faver would later return without the helper.

Milton Faver died of natural causes, and is buried in the nearby mountains he so loved.

27. Fortin El Cienega

Fortin El Cienega is named for the Spanish word for "marshland". A private fort built near the source of Cienega Creek six miles east of Shafter in central Presidio County, it was one of the three private fortresses built around 1857 by early day American rancher, Milton Faver, who had fled Missouri believing he had killed another duelist. In Mexico, he worked in a mill and drove his own freight carts to earn money for a cattle ranch, which he acquired a few acres at a

time around the fresh water springs located north of Presidio.

El Cienega served as a stronghold during Indian attacks and during the many periods of Indian uprisings it was an outpost for patrols from Fort Davis. During the Civil War when Fort Davis was closed, Indian raids were frequent. As strong as the fortifications were they did not stop Indian attacks. One day in 1871, Indians dug a trench under the wall at El Cienega. When Faver and his men discovered the Indians' plan, they killed the first Indian appearing in the hole.

Milton Faver's forts have been restored as luxurious guest ranches. Now, in one of the bedrooms, when you step through a large wardrobe and into the area (that in earlier days was a place for women and children hiding from Indian raids) you are in a modern master bathroom.

28. Fortin La Moritas

This is the third of the private family forts built by Milton Faver. It is located near the old mining town of Shafter between Presidio and Marfa off of Highway 67 along with the other family fortins of El Cibolo and El Cienega. Moritas means "little mulberry" in Spanish.

Abundant water from the area's prominent springs, Cienega, Big

Springs, Cibolo, and La Moritas, allowed Faver to grow vegetables and fruits and raise cattle, sheep, goats, horses, and mules. With this water, the ranches were self-sufficient in a land with little rainfall. Faver constructed walled fortifications at El Cibolo and El Cienega for protection against attacks by Indians and bandits, but for some unknown reason, to his sorrow, he did not fortify La Moritas.

On July 31, 1875, Indians raided La Moritas and carried away Faver's brother-in-law, Carmen Ramirez, Carmen's wife and two small sons. The next day Carmen's brother, Pancho, rode from Cibolo to Moritas. Learning of the Indian attack, Pancho returned to Cibolo and found four men to help him pursue the Indians. Two miles along the trail the five men found Carmen's body. They continued following the Indians, aided by pieces of clothing Mrs. Ramirez was dropping to mark the trail. When they came close enough to see the Indian murderers and kidnappers to determine that the number of Indians was very large, Pancho's companions refused to continue. Feeling it was unwise for him to go on alone, Pancho returned to bury his brother.

During the Civil War when Fort Davis was abandoned and there was no military around for protection, 300 of Faver's cattle were stolen. Left with only 32 corralled calves, he began to rebuild, and eventually built his herd back to more than 10,000 cattle. Although he registered an F-shaped brand, most of his herd ran unbranded and wild in nearly inaccessible mountain canyons. Faver owned only 2,880 acres of land, but he reportedly used up to 25,000 acres of open range. He had inexpensive labor that he paid 12½ cents per day to tend cattle, goats, and sheep, and to cultivate vegetables and fruits in gardens and orchards near the springs. Faver traded for anything he or the workers needed but attempted to build self-sufficient ranches.

Faver later sold the ranch to a man who did not make it as a rancher. The man did, however, discovered silver in nearby Shafter and gladly returned the ranch to Faver.

The November 1999 issue of *Texas Highways* featured Fortin El Cibolo. For reservations at these family forts, call 915/229-3737.

29. Fort Davis (Originally named Post on Limpia)

(See colored pictures in the center section)

Federal military authorities believed a fort on the San Antonio-El Paso road in West Texas was necessary to protect the travelers as well as settlers in the area. In 1854, they selected a site in the foothills of the Davis Mountains to locate Fort Davis. There Indian trails to Mexico intersected the road and there Apache and Comanche raiders frequently attacked travelers.

With the beginning of the Civil War, the Federal troops that evacuated Fort Davis were quickly replaced by Confederate cavalry. After the Confederates later abandoned the fort, the men left in charge had a close brush with death. A band of Indians approached the fort. Lacking anywhere else to hide, seven of the men climbed on the roofs of the buildings waiting silently for two days and nights, with no fire to cook or to provide warmth, for the Indians to finally depart. The California Column, a force composed of 1,500 volunteer troops, organized in 1862 under Colonel James H. Carleton marched east to discourage the invasion of California by the Confederates. An advance party under Lieutenant Colonel Edward E. Eyre sent detachments to reoccupy army posts as far to the east as Fort Davis, where the United States flag was raised on August 29, 1862. Most of the California Column members were discharged in August of 1864, but after the war many Californians decided to remain in West Texas. As new cattlemen from Texas settled in the area in the 1870s and 1880s, the former California Column men lined up with Mexicans living in the area against the newcomers in several civil disturbances.

Federal troops reoccupied Fort Davis in June 1867. After the fort was rebuilt, its troops engaged in more Indian battles than any military installation in the country. This was because the fort lay on a route of Comanches to Mexico, a route for cattle drives, and a road taken by the early stagecoach lines. The fort was finally abandoned in 1891. A restored Fort Davis (open daily from 8 a.m. – 5 p.m. except on National holidays) offers visitors many interesting sights.

Another interesting story about the fort tells of a young woman, Dolores, who became engaged to a goat herder, Juan. While Juan was out tending his goats she would communicate with him by building a fire every Thursday night on the low mountain south of town. Shortly before their wedding day he was killed and scalped while tending his goats. Overcome with grief, she continued to climb the mountain and build a Thursday night fire. Dolores died in 1893 and was buried near a path she walked up the mountain (which became "Dolores Mountain").

30. Fort Quitman (Also Camp Rocky Ridge)

"The country in any direction is a rolling sand prairie covered with stunted chaparral and many mesquite bushes and wild cactus which grow very high. At the fort and on the far side of the mountains are found beautiful specimens of quartz containing small quantities of silver, iron, copper, etc." A soldier wrote this description of Fort Quitman in 1859. A stagecoach passenger obviously had another impression as he described the same site in his remarks that, "there are a few houses and some rude stick tents, deep sand and the sunshine is as hot as I ever felt."

Eighty miles east of El Paso and 20 miles southeast of the site of present-day McNary was Fort Quitman. Captain Arthur T. Lee of the Eighth Infantry established it on September 28, 1858 and named it for Mexican War General, John A. Quitman. The fort was built 400 yards east of the Rio Grande to protect travelers and mail along the San Antonio to El Paso route. Fort Quitman was vacated on January 5, 1877, but soon reopened during a campaign against Victorio, the Apache chief, and his band of 300 braves. During the summer of 1880, Victorio's warriors crossed and recrossed the Rio Grande in the vicinity of the fort, and as the Apaches returned to the reservation they attacked a stagecoach near the fort, killing one man.

Colonel Benjamin H. Grierson, Federal commander of the District of the Pecos in West Texas, was ordered to throw out a screen of troops from the Guadalupe Mountains to the Rio Grande to stop Victorio. Grierson established headquarters at Eagle Spring, a stage stop on the road between Fort Quitman and Fort Davis. There he directed his troops to scout for any sign of the Apaches. The campaign then became a waiting game until late in July when the telegraph between Eagle Spring and Fort Quitman suddenly went dead. Grierson and a patrol proceeded to Quitman to investigate. At Fort Quitman, Grierson received reports from the Mexican soldiers opposite his camp that Victorio was making for the river. Because they were out of supplies the Mexicans could not intercept him. This prompted Grierson to return to Eagle Spring, which was a more advantageous point from which to direct his operations. On the return trip his men sighted one Apache on a small hill. The warrior escaped, but Grierson, realizing Victorio would try to get water at the spring, immediately placed himself and 8 men, including his 19-year-old son Robert, directly in the path the Apaches would follow. Camp Rocky Ridge was established.

Shortly afterward an eastbound stage rolled through. Grierson took this opportunity to send a message to the troops of cavalry at Eagle Spring to come to his assistance. Couriers from Eagle Spring arrived after midnight with information that Victorio and 125 warriors had crossed the Rio Grande where they had skirmished with some scouts, and were moving in Grierson's direction. After forwarding couriers to Fort Quitman to expedite the reinforcements, Grierson had his men put up a fortification on top of Rocky Ridge, and waited. Aware that troops already held the waterhole, Victorio sent some of his warriors to try to outflank the soldiers, but when the Apaches sighted the dust cloud made by the troops riding in from Fort Quitman, Victoria broke off the battle. This setback and a later one at Rattlesnake Spring (August 6) forced the Apaches to go back into Mexico and prevented their return to reservations for sanctuary and additional recruits. This fight in early 1881 led to Victorio's defeat by Mexican troops at Tres Castillos, and consequently to the end of the Apache wars in Texas.

"A person may now walk in the shadows of the fort ruins and reminisce of a bygone year when the rattle of sabers mingled with the creak and crank of wagons," a poet wrote. Rocks in the sands off Highway 192 are the only ruins of Fort Quitman. Any rattles may be from snakes.

31. Fort Hancock (Originally known as Camp Rice)

Generally garrisoned by detachments of infantry and cavalry that rarely numbered more than 60 men, Fort Hancock was established to defended settlers against Indians and prevented bandits and smugglers from crossing the Rio Grande. This was the last Texas frontier fort.

It was built to protect the border from intruders. The fort was later moved from its initial location six miles northwest of Fort Quitman to a site on the Southern Pacific Railroad, and subsequently it was relocated to its final location on higher ground. Commanding General William T. Sherman believed the fort should be permanent because of its proximity to the railroad, and it was one of the few fort sites purchased (and not leased) by the United States in Texas. The name was changed to Fort Hancock in 1886.

The fort suffered at various times from fires and from flooding. In 1885, the soldiers built dikes to protect the post from overflows of the Rio Grande. When on the night of May 31, 1886, the western dike broke, lower portions of the fort flooded. That break was fixed and the dike strengthened, but four nights later a heavy gale pushed water over the retaining wall flooding the entire post for a depth of 18 inches up to nearly 3 feet. Then in 1889, in a series of fires the carpenter and blacksmith shops were burned, and later the wheelwright's shop was destroyed. Another fire burned the post gymnasium, the quartermaster's stable, and the haystack. By then, the fort had outlived its usefulness; the Army abandoned it. Peace was coming toTexas.

A commemorative marker on U. S. Highway 80, 52 miles southeast of El Paso, marks the site. Small ruins may be seen close to the Rio Grande near present-day Fort Hancock.

32. Presidio San Elizario

(See colored pictures in the center section)

Located in the community of San Elizario, 25 miles east of downtown El Paso on State Highway 258, the presidio was named in honor of the French patron saint of soldiers, St. Elzear. The community dates back to 1598 when the Spanish explorer Don Juan de Onate arrived from Mexico to build the presidio on the Rio Grande as a military garrison to protect the mission and settlement that had been constructed earlier. For centuries, soldiers defended the garrison against Apaches, bandits, renegades, and political defectors (from both sides of the river).

Presidio San Elizario is noted as one of the "O'Connor Presidios," which are named after Major Hugh O'Connor, a Spanish Inspector General who in 1767, had built a 1,000 mile line of presidios from La Bahia in Texas all the way to Santa Gertrudis de Altar, which is near the Gulf of California. Each presidio was garrisoned with an average of 100 Spanish soldiers.

Presidio San Elizario has been moved several times, the last time being in 1789 when it was moved 37 miles up the Rio Grande to the site of the town that now bears the same name. The community has been recognized as the site of the first American Thanksgiving, celebrated many years before the commonly accepted date of the Plymouth Rock Thanksgiving.

During the Civil War, the presidio and its grounds became the home of soldiers from Fort Bliss who were a part of the California Column. They named it Camp San Elizario.

In the San Elizario community in1877, local citizens and a few from across the river had a disagreement about the ownership of salt deposits to the northeast of San Elizario, and a small war started, called the Salt War. Before the Civil War, residents of San Elizario obtained their salt from Tularosa in New Mexico, but following a rumor in 1862 that those owners might close the Tularosa supply, San Elizario residents turned their attention to the Salt Basin, 100 miles to the northeast. They created a road from Fort Quitman to the basin, drove their carts there, filled them with salt, and after driving their carts back to San Elizario they sold the salt.

Texas Rangers attempted to intervene in the Salt War but they walked into a den of snakes, as the citizens did not want the Rangers interfering. Ranger Captain John B. Jones was sent to El Paso to quell the war. He was unable to restore order or to overcome the band of Mexican citizens who sought to keep the salt deposits open to the general public. Rangers met overwhelming armed resistance and they surrendered (for the only time in the Rangers existence) to avoid bloodshed.   After giving up their guns, the Rangers were allowed to leave, and San Elizario was then looted by the mob. In a few days several detachments of troops from El Paso and a posse of American citizens descended on San Elizario, killing four men and wounding several others on the way. The leaders of the mob and many of their followers fled to Mexico. After that, no one involved in the Salt War was ever arrested or even brought to trial.

The adobe chapel that was completed in 1883 is still in use. Fire destroyed the original interior in 1935 and it was replaced in 1944 with beautiful interior pillars, detailed in gilt, and connected by arches sweeping across the painted ceiling. Visitors are welcome; please respect any worshippers by treating the facility with respect and remaining quiet during your stay.

33. Fort Bliss (Once known as Camp Concordoria)

For more than 500 miles troops marched in 1849 enduring that summer's 100°F heat to reach El Paso and establish a fort to protect residents and travelers from hostile Indians, bandits, and renegades. They named it the Post of El Paso; it later became Fort Bliss in honor of Captain William Wallace Smith Bliss, who had served during the Mexican War with General Taylor.

After the Mexican War, the need to defend the border, to maintain law and order, and to protect settlers and many California-bound migrants from Indian attacks, the government had been compelled to establish a fort on the Rio Grande. Some soldiers were initially quartered on a ranch in El Paso, and a third occupied the presidio at San Elizario, 20 miles down the river.

It was from Fort Bliss, in 1862, that General Henry Hopkins Sibley, with authorization from Confederate President Jefferson Davis, undertook the westernmost and most ambitious campaign for the Confederacy during the Civil War. With Texas soldiers, who under Colonel John Baylor had already invaded New Mexico capturing Fort Fillmore, Sibley proclaimed his troops to be the "Army of New Mexico." He planned to march north and occupy all of New Mexico, to seize the rich mines in Colorado, to then turn west through Salt Lake City, and then capture the California seaports near Los Angeles and San Diego. With one sweeping bold move, he would make all of the west part of the Confederacy; people in New Mexico, Colorado, Arizona, Utah, and California would join in this grandiose plan by Sibley and Davis.

Sibley's Brigade, as it became known, (not knowing that Union troops were on the mountain watching as they left El Paso) marched up the Rio Grande. At Fort Craig they fought the bloody Battle of Valverde; a defeat for the Union troops when Rebel foot soldiers charged into the Unions' deadly cannon fire. Sibley's troops then captured Albuquerque and Santa Fe, and moved to engage the troops at Fort Union, a Union supply center 100 miles northeast of Santa Fe. This was on the route towards gold mines around Denver City in Colorado Territory.

At Glorieta Pass, Sibley won the battle but lost the war. On the morning of March 28, 1862, Sibley's Brigade opened the Battle of Glorieta with 1,200 Texans encountering Colonel Slough's 850-man Union force at Pigeon's Ranch one mile east of Glorieta Pass. Other units from Slough's troops, including 490 men led by Major Chivington, were pushing across a mesa when the main forces met near Glorieta. As the major battle raged, Chivington's Union troops reached a point some 200 feet directly above the Texans' supply wagons that they had parked at Canoncito. They descended the steep slopes and burned the Texans' reserve ammunition, their baggage, food, and medicines. The Battle of Glorieta ended after dark. Texans had lost 48 killed and 60 wounded and Union forces had taken almost identical casualties. Confederates' supplies had been lost to Major Chivington's raiding party. During Sibley's retreat to Texas he reportedly lost (to heat, starvation and a lack of water, and desertion) a third of the 2,500 men that he started with on the campaign. He then burned Fort Bliss.

There is an earlier Civil War story about the fort concerning Colonel John Baylor, who before Sibley, had invaded New Mexico. His troops met a force of Union troops. Apparently those troops had filled their canteens with brandy, not water because Baylor captured 700 drunk soldier, and 200 horses without a single casualty.

The history of Fort Bliss spans more than a century, from bow and arrow days to the days of guided missiles. Visit the present-day fort and its museum about its frontier military.

34. Mission San Antonio de la Ysleta del Sur

There is a Ysleta legend of a woman in blue, Mother Maria Jesus de Agreda. Jumano Indians related that she had visited them and taught them Christianity. Later, it was discovered she was abbess of a convent in Spain. Though she apparently had dreams in which she visited the Indians, she had never physically left the convent to come to America, nor seen the Indians.

Founded in 1682 for the Tigua Indians whom Coronado had encountered in New Mexico in 1540 and on his retreat reportedly took some of the Indians with him to the El Paso area. This mission was named San Antonio de la Isleta; it was later known as Mission Corpus Christi de la Isleta, then as Missions San Lorenzo del Realito, Nuestra Senora del Carmen and San Antonio de Los Tiguas. The priests are recognized for bringing agricultural methods to the Indians and they also brought grapevines from whose grapes a good wine was later made. This mission church still stands (next door to an official Indian reservation) in the old town of Ysleta in El Paso at the corner of Highway 20 and Zaragosa Street. The sanctuary is open to the public. Ysleta and the nearby Mission Socorro are credited with being the first missions founded in Texas.

Mission San Antonio de Senecu (also known as Senecu del Sur) is in the El Paso area and was established in the spring of 1682 after the Pueblo Revolt in New Mexico (the revolt occurred when the Indians became angry at Coronado's Spanish and drove them from that area). Mission Senecu was probably destroyed by a change in the course of the Rio Grande during the early nineteenth century. The Texas Highway Department has erected a marker that locates the site two miles northwest of Ysleta, which due to change in the river's flow is again located in Texas.

Also in El Paso is the Mission Socorro, officially Nuestra Senora de la Concepcion del Socorro and now called La Purisima. In 1682, it was originally located south of the Rio Grande. The mission was established for the benefit of the Prio, Tano, and Jemez tribes of Indians who were refugees from New Mexico. In 1683, it was moved to a site near Ysleta. The present town of Socorro stands on the ruins, and the modern mission holds services for citizens of the area. The mission interior is beautiful. At a side altar is a statue of Saint

Michael, the Archangel. A legend tells that when the statue was being shipped it bogged down in mud, as it contained a fortune in gold. Mission visitors are requested to please remain silent.

One of several expeditions sent to explore the area between San Antonio and El Paso with the purpose of opening a wagon road to the west was the Neighbors expedition. It was named for Major Robert S. Neighbors, who led the expedition. Neighbors had been one of the Texans taken prisoner in San Antonio in 1842. After being released in 1844, Neighbors became the Indian Agent of Texas, dealing mostly with the Lipan Apache, Tonkawa, and Comanche Indians. Neighbors was therefore familiar with the area and qualified to establish a route to El Paso. Accompanying him was Rip Ford, and three other Rangers and four Indians.

The route he took west was a very indirect one so he could take care of his personal matters. Leaving San Antonio, they passed through Austin and passed near present-day Waco. After leaving the Waco area, they went further northeast up the eastern bank of the Leon River. They then crossed the Leon and proceeded almost due south to an Indian camp on the upper Colorado River. From there the expedition finally headed west using the Horsehead Crossing over the Pecos River. The expedition crossed the northern end of the Davis Mountains and headed for the Rio Grande. Neighbors, believing the last 100 miles up the Rio Grande were unsuitable for a wagon took a more northern route; reaching El Paso after 23 days. The return trip was more direct and followed a more northern route used earlier by a Mexican army between El Paso and the Pecos River. Neighbors' expedition departed the presidio at San Elizario on May 6, 1849, heading towards the Hueco Tanks, the Guadalupe Mountains and the Pecos River. He reached present-day Fredericksburg on May 31 and San Antonio on June 2. He had made it from El Paso to San Antonio in 21 days. A route to El Paso was found, and settlers began to move towards the west; developing Texas along the way.

The return route later became known as the Northern Route and it was the route that the Butterfield Overland Mail followed from the Concho River to El Paso. Neighbors and Ford both estimated they had walked and ridden their horses for a distance of 598 miles on the return route. That distance is close to the 548-mile distance shown on modern maps for a San Antonio to El Paso trip.

35. Butterfield Overland Stage Line Stations

One of the famous stagecoach operations in Texas was the Butterfield Overland Mail. California settlers were unhappy with the time it took for mail from the East to reach them via Panama. They demanded quicker service, namely an overland stage route to the west coast. As a result, on April 20, 1857, the Post Office Department advertised for bids on a new route to California. The contract was awarded on July 2, 1857, to a well-financed group headed by John Butterfield of Utica, New York. He agreed to run a southern route through El Paso. Postmaster General Brown favored such a route because it could provide year-round service as opposed to the mid-continent and northern routes, which might be shut down by weather in winter months.

One particular clause in Butterfield's bid for the route from St. Louis to San Francisco may be the reason the line journeyed through Texas and one of the reasons the bid was accepted. Butterfield's bid contained a clause that gave the Postmaster General the authority to decide the best route, and this was at a time when the disagreements between North and the South were heating up in Washington. The Postmaster at the time had strong feelings for the South. On September 16, 1858, the Butterfield Overland Mail started its first westward trip from St. Louis, Missouri. The last trip on this route started in 1861.

Butterfield's stage coach route headed south to Memphis and then southwest crossing the Red River at Colbert's Ferry in Grayson County. It then continued across Texas for 282 miles to Fort Chadbourne via Jacksboro, Fort Belknap, and Fort Phantom Hill. The long journey then to El Paso swung south across a plain (where water was in short supply) between the Concho and Pecos rivers, past Horsehead Crossing on the Pecos and up the east bank to Pope's Camp. There it crossed the river, hugging the bank running northwestward to Delaware Spring. It then turned westward through Guadalupe Pass to Hueco Tanks and then went on west to El Paso.

Many stations in Texas were established at existing forts. Elsewhere stations were established first and forts were subsequently built, but many stations were independent miles from nowhere. For many of the stations, the nearest settlement was a hostile Indian village.

A station was located at Pine Springs near El Capitan in the Guadalupe Mountains. This station is now being reconstructed. One stage coach passenger poet wrote, upon seeing the mountain. "No sunrise at sea or from the mountain's summit could equal in grandeur that which we now beheld, when the first rays struck the snow-clad mountain, which reared its lofty head before us. The projecting cliffs of white and orange stood out in bold relief against the azure sky, while the crevices and gorges, filled with snow, showed their inequalities with a wonderful distinctness. At the same time the beams of the sun playing on the snow produced the most brilliant and ever changing iris hues. No painter's art could reproduce, or colors imitate, these gorgeous prismatic tints."

Thirty miles to the northeast of El Paso, a station was built near the Hueco (pronounced "wayco") Tanks. This station site is now within the Hueco Tanks State Park. This park is noted for its prehistoric Indian rock art with an estimated 5,000 pictographs and petroglyphs that are scattered throughout the park. The Park provides camping and rock climbing opportunities.

When the Civil War began on March 2, 1861, the United States Congress passed the legislation transferring the Butterfield line from Texas to a northern route. Confederates seized all of the Butterfield stations and many coaches. Thus, a spectacular period in the stagecoach history of Texas ended. Settlers, wagon trains heading west and cattle drives followed portions of the Butterfield route through Texas.

36. Pope's Camp (Also known as Pope's Fort)

Captain John Pope established the camp as a base of operations near the New Mexico border and the bank of the Pecos River. Pope was in charge of a government-sponsored water well drilling project in 1854. Charged primarily with finding a route for the railroad from the Mississippi River to the Pacific Ocean, Pope knew it was vital to find water along any train route. Unbeknown to Pope was that east of his camp is an area named the Monahans Sandhills. There pygmy Oak trees now grow to a height of only 3-to-4 feet, with a root system that may go down 90 feet looking for water (the water table being that far down in the earth).

Pope's well drilling operation was not a small task. It reportedly cost nearly $160,000 plus the cost of having a quartermaster's department and two companies of troops for protection. Troops provided protection from Indians until 1858. Adobe was used for the building walls, as it made a good protection against both bullets and arrows. The fort walls ran 200 feet by 150 feet by 200 feet and resembled an oddly shaped five-point star. Within the walls were ten limestone-and-rock houses, a guardhouse and tents. Each house had a fireplace as the temperature in this area frequently drops to near freezing in the wintertime.

The Butterfield Overland stage made a station at the camp to rest and water its horses. Across the river from the camp had been a large Indian camp and many artifacts have been found near the camp at what was earlier called "Pope's Crossing." Remains of the original camp are now under Red Bluff Lake near where the Pecos River crosses the New Mexico border.

37. Fort Stockton

The Comanche Trail has a long history in the Southwest. A map of West Texas made in 1857 by J. H. Young shows the lower portion of the trail with two prongs: one that crosses the Rio Grande in the vicinity of Boquillas, Mexico and the other at Presidio. The two converged at Comanche Springs on the San Antonio-El Paso-San Diego roads, the Butterfield Overland Mail route, and the San Antonio-Chihuahua Trail, and near the Pecos River-New Mexico road. It was near the site that the United States Army would established Fort Stockton in 1859 for the protection of the mail service, travelers, and freight wagons heading west toward California.

Confederates took possession of the fort at the outbreak of the Civil War but abandoned it the next year. With a shortage of men during the Civil War, the Confederacy never again tried to man a fort between Fort Clark and Fort Bliss. Apaches, without opposition, then controlled the area. What fights there were during that period was mainly between the Apaches and the Comanches. Most traffic across West Texas was by deserters, new emigrants, and an occasional guarded freight caravan. The first cattle drive may have occurred nearby in 1866 when 10,000 head were driven on what was to become the "Goodnight – Loving trail."

In 1866, beef steak was selling for thirty-cents a pound in New York and Texas cattle could be bought for $5 a head, since during the war herds that had gone unattended multiplied. Charles Goodnight, in late 1865, had collected a herd to take to market, but Indians stole the cattle. The next year he joined his herd with that of Loving, and together they drove a large herd through Indian country. Cattle drives became big business, and a belief existed that a large herd had a better chance of crossing the wild country. Drives were hard work and dangerous, so the Cowboys were paid a handsome wage of $15-to-$25 per month and food and horses were supplied by the owners. Cowboys provided their own saddles, blankets, ropes, and clothing.

The life of a cowboy on a drive was up at sunrise, and to bed after all the work was done. During the night while the herds rested, the cowboys took turns riding patrols and watching for rustlers. Cattle stampedes were a constant threat because thunder, lightning or any sudden noises could cause cows to start running, and when one ran, they all ran. Often Indians would deliberately cause stampedes to separate the herd from the cowboys. While the cowboys tried to stop the stampedes, the Indians would steal the cattle.

On one drive, during an Indian attack, Oliver Loving and a cowboy named W. J. Wilson were trying to round up strays from the herd when they were separated from the rest of the crew. Sighting an estimated 600 Indians, Loving and Wilson took shelter in a cave. Armed with only six-shooters and a Henry rifle capable of sixteen to eighteen shots, the two held off the Indians. Loving was wounded when the Indians called for a peace talk but they shot him when he stepped out of cave. After darkness, Wilson was sent to find help. While he was gone the Indians tried to drive Loving from the cave by digging tunnels but Loving was able to still fire his guns, so the Indians were unable to enter the cave. Only after the Indians gave up their attack would Loving make his way to safety.

Fort Stockton was revived again in 1867 when the army rebuilt the fort on a larger and more permanent basis to protect travelers and settlers from Indians. Until it was abandoned in 1886, the fort provided employment for freighters and laborers and a market for local farmers, stockmen, and merchants.   It was also the basis for building the city of Fort Stockton.

The city of Fort Stockton has reconstructed three officers quarters, the guardhouse, two of the enlisted men's barracks, a kitchen and the parade ground. One house contains a museum. Tours of the fort and many historic homes in the city are available to the public.

38. Camp Melvin (Also known as Camp Melbourne)

Camp Melvin was a little-known temporary outpost established in 1868 on the Pecos River "in the middle of no-where" two miles west of State Highway 349 in northwestern Crockett County. The site was significant as a river crossing. In May of 1684, Spanish explorer Juan Domínguez de Mendoza crossed the river there. His expedition camped near the crossing.

Camp Melvin operated as an outpost of Fort Lancaster from 1868 to 1871. From 1868 to 1881, stagecoaches crossed the Pecos at the site on the road from San Antonio to El Paso. One stagecoach company maintained a station there even though this crossing was dangerous as it was subject to many Comanche attacks in the 1870s.

This location was   called by many different names after 1864: San Pantaleon, Connelley's Crossing, Camp Melbourne, Fennelly's Crossing, Pecos Crossing, Camp Melvin, Camp Milvin, Pecos River Station, Ficklin, Crossing of the Pecos, Pecos Bridge, Pecos Stage Station, Pecos Station, Pontoon Bridge Crossing, and Pontoon Bridge. Between 1892 and 1926 the site was called Pontoon Crossing. A few stone ruins may remain, but the site is now on private property.

39. Fort Lancaster (Originally named Camp Lancaster)

This post was established as Camp Lancaster far out on the edge of the frontier in hostile Indian territory with no settlements anywhere close. It is now in a park off of U. S. Highway 290 at a historic site 10 miles east of Sheffield in Crockett County. Captain Stephen D. Carpenter built the post on August 20, 1855 on the left bank of Live Oak Creek where it meets with the Pecos River.   Manned by companies H and K of the First United States Infantry it became Fort Lancaster on August 21, 1856.

Captain R. S. Granger, who served from February 1856 to March 31, 1858, succeeded in command and he commanded until the removal of the Federal troops in March 1861 after the secession of Texas from the Union. During the Civil War, Walter P. Lane's Rangers that later became a part of Company F, Second Regiment of the Texas Mounted Rifles occupied the post from December 1861 to April 1862. After the Civil War a company of Federal infantry and a detachment of cavalry reoccupied the fort in 1871 as a subpost.

Fort Lancaster protected the road from San Antonio to El Paso in the years following the discovery of gold in California. The duties of the men were to escort mail and freight trains, pursue Mescalero Apaches and Comanches, and patrol their segment of road to keep track of Indian movements. Originally constructed of picket canvas and portable prefabricated buildings, by the time it was abandoned, all its major structures were made of stone or adobe. The post was abandoned in 1873 or 1874 and much of its masonry was used for buildings in nearby Sheffield.

Butterfield Overland Mail started coming through the territory of the fort's protection in August 1859 with three coaches per month passing over the road. There was a stage stop at Fort Lancaster and another twenty-five miles away at Howard Springs. Troops from the fort patrolled the route and provided protection to the station at the springs. One time when the east and a west bound wagons met at the springs, Indians led by Chief Lone Wolf (considered to be the most dangerous of the Kiowas) attacked and killed 17 teamsters. Soldiers came to the rescue, but the odds were against the troops. Their sergeant, who had been wounded, ordered the troops to give him a pistol and leave. When reinforcement troops from the fort returned the next morning their sergeant lay dead. The Indians had cut his heart out and laid it on the man's chest with a wreath around it in admiration of the heroics and courage displayed by the dead soldier.

In 1968, the Texas Parks and Wildlife Department began an archeological exploration project that involved excavating one barracks and three latrines and test drilling for two other barracks and two commissary structures. An officers' quarters, the commissary, the hospital's kitchen, and the flagpole location were entirely excavated in 1971. In 1974, two enlisted men's barracks and two officers' quarters were excavated. The excavations produced artifacts and architectural information. Today, much of the material is at the Fort Lancaster visitors' center (open Wednesday – Sunday from 8 a.m. to 5 p.m.), and in state archeological reports in Austin.

40. Fort Terrett (Also known as Camp Terrett, Post on the Rio Llano, Camp Lugubria and Camp Bainbridge)

Added to the second Federal line of forts in 1852, Fort Terrett was located 14miles west of Roosevelt. This was during the period when the Federal government tried to contain Indian raids by building small fortification across the frontier. It was not until after the Civil War that the powers in Washington decided that the Indians were "savages, mounted on fleet and hardy horses, making war their business and the pastime of their lives", and that mounted troops would be the only effective way to combat the Indians. Fort Terrett had a short and dull life.

One interesting fort story, however, concerned Second Lieutenant R. W. Johnson who, with his young wife, reported there for duty. The quarters for junior officers were not complete, so the couple established a home by pitching two tents, ten feet apart and facing each other. One tent was their living quarters and the other their bedroom. Not being familiar with the west, the couple failed to notice the selected site was also the home for rattlesnakes. After finding one outside their bedroom tent, they eradicated the rest of the nest. But they had another problem; fleas. Being an enterprising couple and not wanting fleas in their bed, they improvised a system where they stood on chairs to disrobe and after putting on their nightclothes they jumped into their beds without touching the ground.

The fort was closed by the time of the Civil War, but Texan's found it was needed since it was located 100 miles west of any Confederate frontier forts and Indians raided at their own pleasure. Hostile Indians took advantage of the war to regroup, rearm, and hunt unchecked. A band of Kickapoos, from a safe haven in Mexico, stole 15,000 head of cattle in August of 1866.

A few of the buildings of the fort are now used on a private ranch near Sonora.

41. Camp Ives

This camp was built on Turtle Creek four miles north of Camp Verde in Kerr County. Second Lieutenant Wesley Owen, commanding Troop I, Second U. S. Cavalry, established this camp on October 2, 1859. Although built in answer to requests from settlers for protection against Indians, the camp saw little use, though ladies at Camp Verde and Ives appreciated each other's frequent visits. On March 13, 1860, it was evacuated temporarily when soldiers stationed there escorted Lieutenant Colonel Robert E. Lee, then in temporary command of the Second Cavalry, to the Rio Grande. The camp was reoccupied on October 20, 1860, but remained in operation only until January 28, 1861 when the troops abandoned Ives and moved to Camp Verde, as Texas moved towards secession.

42. Camp Verde

Camp Verde was a United States Army post that was established in 1855 in Kerr County three miles north of Bandera Pass. Jefferson Davis, then a United States Senator, believed the "Great American Desert Thesis" that much of the southwest was not habitable. He urged the Army to purchase camels to be used in this wasteland. Thirty-three camels (along with three Arabs and two Turks) were brought from North Africa to Texas. In 1856, the camp became famous as the "Camel Camp," as it was headquarters for 40 camels used in providing overland communications to California. After an initial success with the camels, the army decided to buy more camels for the frontier.

Camels carry 600 pounds and travel miles without water, and the beasts survive by eating almost any type of plant. The camels adapted to their Texas home and were used for projects including a survey for a wagon road to New Mexico. A few ended up on salt trains and some were used to carry cotton bales. One enterprising captain in Arkansas even used a camel to carry his luggage. The failure of the camel was not due to its capacity; its work was superior to mules.

The failure was due to its horrible smell. Mules, horses, and the camel handlers detested the terrible stench of the camel and rebelled against it.

During the Civil War, Camp Verde served as a Confederate prisoner of war camp. The life of even the Confederate soldiers stationed to protect settlers was far from pleasant. One wrote: "there are inadequate rations, no shoes or clothing, no beans or rice, no coffee or sugar, and most demoralizing is that the weapons we are supplied would not kill a man at ten paces."

Indians continued to attack so Texans formed a militia and camped at a second Camp Verde two miles from the first. They later established Camp Montel near Bandera.

The community of Camp Verde started shortly after the first camp was established and grew around a community store adjacent to the camp. It was reported the primary purpose of the store was to provide liquor to the soldiers because regulations prohibited the sale of intoxicants within the camp. The store was only open on the soldiers' payday, and the owners supplemented that income by contracting to supply the government with wood and beef. A store and a post office continued to provide service to area inhabitants after the military camp was abandoned. Camp Verde's first post office was established in 1858, and probably operated from the same store. Today, area mail service is probably provided by that same store off of Highway 173. A commemorative marker placed in 1936 is west of the highway across from that store. Old fort structures are on private property, and after abuses, the public is not welcomed.

43. Camp Montel

Charles De Montel established a Texas Ranger station named Camp Montel in March of 1862 with 112 men divided between this camp and Camp Verde. Later, after the Texas Frontier Regiment was reorganized in 1863 they were stationed at Camp Montel. Then in early 1864 that regiment (called the Mounted Regiment) was turned over to the Confederacy as the 46th Texas Cavalry Regiment. Stations were established at the head of Seco Creek as Lipan Apaches and Comanches drifted into the area. Settlers in the area lived in constant fear of Indian raids.

The route from Camp Montel to Camp Verde became known as Bandera Pass. Bandera is Spanish for "flag," and there are a number of colorful accounts as to how the pass was named. One account says a flag was placed to mark a battle between the Spanish and Indians. Spanish Captain Jose de Urrutia in 1739 found the pass while fighting the Apaches who were threatening the settlements at Bexar. Urrutia, in route to the Presidio San Saba and Mission de la Santa Cruz, surprised the Apaches and took captives. A flag was placed as a warning marker. Another story has it that a Spanish General named Bandera led a punitive expedition in the area against Apaches after the Indians raided San Antonio. A third legend relates that after pursuing Indians to Bandera Pass the Spanish left a flag or flags to warn them against making future raids.

A fourth story claims that in the mid-1700s a meeting was held between the Spanish and Indians, whereat the Spanish pledged never to go north of Bandera Pass if the Indians agreed to cease raiding in the south. A red flag, a bandera, was then placed on the pass as a symbol of the treaty. Whatever agreements may have been made, they were all broken. Apaches continued to raid to the south and the Spanish continued expeditions to the north.

In 1843, there was a battle at Bandera Pass between the Comanches and a band of Texas Rangers led by John Coffee Hays. The ambushed rangers used new Colt revolvers in defeating the Indians. In the 1850s, Bandera Pass saw a stream of soldiers and settlers passing between the lumber camps on the Medina and the post at Camp Verde in the valley of Verde Creek.

When the Frontier Regiment was consolidated in 1861, the 1st Texas Volunteer Cavalry was organized and named the Montel Guard. It was stationed at the old camp. Bandera County maintained its frontier character until well after the Civil War. Indian attacks were frequent. In one attack horses were stolen and settlers killed. Volunteers under famous Texas Ranger Bigfoot Wallace chased the Indians into Bandera County, but the Indians escaped. The volunteer group did recapture 200 horses before returning to their homes.

Due to its distance from the battlefields and the fact that there were so few slaves in the area, the county was spared much of the trauma of the Civil War and Reconstruction. After the abandonment of Camp Verde by both Union and Confederate forces, local minutemen and the vigilantes stood guard at the Bandera Pass throughout Civil War and Reconstruction years. Their duty was to intercept carriers of contraband and livestock rustlers taking advantages of wartime breakdowns of law and order in the area. In 1870s, this was an area for long cattle drives. Boys became cowboys, storekeepers contracted as outfitters, and ranchers became trail bosses. The Pass saw heavy traffic when cattle were later driven north towards Kansas on the Western Trail.

44. Camp Wood

This camp was established in May of 1857 on the Nueces River on the site of Mission San Lorenzo de la Santa Cruz near the present-day town of Camp Wood in Real County. Its water was supplied by the same spring that had earlier served the mission and its silver mining. One of the soldiers first stationed at Camp Wood reported there was a mile-long ditch leading to the site of the mission. Could the early Spanish have discovered a silver vein near the surface? Records show the mission did mine silver, but there is no further description of that activity.

Camp Wood was a United States military outpost occupied by Lieutenant E. D. Philips and a company of the First Infantry assigned to protect the San Antonio-El Paso route and the entrance to the Rio Grande valley from Indian raids. The camp was named for Brevet Major George W. F. Wood. The camp was temporarily abandoned on October 29, 1857. Lieutenant John Bell Hood, later commander of Hood's Texas Brigade, reestablished the post in 1858 with a company of the Second Cavalry. The post was abandoned by Union troops in the spring of 1861 and afterward occupied by Confederates. Walter Paye Lane's Rangers arrived in 1861.

A Civil War skirmish known as the Battle of the Nueces took place not too far from Camp Wood on the morning of August 10, 1862. Many of the German settlers in the region sided with the Union. A group of about 65 of these Union sympathizers started for Mexico and camped on the west bank of the Nueces River. They were attacked by 94 mounted Confederates, and about half the Unionists were killed. Of the German survivors, 11 reached home and most of the others escaped to Mexico and eventually joined the Union forces in New Orleans. After the war, the remains of the Unionists killed at the battle site were gathered and buried.

Following the Civil War, both United States troops and Texas Rangers periodically were stationed at Camp Wood, and the influx of settlers began. During a full moon in 1876, Kickapoo Indians from Mexico crossed the Rio Grande and raided ranches killing several people, including a young boy named Allan Lease. The troops of Camp Wood, under Lieutenant John Bullis, gave chase down the Nueces Canyon hoping to catch the Indians before they reached the border. The Indians, however, had fresh stolen horses and beat the troops there. Bullis did not stop at the border, however, and ordered his troops to cross the river. They rode all night following the trail of the Indians and the next morning found the Indians' camp. Nearly 170 Indians were killed, but only 3 soldiers were lost. The troops recovered about 150 of the horses. In appreciation of the troops' actions, people of West Texas gave Bullis a sword with a seed-pearl-covered hilt.

The camp's buildings have since disappeared, but the camp cemetery continued to be used until the early twentieth century.

45. Mission San Lorenzo de la Santa Cruz

The Spanish had established a mission and fort called Santa Cruz de San Saba in North Central Texas, near present-day Menard in March 1758. That mission was soon attacked and destroyed by Comanches. All that was left of the Spanish presence in that area was the military outpost of San Luis de Las Amarillas. The new commander there had instructions to explore lands between the San Saba River and New Mexico, with the objective of establishing a presence in a region not threatened by the French. The commander, however, decided instead to start a new settlement on the upper Nueces River. This created a problem because the Viceroy who issued the orders refused to provide the settlement with any support.

This site, halfway between San Saba and San Juan Bautista, was called El Canon. At the site on January 23, 1762 the settlement of San Lorenzo de la Santa Cruz and a mission with the same name were founded. A garrison of 20 soldiers was provided by the presidio at San Saba. The mission attracted 400 Indians within a week, but the priests soon learned that the Apaches had no real interest in conversion. Rather, the natives viewed the site as a haven from their enemies, the Comanches, with the Spanish as their defenders. The mission complex itself included a 64-yard square plaza surrounded by walls that provided some security. The mission came under attack by 300 Comanches and their allies in October 1766, followed by a second assault the following month. Both attacks were turned away, but in July 1767, it was determined that there was no hope for converting the Apaches, and the mission was abandoned.

Remains of mission San Lorenzo have been excavated. They are located at the north edge of present-day Camp Wood on a low ridge running parallel to the east bank of the Nueces River. Camp Wood citizens are now trying to raise the funds to complete reconstruction of this early mission. History of the mission accumulated from documents of the church does not mention any of the silver mining activities at the mission that other sources have reported as having taken place. Commemorative historical markers have been placed along Highway 55 near the town.

46. Mission Nuestra Senora de la Candelaria del Canon

The third of three San Xavier missions, which also included San Ildefonso and San Francisco Xavier de Horcasitas, was founded on the south bank of the San Gabriel River (then known as the San Xavier) about 5 miles from the present-day site of Rockdale in Milam County.

The San Gabriel River location was abandoned after a severe drought and epidemic. Following the 1758 destruction of the mission on the San Saba River, efforts to find a new mission for the Lipan Apaches centered on the upper Nueces River. On February 6, 1762, Mission Nuestra Senora de la Candelaria was moved from the San Gabriel River to this site near present-day Montell in Uvalde County. Candelaria attracted 400 Apaches within a week of its founding, but as occurred at other missions, the Indians were not interested in being converted. They viewed the site as a refuge from their Comanche enemies, and wanted the Spanish soldiers stationed at the mission to protect them. Problems plagued the mission from the time of its inception. It had been set up before the threat of French invasion of the frontier disappeared in 1763. Spain was no longer interested in sending money so priests were transferred to missions in Mexico in 1771. Remains of the buildings were taken by settlers to build homes after the 1800s.

The area near the mission was the site of an Indian attack in 1861 that claimed the lives of two well known Indian fighters, Henry Robinson and Henry Adams, and Adams' daughter's fiance. Robertson was so famous among the Indians that a picture of him with his red hair and beard was painted on a rock on the Llano River. The men were enroute to Camp Wood when Comanches killed and scalped them, and even took Robinson's famous red beard.

47. Fort Inge (Initially named Post on the Leona, or Fort Leona)

Fort Inge is on the Leona River where Mount Inge, a 140-foot volcanic plug of Uvalde phonolite basalt, dominates the site. It was one of the earliest western frontier forts when it was established in 1849 by U. S. troops to protect travelers between San Antonio and El Paso. The fort was named for Lieutenant Zebulon Inge who was killed in the Mexican War. It was located near Uvalde on the route Mexican General Woll followed in 1842 to recapture San Antonio, and which Woll used after the Dawson massacre to retreat from San Antonio back into Mexico.

Troops from the fort in 1861 participated in an interesting battle when a patrol was sent to chase a band of Apaches. The Indians led the troops on a route that crossed the Barosito Creek several times, causing the soldiers' rifles and ammunition to get wet. On top of all the water that the soldiers had endured while crossing the creek, it had rained all day. When the troops found the Indians (or more accurately, when the Indians found the soldiers), the Indians, out-numbering the soldiers, attacked. When the soldiers pulled their rifles and prepared to fire, they found the firing caps were too wet and their rifles impossible to fire. The troops resorted to hand-to-hand combat while many drew their sabers to fight. Three soldiers were killed before the patrol could withdraw. This battle was one of the few times the soldiers used only their swords.

Another interesting story in the history of Fort Inge concerned the legend of John Bell Hood, who was once stationed at Inge. He pursued a band of hostile Indians, rescued a scalped white girl, and received the *Sword of Thanks* from the Confederate Texas Legislature for his bravery even though Hood was a Union officer at the time. There is another legend concerning a Texas Ranger named Ed Westfall. He was attacked by Comanches, shot through the neck, and blinded. He then crawled for a week (30 miles) without food to reach Fort Inge. To the surprise of the doctors at the fort, Westfall not only lived, but he later recovered his sight. Also while stationed there, General Lew Wallace started to work on a draft of his famed novel, <u>Ben Hur</u>.

The purpose for the Fort Inge soldiers included protecting the construction of the San Antonio-El Paso military road, escorting supply trains, and protecting frontier settlements from bandits and raiders. The fort was a typical one-company, 50-man, post for most of its history. For a period in 1854 it was the headquarters for the 200-man U. S. Mounted Rifle Regiment. During the Civil War, Walter P. Lane's Rangers, Confederate Company A Cavalry, and John J. Dix's Norris Frontier Regiment occupied the post. Federal troops reoccupied Fort Inge in 1866.

The fort's dozen buildings were arranged around the rectangular parade ground with an enclosed stable at the south end. The most substantial building was constructed of cut limestone and used as a hospital and later as a storehouse. Other structures were built from upright log pickets plastered with mud and whitewashed. A low, dry-stacked stone wall was built later.

Uvalde's Historical Commission rescued the 42-acre site and started reconstructing the structures and upgrading an interpretive trail. When the wild flowers start to bloom along that trail, Fort Inge has the potential of being one of Texas' prettiest reconstructed fort sites.

48. Camp Blanco

In 1864 the Texas Legislature authorized the formation of a Frontier Regiment which would be divided into three districts of Texas Militia to protect settlers from Indian attacks. As one of the operational bases, Camp Blanco was established on the Little Blanco Creek in northeastern Uvalde County. General Order # 2 issued that year to the volunteers read:

Section 1. Requiring members to meet their respective officers armed and equipped, horses shod, rations and ammunition for at least 15 days to report to Camp Blanco ... or be fined.

Section 2. Officers will meet with their respective squads ... and on no occasion leave their squad without consigning it to the care of some officer.

Section 3. No substitutes will be received only by the officer to command the same and not unless the substitute be a member of the company which the squads are a part.

Section 4. Privates are required to comply cheerfully to orders given and in any case they feel mistreated file their complaint in writing that they may be heard and amendments made.

This order was dated September 18, 1864, from Camp Blanco, Uvalde County. The story and future of Camp Blanco, after this order, have escaped from written history.

This was a period of high inflation with shoes selling for $30 and coffee for $10 a pound. There was a shortage of salt, paper, weapons, and labor. The Union army had not brought Texas to a point of surrender, but the economy and hardships at home took a toll that would last for years after the Civil War was over.

49. Camp Dix (Also known as Camp Lawson)

A Confederate outpost was established by James M. Norris on April 4, 1862, at a spot on the river known as Black Waterhole, 7 miles east of Uvalde. The camp was a Frontier Regiment post (See "Camp Blanco" for more information on the regiment) under the command of Captain John J. Dix, Jr. It was at the crossing of the San Antonio-Eagle Pass road and the Frio River. The road was vital as a commercial route for hauling Texas cotton to Mexico after the Union forces gained control of the entry points to Mexico along the lower Rio Grande. Camp Dix was one of 16 encampments established to protect the Confederate wagon trains hauling cotton on the way to Mexico, and provide protection for settlers against the Indian raids after nearby Fort Inge was abandoned by the Union soldiers at the beginning of the Civil War.

The camp was not popular with the local settlers because the troops lived off of the community and did very little chasing of Indians. In 1863 a grand jury was convened in Uvalde to charge the troops with theft. It was found that Company H had taken $2,450 (a small fortune at that time) in hogs, cattle, and beehives without paying a cent. The court stated "that the removal or withdrawal of the company from this county and from the frontier is essentially necessary to the future peace and security in this county."

Camp Dix was abandoned after the consolidation of the Frontier Regiment in 1864.

50. Camp Sabinal

On the Sabinal River near the present-day town of Sabinal in Uvalde County, Captain Albert G. Brackett founded Camp Sabinal in 1856 to protect the settlers traveling from San Antonio to El Paso. At the time, the 2nd U. S. Cavalry stationed at Fort Mason were the only Federal mounted troops remaining in Texas. Nothing remains of this camp.

51. Fort Lincoln

In 1848, at the conclusion of the Mexican War, a Texas Ranger company commanded by Charles S. DeMontel established a camp on Seco Creek a mile north of D'Hanis in Medina County. In 1849, Fort Lincoln was built at the site on a 1,476-acre plot that had been granted to the heirs of Milton Anderson on August 27, 1846. Like many forts in early Texas it was built on leased property. Buildings were of logs or poles, with roofs of shingles, thatch, or tarpaulins.

The settlement of D'Hanis was settled in 1846 by Germans that were attracted to the area (which at the time was wilderness) by the offer of 320 acres of land for which they had to pay a piddling sum over 15 years. The price included transportation to this land of opportunity, but it did not include any supplies such as nails and the settlers arrived without money. Not that there were any stores, but they endured a hardship building their homes from short mesquite poles using only tall grass to tie the poles together. The few guns they had were harmless bird guns.

Everyone in the settlement was frightened when the Indians first came to visit. The war paint and spears that the Indians carried were unexpected. The Indians did arrive under a white flag and did not harm anyone; but they took all of the settlers' provisions when they left. Texas Rangers came to the rescue shortly thereafter by shooting game to feed the settlers and teaching them self defense.

Fort Lincoln was named for Captain George Lincoln, an officer of Company E, Eighth Infantry, who lost his life in the Mexican War at the Battle of Buena Vista. The fort was one of eight that formed the first line of permanent Federal frontier defenses in Texas from Eagle Pass on the Rio Grande to Coffee's Bend (Fort Preston) on the Red River. The fort was built on the west bank of Seco Creek on high, open ground that provided a commanding view of the area. Water was hauled from the creek, at that time no more than a series of standing pools. In 1851, builders made use of local gray limestone in building facilities for two companies, a commissary store, a storehouse for company property, a quartermaster's depot storehouse, and a hospital.

Companies E and G, U. S. Eighth Infantry, commanded by Major James Longstreet, were stationed at Fort Lincoln to repel and track down Indian raiders in protection of the newly arrived European and American settlers. The troops also protected the commercial and military property transported on the Woll Road, an important trade route from San Antonio to Fort Duncan on the Rio Grande and points west. Fort Lincoln was abandoned on July 20, 1852, after the early frontier advanced westward. The buildings remained intact for some time, and the Texas Rangers made headquarters near the site. None of the fort buildings now remain. The barracks were torn down and transformed into constructing residences east of Seco Creek at D'Hanis. An Irishman, Richard Reily, purchased the old hospital and used the building as a home for his family. On May 26, 1936, a dedication ceremony was held for the unveiling of a commemorative marker placed at the site by the Texas Centennial Commission.

Another community, Seco Settlement, was established near Fort Lincoln and a mile north of D'Hanis. For protection from Indian raids, settlers from Old D'Hanis moved to sites near the fort soon after its establishment in 1849. Most of the communities' settlers were from Germany, France, and Ireland. Latter-day accounts describe the country at the time of settlement as "one vast prairie of sage grass." The settlers built a school, homes, and several stores and other small businesses and engaged in farming and the raising of cattle and sheep. Seco Settlement is no longer evident as a separate community. By 1984, the settlement had become part of D'Hanis.

52. Camp Nueces (La Salle County) (And Camp Cook)

Camp Nueces, in La Salle County, was the headquarters for the Somervell Expedition of 1842. Texans mounted this expedition in retaliation for Mexican raids in Texas earlier that year. Mexico had refused to recognize the Treaty of Velasco (signed in 1836), which ended the Texas Revolution and sent 12,000 troops to capture Fort Lipantitlan, Goliad, Refugio, Victoria, and San Antonio. Texans in San Antonio were caught by surprise (though they were warned two months earlier that Mexico planned to take back the town) and surrendered because it was impossible to immediately find men for a defense for the city.

Following the loss of San Antonio, a company of 55 Texas scouts under Captain Mathew Caldwell engaged the Mexican soldiers at the Battle of Salado Creek. As the fight proceeded, another company under Captain Nicholas Dawson approached to give support to Caldwell's forces fighting against Woll. Only a mile and a half before reaching the battle, Dawson's troops were attacked by cannon fire as the Mexicans took advantage of their position above the creek bed and shelled the Texans until all were thought to be dead, in what became known as the Dawson Massacre. Woll later retreated to Mexico, with a reinforced group of Texans in pursuit.

Cash poor and land rich, the Texas Congress then authorized selling 10,000,000 acres of land for money to finance a force to invade Mexico, but President Sam Houston vetoed that bill.

In October 1842, Sam Houston ordered General Alexander Somervell to organize troops and volunteers, and then invade Mexico "if the strength, equipment, and the discipline of the volunteers indicates a reasonable possibility of success." Almost 700 volunteers came to San Antonio ready to fight the Mexicans troops, and invade Mexico, for glory and plunder. In November, 13 miles from San Antonio, the Somervell Expedition stopped at Camp Cook (only the camp's name is now remembered) near the Medina River at the crossing of the San Antonio–Presidio Del Rio Grande Road.

The Somervell expedition captured Laredo then moved to recapture the town of Guerrero, in present-day Mexico. On December 19, however, Somervell, noting his insufficient supplies and a lack of discipline among the volunteers decided it would be a disaster if he tried to invade Mexico. He gave orders (as Sam Houston had directed) to disband and return home.

Many Texans were disappointed with the order to disband and 308 men and five of the captains decided to continue the fight as the Mier Expedition, commanded by William S. Fisher, (Ranger's Headquarters in Waco, Fort Fisher, is named in his honor). (See the information in this region about the "Mire Expedition" for more information on the results of that expedition.)

One of the members of Somervell's expedition was named Flacco the Younger, a Lipan-Apache chief who had acted as a scout. He was among those who obeyed Somervell's order to return home, but on the way he was attacked near San Antonio and killed by Mexican bandits. Some reports say Cherokee Indians killed him, but his murderers were never found. Flacco's father, Flacco the Elder, also a chief, thought the Texans did not try to find the killers. Some historians speculate this was the reason that the Apaches were almost constantly at warfare with the Texans after the murder.

53. Fort Ewell

Following the Texans fight for independence in 1836, the border between the Republic and Mexico was in controversy. Texans said the southern border was the Rio Grande while Mexico claimed the land south of the Nueces River. Instead of two sets of laws being enforced, the area was basically lawless, and without law comes the bandits who venture outside the law.

A renegade, King Fisher, ruled the country south of San Antonio to the Rio Grande, was one such outlaw, and his actions brought Texas Ranger L.H. McNelly to Fort Ewell to establish Ranger headquarters. More than 100 outlaws camped in the surrounding area, seized control of any civil governments and even fenced in corrals to keep the cattle and horses they stole. Vigilante groups composed of law abiding citizens had been formed in some areas, and they were as much a problem in keeping the peace as outlaws, as they employed gunmen to protect their herds. Average citizens reported suffering as much, or even more, from the rustlers, and hired gunmen, then they did from the earlier Indian raids.

McNelly brought peace and law to the area by spreading the word that the governor had sent him to the area to stop all the nonsense, and that the next person that killed anyone, would be shot within two hours of his crime. Captain McNelly was the ideal Texas Ranger. He was courageous, blunt, and confident, and his legend persists though his life was short. He died, not from gunshot, but from an unnamed illness at the age of 33.

Fort Ewell was on the south bank of the Nueces River at the crossing of the San Antonio road to Laredo. It was established on May 18, 1852, after the U. S annexed Texas but the state was still trying to protect the new settlers. Companies E, G, and I of the Texas Mounted Riflemen under Captain John Smith Simonson garrisoned the fort.

An inspection report in June 1853 stated that the fort was in a poor location. The river was 75 feet wide but only 4 feet deep. This caused it to frequently overflow its banks during heavy rains and flooding made the fort inaccessible at times. The buildings were constructed by troops using soft adobe that was not strong enough to support a roof. Due to a lack of rain most of the year, grazing for their animals was not good, and attempts to grow kitchen gardens were unsuccessful. Food and clothing were sometimes at a premium, and troops were often sick. For two years after July 1852, every officer and man was sick on the average of once every three months. Soldiers deserted and went to Mexico. In December 1853 the base was abandoned, and by October 1854 the fort was abandoned though Rangers frequently used the site as a camp.

In the mid-1860s, Indian raids became frequent in this area, and one Indian battle took place not far from Fort Ewell, between San Miguel and Cesadara Creeks. About 35 Indians had attacked a ranch and stolen horses, killing one man. Other settlers, giving chase, found they were themselves out-numbered and so they withdrew into a densely treed area. One settler took off for the old fort and help. The Indians also dismounted so they could attack the settlers in the thick timbers. After a seesaw fight, the Indians left after their chief was killed. When the Texas Rangers arrived from Fort Ewell, they gave chase to the Indian party, but without luck.

Tales of buried treasures also proliferate in the area around the county. A marker stands on inaccessible private property southeast of Cotulla.

54. Fort Merrill (Also Fort Ramirez)

On high ground commanding a fine view of surrounding country where the road from Corpus Christi to San Antonio crossed the Nueces River, Captain Samuel M. Plummer and companies H and K of the 1st United States Infantry founded Fort Merrill on March 1, 1850.

Using lumber shipped in from New Orleans and logs cut from along the river the soldiers of the garrison erected a dozen buildings. The garrison was so small that it could do no more than sentinel duty as the frontier had moved west. It was probably named in honor of

Captain Hamilton W. Merrill of the 2nd United States Dragoons who was killed in the battle during the Mexican War. Texas Mounted Rifle Regiment Companies I and E were the regular garrison until April 26, 1853. Then they were transferred to Fort Ewell, leaving two noncommissioned officers and thirteen men at Merrill. It was abandoned on December 1, 1855.

Around the fort was a deep, black, rich soil: "it is the best stock raising country in Texas and the extensive prairies afford the best pastures in the world" noted passing travelers. Future United States President, Ulysses S. Grant, noted 1,500 to 2,000 wild horses, when he toured this area. Early Spaniards had introduced horses to this land and those horses multiplied forming large herds of wild horses. Indians soon learned that by chasing the horses away from the Spanish, the Mexicans and later the settlers they created a great advantage by having their enemy on foot, unable to give chase to the Indians' raiding parties. Texas Rangers and United States soldiers later adopted the Indians practice of stampeding horses and putting Indians a-foot.

After Fort Merrill was abandoned all of its lumber was carried off. There are portions of the sandstone foundation remaining, but on private property that is not accessible to the public. Site of the fort was off U. S. Highway 281, three miles northwest of Dinero in Live Oak County. The nearby George West museum includes artifacts of the era.

Also in the county was Fort Ramirez, Rancho del Ojo de Agua Ramirena, a fortified ranch house built by the Ramirez family along the Nueces River in southern Live Oak County. The building was never an official fort, but it was the first permanent structure in the county and provided protection for the Ramirez family and their workers until the family left the area in 1813. The brothers Antonio Ramirez and Victoriano Ramirez had cleared land and built a corral and the ranch house before receiving their land grant. When the promised grant did not come, the family moved away. A rumor of buried treasure resulted in destruction of the house.

Region Two

This section of the guide commences in East Texas at San Augustine, home of an early day mission once involved in a ridiculous conflict named the "Chicken War". Then we explore the area of Nacogdoches, which has the distinction in its history of having nine different flags flown above its roofs. Some of the flags represented countries but others represented the rule of men called "filibusters" who tried to make Texas their private domain. One was Doctor-General James Long who wanted to set the area free from Spanish rule. He entered Nacogdoches with an army of ruffians and announced himself as liberator, raised a flag of freedom, and issued a decree that Texas was an independent Republic. However, 500 citizens of Nacogdoches ran and hid from their self-proclaimed liberator when the mob he called his army plundered the town.

After the Louisiana Purchase, the United States and Spain were unable to agree on the boundary between Louisiana and Texas. To avoid armed clashes the two military commanders agreed in 1806, to declare the disputed territory along the Sabine River to be "Neutral Ground". The agreement prohibited settlers in the Neutral Ground, but settlers from both the Spanish and United States' side moved in along with outlaws making travel and trade dangerous. The U. S. was in a depression and the almost-free Texas land brought many families seeking a new life.

One group that was allowed was the Cherokee Indians. The Spanish viewed the Indians as a buffer against American expansion and approved the settlement. Cherokees first settled in 1807 at the site of present-day Dallas, but pressure from the prairie Indians forced them to move eastward along the Red River into an uninhabited region north of Nacogdoches. When Texas passed from Spanish hands to the Mexicans, they, like the Spanish, welcomed the presence of Cherokees in Texas. While the Mexican government delayed granting the Cherokees title to the land, the population of East Texas swelled. By the mid-1820s, Americans were drifting to the area near the Cherokees, and distrust developed between the two, as each felt threatened by the other. Family forts called blockhouses were built, particularly in the lawless Neutral Ground.

The tour of this region ends near Washington-on-the-Brazos (first capitol of the Republic of Texas) where Texans in 1836 signed their Declaration of Independence from Mexico.

Region Two Map
(Numbers are as the sites are listed in the text for this region)

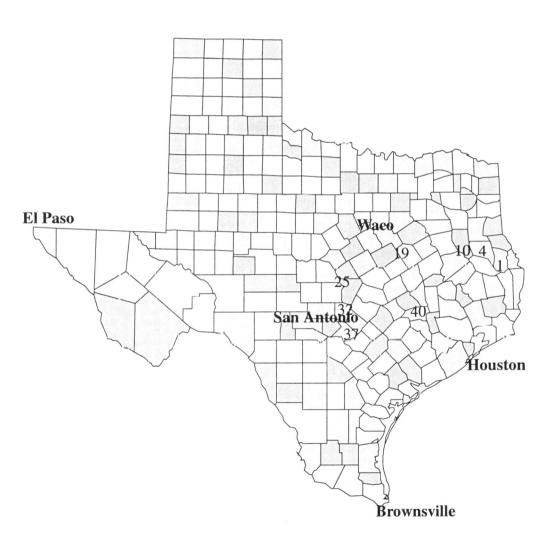

Location
Region Two

1   Mission Nuestra Senora de Los Dolores de Los Ais – in San Augustine
2   Fort Teran – near Colmesneil
3   Mission Nuestra Senora de Guadalupe de Los Nacogdoches – in Nacogdoches
4   Stone Fort – in Nacogdoches
5   Presidio Nuestra Senora de Los Dolores de Las Tejas – near Douglas
6   Mission Nuestra Senora de la Purisima Concepcion de Los Hainai – near Douglas
7   Mission San Jose de Los Nazonis – near Cushing
8   Cook's Fort – in Cherokee County
9   Lacy's Fort – near Alto
10   Mission San Francisco de Los Tejas – near Weches
11   Brown's Fort – in Houston County
12   Fort Henderson – in Robertson County
13   Fort Trinidad – in Houston County
14   Fort Boggy – near Centerville
15   (Mission) Nuestra Senora del Pilar de Bucareli – in Madison County
16   Dunn's Fort – near Wheelock
17   Fort Sullivan and Fort Nashville – in Robertson County
18   Fort Oldham – in Burleson County
19   Fort Parker – near Groesbeck
20   Fort Tenoxtitlan – in Burleson County
21   Camp Chambers – in Falls County
22   Fort Milam – near Milam
23   Little River Fort – near Little River / Academy
24   Black's Fort – in Burnett County
25   Fort Croghan – in Burnett
26   Fort Tumlinson – in Williamson County
27   Camp Cazneau – in Williamson County
28   Kenney Fort – in Williamson County
29   Camp Austin – in Travis County
30   Fort Colorado in Travis County

1. Mission Nuestra Senora de Los Dolores de Los Ais

(See colored pictures in the center section)

This was one of the earliest missions in Texas (along with one in present-day Louisiana) when the Spanish started to discourage the French from settling in East Texas. First located about a mile south of present-day San Augustine in 1717 by the Domingo Ramon expedition, it was abandoned due to the French invasions in 1721 and then re-established at its current site. The mission failed for various reasons. Blame was cast on the Indians for being lazy, on the French for buying the clothes and other gifts the Indians received from the Spanish (under mining the purpose of the gifts), and on the soldiers for being friendly with the Indian women.

Alliances and disputes in Europe in this era were continued in the New World. One fight, known as the Chicken War, caused the abandonment of Spanish missions in eastern Texas in 1719. When news that Spain and France were on opposing sides reached Lieutenant Philippe Blondel of the French post at Natchitoches, Louisiana, he immediately attacked the nearest Spanish outpost. This was at a site near present-day Robeline, Louisiana at the Mission

San Miguel de Linares de Los Adaes. Finding only one lay brother and one soldier at the mission, Blondel and his detail then raided the henhouse. As Blondel mounted his horse, after tying chickens to his saddle, the chickens flapped their wings, the horse reared, and the Lieutenant was spilled in the dirt. Thus this momentous battle was given the name "Chicken War."

June 22 1719, Blondel's troops reached Mission Nuestra Senora de Los Dolores and told the priest that Pensacola had been captured, and a hundred French soldiers were on their way from Mobile with the East Texas settlements their objective. Father Margil, viewing retreat as the only alternative, packed his belongings and headed for Mission Nuestra Senora de la Purisima Concepcion (in the area of present-day Douglass). Upon hearing the report, Captain Domingo Ramon of nearby Presidio Nuestra Senora de Los Dolores de Los Tejas heeded the desire of his soldiers and their wives and withdrew to San Antonio. Father Margil and two soldiers remained at Mission Concepcion for 20 days "consoling" Indians, who were reluctant to let them leave. On October 3 the entire camp marched for San Antonio.

The Chicken War represented a costly overreaction (and another reason for the name "Chicken War") by Spanish religious and military men to a feeble French gesture. The French made no aggressive move against Texas after Blondel's fiasco. In addition to causing a two-year hiatus in the Spanish missionary effort, the episode disrupted the commercial aims of the French Company of the West. The Chicken War left no one with whom the French might make trade.

In 1722, the Aguayo expedition reestablished six Spanish missions and two presidios. Los Adaes Presidio, 70 miles from the French at Natchitoches, was designated capital of the Province of Texas. By 1763, Mission Dolores de Los Ais, was closed.

When Dolores was reestablished a few years later its structures were built of native stone and the wall made by settling wooden poles or logs vertically in the ground and plastering the walls with mud. The buildings and walls were both whitewashed. The mud pits for plaster were apparently used later as cooking pits or refuse dumps. Mission Dolores was abandoned again in 1773. The Indians wishing to remain with the mission were moved to missions in San Antonio.

Stone from the original mission has gone into many of the buildings in present-day San Augustine. The city has reconstructed part of the mission and has opened a museum with items found during the reconstruction on display. Also in the museum is a beautiful mural depicting the original mission. Museum hours are 8 to 12 weekdays or by appointment (409-275-3815).

2. Fort Teran

The Liberty-to-Nacogdoches Trail was a route early missionaries traveled from El Orcoquisac (an early settlement once located near present-day Wallisville) to missions around Nacogdoches. It was on this trail that the Mexican government in 1831 erected Fort Teran at the Coushatta Trace crossing of the Neches River. Some accounts say the fort was located on the south side of the river and others say it was on the north, but all accounts agree that the fort was built for one purpose—to stop the flow of illegal Anglos entering Texas. A man named Peter Ellis Bean was placed in charge of building the fort and commanding the Mexican troops.

Bean's story is an interesting one and reflects the opportunity for adventure that young men of the time came to Texas to find. He first came to Texas in 1800 when he was only 17, as part of the Philip Nolan expedition. Nolan was one of the early filibusters from the United States who ventured into Texas. Bean was a young lieutenant with Nolan, who captured wild horses, but the Spanish government became suspicious that was not his true purpose. There is some speculation Nolan was there, possibly under directions of U. S. President Jefferson, as part of a plan to seize land in Texas. The Spanish decided to arrest Nolan, and on March 21, 1801, they attacked the camp. Nolan was killed in the fight, but the others who survived were captured and taken to Mexico. Peter Ellis Bean, in route to becoming a Texas legend, was among this group.

The Spanish condemned one man from the group to die and sentenced the rest to prison. The man sentenced to die was chosen among the survivors by a roll of the dice. Bean survived this ordeal as well, although unlucky Ephram Blackburn did not. Bean took advantage of a Revolution in Mexico in 1810 and volunteered to fight for the Mexican Royalists to gain his freedom from prison. As soon as he was free, he joined the revolutionaries and persuaded them to send him to the U. S. to ask for aid for the revolutionaries' cause. Back in his own homeland, he fought with General Andrew Jackson at the Battle of New Orleans.

Thereafter, Bean was a man of split loyalties, dividing his time between visits to Mexico and the United States. In 1823 he returned to East Texas and served the Mexican government as an Indian agent when he persuaded the Cherokees to remain neutral during the Fredonian Rebellion in Nacogdoches. Then in 1831 he directed the construction of Fort Teran.

The role Bean, or Fort Teran, played in the development of Texas, the Texas Revolution or in the Civil War is not documented. Its location may have been too isolated to be involved.

One of the stories told about the fort was that Mexican soldiers, under attack, put gold in the mouth of a cannon and pushed it into the river. Who the attackers were and why the soldiers threw gold away are questions unanswered. If the gold was nuggets, ore, or the golden coins that Mexico used to pay its soldier, are facts lost over time. Other stories connected with the area around Fort Teran also involve lost gold, silver and copper mines. One tale is about a group of Portuguese who searched for gold. After camping near the fort for days they just disappeared, leaving their camp belongings behind. Did they find gold and if so had no need of their supplies or were they victims of foul play? That mystery also remains without an answer.

Even today, along the riverbank, there are holes dug by someone in search of something. If they found anything, they are keeping their secrets. But beware if you venture to the area as there is a deep, uncovered shaft that cannot be seen after dark, and rattlesnakes are plentiful.

A commemorative marker north of Colmesneil off County Road 1745 is near the site.

3. Mission Nuestra Senora de Guadalupe de Los Nacogdoches

Workers were digging a foundation for a building in the center of Nacogdoches in 1999 and discovered what may be the ruins of Nuestra Senora de Guadalupe de Los Nacogdoches

The earliest Europeans to reach the area that is now Nacogdoches County were probably in a Spanish expedition led by Luis de Moscoso Alvarado, who traveled in this area as early as 1542. The Spanish, however, largely ignored Texas until the French explorer Rene Robert Cavelier Sieur de La Salle established a fort on the coast in 1685. This caused the Spanish to return to the area. They came with an intent to stay when their expedition arrived in 1716. They found several villages of Indians and in the midst of these tribes the Spanish then built Nuestra Senora de Guadalupe de Los Nacogdoches (named for the Nacogdoche Indians). The mission however, was unsuccessful in its goal of converting the local Indians, but it did provide an important presence to offset the French influence, which in 1773 permanently withdrew.

The abandoned missions' deserted buildings formed a center for the settlement of Nacogdoches by Antonio Gil Ibarvo in 1779, when settlers from a mission at Bucareli returned to East Texas. Ibarvo began making informal land grants to the early settlers. With the arrival of many Americans into the area, families wanted the grants legalized in order to preserve their rights. In an effort to populate the area, Spain experimented with a policy enticing settlers to enter Texas with promises of land, religious tolerance, and special privileges. Spain issued new laws opening Texas to any foreigners who would respect its laws and abide by its constitution.

Nevertheless, many of the arriving Americans were not willing to abide by the laws of Spain. In the course of Nacogdoches history, nine flags were to fly over the town. Some were the flags of countries and other the flags of individuals seeking power or personal wealth. Philip Nolan, who began trading in Texas as early as 1791, was the first filibuster. In 1801, he illegally entered Texas and established an unnamed fortress near present-day Nolan Creek. After Spanish soldiers killed him, papers were discovered implicating him in a plot to seize the region from Spain. During the Mexican War of

Independence, Nacogdoches was the target of a filibustering expedition led by Augustus W. Magee and Jose Bernardo Gutierrez de Lara. Accompanied by a force of Mexican revolutionaries and Anglos, their expedition took control of Nacogdoches in August of 1812. Nacogdoches again was the scene of bloody fights, during which authority was reestablished through execution and confiscation. But a year later, Spanish Royalists led by General Joaquín de Arredondo crushed that revolt. Most of the residents fled east, and by 1818 the area was virtually deserted.

American James Long led his filibustering troops to the area in 1819. When the Long expedition was defeated in October 1821, many settlers were again driven out of Texas, and Nacogdoches was again virtually abandoned. The population began growing following the passage of the Mexican Colonization Law of 1825. Empresario grants were given in the area surrounding Nacogdoches, including to men such as Frost Thorn and Haden Edwards. When Edwards challenged the validity of many previous land titles, he alienated many of the older settlers of the region. In 1826, in their effort to assert claims, Edwards' brother, and 30 followers rode into Nacogdoches, seized the Old Stone Fort, and declared the independence of Texas in a revolt known as the Fredonian Rebellion. Mexican militia defeated the revolt, and the Edwards brothers and the others were forced to flee.

Dissatisfaction with Mexico's immigration laws and problems with land titles started another revolt by Anglos and Mexicans living in the area, which resulted in a victory for the anti-government forces in the Battle of Nacogdoches in 1832.

The final and most successful revolt occurred in 1836 with the Texas Revolution. During the conflict, Texans fled in front of the approaching Mexican Army. Nacogdoches was virtually abandoned. But, with the defeat of General Santa Anna at the Battle of San Jacinto the residents of Nacogdoches returned en masse.

4. Stone Fort

Built in the 1700s by the Spanish (and named La Casa Piedra), this fort is reconstructed on Stephen F. Austin University's campus in Nacogdoches. Old Stone Fort is its modern name.

During the 1832 Battle of Nacogdoches, sometimes referred to as the opening gun of the Texas Revolution, Anglo settlers defied an order to surrender their arms to the commander of the Mexican troops, Colonel Piedras. Tension had been building since a law was passed in 1830 stopping immigration from the U. S. to Texas, and Mexican soldiers had been sent to East Texas to enforce that law. Texans in Nacogdoches, resisting changes in the law, organized a "National Militia." Colonel Piedras, fearing a disturbance in Nacogdoches similar to one that recently broken out on the Gulf at Fort Anahuac, garrisoned Mexican soldiers in the Stone Fort.

Texans from the Neches, the Sabine, and Shelby settlements met near Nacogdoches and elected James W. Bullock their captain. He demanded that Piedras rescind the law changes; but Piedras refused. When Bullock's militias entered the city they were shot at, and as they withdrew, Mexican cavalry attacked, charging up the main street. About 100 Texans remained, fighting house-to-house and capturing Stone Fort. The running gun battle that followed ended with the Texans capturing and disarming Piedras' troops at Douglass and sending them back to San Antonio. The battle was an important conflict. It cleared East Texas of Mexican rule and allowed citizens to live without that interference.

This fort had seen other important events. In 1800, the Spaniards used Stone Fort as a headquarters for operations against the filibusters, and after Philip Nolan was killed, some of his men were briefly jailed there. When the Gutierrez-Magee expedition entered Texas in 1812, their first stop was the Stone Fort. It was here also that General James Long proclaimed Texas' independence, sending the residents of Nacogdoches into hiding from his ruffians.

In the summer of 1838 a group of Nacogdoches citizens uncovered a plot of rebellion against the new Republic of Texas. This incident, known as the Cordova Rebellion, at first appeared to be nothing more than an isolated insurrection by local malcontents. Later evidence indicated the existence of a web of conspiracy.

The story commences on August 4th when a party of Hispanics fired on a group of Nacogdochians that were searching for stolen horses. It was found that 100 Mexicans led by Vicente Cordova, a wealthy Nacogdochian, were camped on the Angelina River. Thomas J. Rusk called up the Nacogdoches militia and sent runners to nearby settlements for help. Upon receiving news of this plot, President Houston issued a proclamation prohibiting unlawful assemblies and the carrying of arms. Two days later the leaders of the rebellion replied with their own proclamation, signed by Cordova and 18 others. It stated that they had taken up arms, were ready to die in defense of those rights, and only begged that their families not be harmed. On the same day Rusk learned that Cherokee Indians had joined Cordova's force, bringing that force to 400 men. This was bad news for the Texans as in the late 1836 President Sam Houston had learned that the Cherokees made a treaty with Mexico for a combined attack on Texas. If this was that attack, it would be a war of extermination. The Indians would receive title to their land from Mexico in return for their allegiance.

Major Henry W. Augustine of the Nacogdoches militia with only 150 men overtook the rebel army near Seguin and defeated it. The leaders of the insurrection escaped arrest and went into hiding. Cordova eventually made his way to Mexico. The capture of two Mexican agents after the rebellion produced evidence of an extensive Indian and Mexican conspiracy against Texas. Then, on August 20, 1838, a Mexican, Julian Pedro Miracle, was killed near the Red River.

On his body was a diary and papers indicated that it really was an official project of the Mexican government to incite the Cherokee Indians to fight against the Texans.

5. Presidio Nuestra Senora de Los Dolores de Las Tejas

According to some historical writings, the site of this presidio was never located after it was abandoned, but a commemorative marker erected in 1936 by the State of Texas is approximately 5 miles south of Douglass on Highway 225 at a dangerous, 10-mph curve.

The presidio was originally built along the east bank of the Neches River to protect Mission Tejas. A drought resulted in a poor harvest and hunger, and when a serious epidemic broke out, hundreds of Indians died. That mission and presidio had to struggle two years without receiving any supplies from Mexico because one supply train had to return to San Antonio when a hurricane blew in from the Gulf and made the journey impossible. Rumors of an imminent French attack following their assault (the "Chicken War") on the East Texas missions in 1719, caused the mission and presidio to be abandoned.

Presidio Nuestra Senora de Los Dolores de Las Tejas was reestablished in 1721. It was located four miles from the Angelina River and ten miles from the Mission de Nuestra Senora de la Purisima Concepcion de Los Hainai where the missionaries continued having difficulty in attracting Indians to come to the mission. Indians welcomed the small gifts Spanish missionaries frequently handed out, but they did not like the work that they were required to perform. The missionaries had to make frequent visits to the small Indian farm villages that dotted this area to encourage the Indians to return to their mission studies, and work. After an official inspection tour in 1727, it was recommended that partial abandonment of East Texas be made, and totally abandoning the Presidio Nuestra Senora de Los Dolores de Los Tejas.

Once the presidio was abandoned, there was no longer any protection for the missions of San Francisco de Los Neches, Nuestra Senora de la Purisima Conception de Los Hainai, and San Jose de Los Nazonis. These missions were moved to San Antonio.

6. Mission Senora de la Purisima Concepcion de Los Hainai

Mission Concepcion was first established in East Texas in 1716. Site of the mission is near springs of the Angelina River in a wooded area 7 miles east of Nacogdoches. To reach the site from Douglass, take Highway 225 approximately five miles south to a dangerous, 10-MPH curve. Follow CR 789 east 1.6 miles to Goodman's Bridge; turn left up the hill following the dirt road 100 yards. The marker on the left side of the road commemorates the mission site and the site of an old township, which has subsequently vanished. There may be another marker in the area, but it is now located on private property.

In 1731, when notice of the war between Spain and France reached the mission the French had already launched an attack on the Spanish holdings in East Texas. The commander of the French garrison on the Louisiana border had crossed into Spanish territory seizing San Miguel de Los Adaes (the most remote mission, and at that time the capital of the Texas territory). The nearby presidio was not garrisoned with sufficient troops to battle any formidable army, so the Spanish soldiers retreated to San Antonio. Friars at the missions in East Texas, including those at Concepcion, joined in the retreat with the soldiers. Any of the Christianized Indians who wanted were allowed to relocate with the missionaries, and many did.

7. Mission San Jose de Los Nazonis

Founded in 1716 by the Captain Domingo Ramon expedition, this mission was located north of the present town of Cushing on a branch of the Shawnee Creek. A marker on the site (now private property) designates its location. The mission had the same fate as that of the other East Texas missions. It was moved to a site at Barton's Springs near present-day Austin, then moved to San Antonio, and combined with two missions. There it was renamed as the Mission San Juan Capistrano (see region three), and may be seen in San Antonio on the Mission Trail.

A legend surrounding the missions in East Texas, is the story of Angelina (the "Little Angel"). When a 1693 Spanish expedition came into this area they found a little Indian girl who was so gentle that the expedition named her Angelina. The girl was interested in learning and when the Spanish left the area they took the girl with them to Mission San Juan Bautista on the Rio Grande where she studied and learned Spanish. Angelique, as the missionaries called her, later returned to East Texas and was there when the Spanish came again establishing missions. Because she could speak both the dialects of her tribe and fluent Spanish, the missionaries made her their interpreter. One of the first missions that they founded was Mission Concepcion in Anglique's village, which places the mission on the Angelina River.

8. Cook's Fort

Joseph Thomas Cook, a veteran of the War of 1812, received a Spanish land grant of 4,000 acres in 1835 in present-day Cherokee County. In 1836, after serving in the revolution and as a Texas Ranger he received another land grant for his services. Two years later, he employed men in a militia to build a fort and stockade on a major roadway on land adjacent to his home. The fort was to be used for his family and passing travelers as protection against raiding Indians. After the fortress was torn down, as Indian raids decreased, the site became the location of a settlement, "Cook's Fort." In 1846, residents of the new settlement moved to Rusk.

Reports that the Confederates had a gun factory and ironworks built near the fort are contradicted by the dates of the fort's existence. There is a 1936 commemorative marker 3 miles southeast of Rusk on FM 241.

9. Lacy's Fort

The Killough Massacre in October 1838 was reported to have been the largest single human slaughter by Indians in East Texas. Victims included Isaac Killough, Sr. and 17 members of his extended family who had immigrated to Texas the year before. Only a few of the whites survived and they eventually made their way to Lacy's Fort for refuge.

Killough, his four sons, his two daughters and their husbands, and two single men had settled seven miles northwest of Jacksonville on land that was part of a larger tract originally granted to the

Cherokees under the Sam Houston and John Forbes' treaty in 1836. However, the Republic of Texas' Senate had nullified the treaty in December 1837, and portions of the land were sold to the Killoughs and other settlers. Cancellation of the treaty and the arrival of new settlers caused resentment among the Indians. Also the Cordova Rebellion (see Stone Fort for more information) contributed to tension between the settlers and the Indians in the area.

News of the massacre quickly spread, and a militia led by General Thomas Rusk set out to find the attackers. After reaching Fort Houston, they received word that the band was camped at an old Kickapoo village near Frankston. The next day Rusk and his men attacked. During the skirmish that followed 11 members of the Indian group were killed. This massacre was the final chapter of the Cordova Rebellion, where deep-seated resentments aroused by the cancellation of Houston's treaty and the constant arrival of settlers led to the Cherokee War the following year. That war would make Lacy's Fort an active site once again as hundreds of militia and volunteers met at this fortress on their way to fight at Fort Houston, Camp Johnston, and Fort Kickapoo (which was located in present-day Louisiana).

The site of Lacy's Fort is located two miles from present-day Alto. The fort was only a defensive fortification most likely consisting of a stockade and log blockhouse. An Indian Agent, Martin Lacy, built it around 1835, to guard against Indian uprisings. After Alto was founded nearby in 1849 most fort settlers moved there.

A stone marker commemorating the victims of the Killough massacre was erected at the site in the late 1930s, and in 1965 a state historical marker was placed there. West of Alto on Highway 21 is a 1936 state marker commemorating Lacy's Fort.

10. Mission San Francisco de Los Tejas (Also Mission San Francisco de Los Neches and Mission Santisimo Nombre de Maria)
(See colored pictures in the center section)

As discussed in the descriptions of the previous East Texas mission in this region, the Spanish began to settle Texas in order to block French efforts to move westward. Mexico and New Mexico were then considered by Spain to be more valuable than Texas and

Spain did not want the French advancing towards those provinces. Spanish soldiers and missionaries venture here into the woodland home of the Caddo Indians was far beyond their existing settlements.

The Caddos were composed of 25 to 30 different groups that shared a language, political structure, and religious beliefs and ceremonies. The westernmost of these tribes in the 1690s were the Hasinai Indians, whom some historians believe may have had a civilization as advanced as that of the Spanish. Hasinais included a tribe named Tejas, from whom Texas got its name. The Tejas had villages on the present-day Angelina and Neches rivers.

When news that the French explorer LaSalle had established a settlement near the Texas Gulf coast, the Spanish accelerated their efforts for colonizing the area in the eastern portion of Texas. Mission San Francisco de Los Tejas was the first mission established in eastern Texas in 1690-93. Initially the Indians had welcomed the mission, but following their crop failures and epidemics, their hostility grew.

Father Damien Massanet, the founder of Mission Tejas, once mounted a cannon in its doorway to resist Indian attacks. The priest was instrumental in establishing other missions in East Texas: in Nacogdoches, near Douglass, near Cushing, and further to the south at San Augustine. All of the original East Texas missions were later abandoned, and the Indians who had converted to Christianity were allowed to move with the missions. When Mission Nuestra Padre San Francisco de Los Tejas was moved and reestablished in 1721 at a new site to the east of the Neches River, six miles west of the site of present-day Alto, it was renamed Mission San Francisco de Los Neches.

In 1730, after the abandonment of the Presidio Nuestra Senora de Los Dolores de Los Tejas, Mission San Francisco de Los Neches was moved at the request of the missionaries to the Colorado River in the vicinity of present-day Zilker Park, in Austin. A year later it was moved to its final location in San Antonio River and renamed the Mission San Francisco de la Espada.

In Mission Tejas State Park, near Weches off Camino Real Trail (Highway 21), is a reconstructed version of the Mission San Francisco de Las Tejas. The original mission was built of poles, mud, and grass (see an artist interpretation in the Visitors Center in

Nacogdoches).

Nearby was Mission Santisimo Nombre de Maria that was founded in 1690 along the Neches River. Maria lived a very short life, as a flood destroyed it.

11. Brown's Fort

Possibly the earliest settlement fort in Texas was Brown's Fort, built around 1833 in northeastern Houston County by Reuben Brown. It was built for his wife Sarah and his family, and for members of Daniel Parker's family. Sarah Brown was one of the Parker's daughters.

The Browns and Parkers came to Texas from Illinois intent to establish a Baptist Church, but a Mexican colonization law prohibited anything but the organization of a Catholic Church (one of the steps the Mexican government had taken to decrease the number of new Anglos). However, Brown went on to form Pilgrim's Church at Elkhart, the oldest Protestant church in Texas, as part of the Primitive Baptist faith in Texas. After the Parker congregation moved on to establish Fort Parker, Brown became a founder of the Belle Brown Farm in 1837, five miles east of present-day Grapeland. There the Brown family established a community named Refuge.

In 1836, Indians attacked Fort Parker and several settlers were killed. In addition, one of the most famous Indian kidnappings of frontier times occurred when the Indians took 9-year old Cynthia Ann Parker. (Her story is told in this region, see "Fort Parker.") After the Fort Parker massacre, members of the Parker family returned to Brown's Fort for protection.

The Refuge Cemetery still remains. Reuben Brown and his wife, Sarah Parker, and other settlers of Brown's Fort are buried there. Turn right off of Highway 21 on to Highway 227 two miles west of Weches. The cemetery is on the north side of the road 5 miles east of Grapeland.

12. Fort Henderson

This Texas Ranger fort was built by Major William H. Smith's battalion early in 1837 and commanded by Captain Lee C. Smith as part of the defensive line established by the Republic of Texas against marauding plains Indians. The fort was named for General James Pinckney Henderson. It was on the upper Navasota River near the present boundaries of Robertson and Leon counties. At that time this area was deep in Indian country. The fort was difficult to supply and of questionable defensive use. For those reasons the fort was abandoned soon after its construction, probably in the fall of 1837. There are no visible ruins.

13. Fort Trinidad

Established around 1805, along the Trinity River on Camino Real highway (now Highway 21) between Midway and Crockett, the settlement of Trinidad (also a fort) was an important location in the early history of the development of Texas. While Mexico and Latin America were in revolt against Spain, Texas was also occupied by war. The filibusters Jose Bernardo Gutierrez de Lara and Augustus William Magee, aided by the United States, organized their own "Republican Army of the North" to take control of Texas. With a green flag for a banner, they entered Texas through the Neutral Ground on August 7 1812, then marched west capturing Nacogdoches, Trinidad, and La Bahia (present-day Goliad).

The Republican Army of the North then marched in the direction of San Antonio. When news reached Mexico, a Spanish Royalist army under General Joaquin de Arredondo was sent from near Laredo on the Rio Grande to put down the rebellion. Arredondo's force of 1,400 men included Anglos, Texans, Indians, and Spanish Royalists.

The Army of the North, led by General Jose Alvarez de Toledo y Dubois, planned to ambush the Royalists as they traveled and camped his forces about six miles from Arredondo's camp between the Atascosa and Medina rivers. On the morning of August 18 1813, however, General Arredondo's scouts located the Army of the North and prepared an earthwork defense. Arredondo ordered his men not to shoot at the rebels until they were within 40 paces. After the four-hour fight between infantry, cavalry, and artillery, the Army of the North broke and ran.

At Fort Trinidad, Arredondo's forces caught the troops of the Army of the North. The Royalists killed all but fewer than 100 who escaped in the bloodiest battle ever fought on U.S soil, the Battle of

Medina. Arredondo troops then butchered all of the Trinidad settlers. This action and Indian raids that followed destroyed Trinidad. A small community named Spanish Bluff was later built on the site, but it has also vanished. A commemorative marker is placed along the south side of Highway 21 between Midway and the Trinity River.

14. Fort Boggy

In 1840, minutemen under the command of Thomas N.B. Greer established Fort Boggy near Centerville as the headquarters of the Boggy–Trinity Rangers. Fort Boggy was a typical blockhouse that protected the area's settlements. The fort was originally located 5 miles south on Boggy Creek at a site that was destroyed with the building of Interstate 45.

Greer had served at San Jacinto during the Texas Revolution where he manned the famous Twin Sisters cannon. Later he served under John H. Moore in a victory against the Comanches on the upper Colorado River in 1840s. Indians killed Greer while he was serving as a Texas Ranger in 1842.

A State Park is being built on Boggy Creek south of Centerville to commemorate Fort Boggy. Further south along the Trinity River is the sight of several ghost settlements including the settlements of Brookfields Bluff and Halls Bluff where sternwheelers moving up the river brought the area supplies from Galveston.

15. (Mission) Nuestra Senora del Pilar de Bucareli

History does not refer to this as a mission, but it had all of the characteristics of the early missions. It had a name similar to a mission, a chapel, a guardhouse, and settlers, and it played an important role in the development of East Texas.

Bucareli was a Spanish settlement on the Trinity River, probably near the Robbins Ferry crossing in Madison County, northeast of present-day Midway. Spanish colonists dissatisfied with the law that prohibited their trade with the French in nearby present-day Louisiana had been accused of smuggling and ordered from their East Texas homes. They lived for a brief time in San Antonio until they persuaded the Viceroy, Antonio María de Bucareli y Ursua, to permit their returning to East Texas. Permission was granted for a settlement at the site where the San Antonio Road crossed the Trinity River. The settlement was named Nuestra Senora del Pilar de Bucareli, and it was exempted from civil taxation and church tithes for ten years.

Bucareli was founded in September 1774, and soon had 20 houses of hewn wood, and numerous huts. The community prospered, reportedly because of its illicit trade with the French. Nevertheless, raids by Comanches and epidemics in 1777 and 1778, caused the settlers to desert Bucareli and move back to East Texas without official permission. Another version of this sites' history reports that the Spanish, after defeating the filibusters near La Bahia, came to Bucareli, burned the town, and killed many settlers. The surviving settlers led by Antonio Gil Ibarvo established what is present-day Nacogdoches.

The probable version of this story has the Spanish settlers being exiled from a mission near Louisiana because they were illegally trading with the French and other settlers in Texas. This was a practice that Spain did not allow because of the monopolies it had established in trading and freighting goods from Spain to Texas. The monopolies made the costs of goods almost prohibitive to the settlers in East Texas. Bucareli's settlers were allowed to move to Nacogdoches at a later date because of the hardships they suffered here.

The fact that the settlement had a church and sanctions from the church indicates it was truly a mission. The guardhouse, probably a blockhouse that was common in that era, was indeed a fortification to protect the settlers.

Also of historical importance was the nearby Bedias Road or Bedias Trail, an Indian trail at the time of Spanish and French exploration, connecting a Bidai Indian village on Santo Tomas Creek with another settlement at or near present-day Nacogdoches. The trail crossed the Trinity River at Paso Tomas, the site of Bucareli, passed the Bidai village at the Don Joaquín crossing of the Angelina River, 10 miles south of Nacogdoches, and then turned north toward Nacogdoches.

A state commemorative marker for Nuestra Senora del Pilar de Bucareli is located only a few yards west of the Trinity River bridge on the north side of Highway 21.

16. Dunn's Fort (Also Fort Welch)

Dunn's Fort was established southwest of Wheelock in 1832. It was a combination land office-courthouse, but it was initially built for defense. A state commemorative marker is at the original site southwest of Wheelock close to the Robertson-Brazos county border.

Not too far from Wheelock was a Fort Welch, of which nothing but the name remains. It was probably a family blockhouse as the Welch family name is prominent in the area. This was also near the area where the 1836 massacre of the Harvey family occurred one Sunday night. An Indian raiding party attacked the family of John Harvey while they were at prayer. Mrs. Harvey's Bible was later found, blood stained. Mr. and Mrs. Harvey and their son were all killed. A servant girl and the Harvey's daughter, Ann, were taken captive. Ransom requested for Ann was only a few blankets. An uncle found the girl in Mexico four years later and brought her home. Nothing was ever heard of the servant girl.

A state commemorate marker is located on the west side of Highway 6 between Hearne and Calvert near the site of the Harvey massacre.

17. Fort Sullivan and Fort Nashville

In the vicinity of where Highways 79 and190 and FM 485 cross the Brazos were the now ghost towns Nashville (it had a fort) and Fort (Port) Sullivan. Both have disappeared leaving an interesting history. As early as 1843, the settlements' developers dreamed of establishing Fort Sullivan as a port for steamboats moving up the Brazos River, and by 1845, a steamboat was driven up to the mouth of nearby Little River. It is recorded that even a piano was brought up the river on a steamboat from Galveston. In nearby Nashville, there were more than 20 stores and a population of 1,000. Then both of the communities vanished without a trace.

A former resident, George B. Erath, wrote: "It is well that Nashville is wiped from the map, and it would be well if its scenes could be entirely forgotten and the vapors carry the stench of the bloody barbarism to the four winds." Remembering when neither the Texas Rangers nor the government could protect settlers from

Indians, Erath was also to remember and write in his journal: "at the end of one religious service conducted by a Baptist preacher, Indians raided the fort and killed two men in the congregation."

18. Fort Oldham

The home of William P. Oldham served as a temporary fort and refuge for settlers in the area during Indian alarms. Oldham had been a Major in the war for independence, where he had participated in the Siege of Bexar. He then served in the First Company of Texas Cavalry and later joined the Somervell and Mier Expeditions to counter Mexican raids in 1842. Captured by Mexicans while on the Mier expedition, William Oldham escaped and fought his way home.

After the escape, the Mexicans punished the remaining prisoners in what is remembered as the Black Bean Episode. Under Santa Anna's orders, every tenth man was to be executed. There were 176 beans placed in a jar, one for each prisoner. Seventeen of the beans were black and the remainding beans were white. Each prisoner selected a bean from the jar. Lucky prisoners who selected white beans were eventually released, though many died in prison before that happened. One prisoner, Big Foot Wallace, noticed that the black beans were poured into the jar on top of the white beans, so when his turn came, he picked a bean from the bottom. It was a white bean. Prisoners who selected the black beans were executed by a firing squad.

Oldham's sons Giles, Henry, Hugo and Otho Oldham and a son-in-law, James Early are buried behind a barbed wire fence in "Old Oldham Cemetery". Visitors beware that behind that fence is also a bull that has been known to express his displeasure at anyone climbing that fence, but he apparently enjoys having his picture photographed as he poses by the big kettle.

A coincidence: While escaping from Mexico after the Mier Expedition, 5 of the escapees, died of starvation, 3 were never heard from, and 4 made it back to Texas. Oldham was among the lucky four. The escapees had to eat snakes and grasshoppers and do whatever it took to find something to drink to survive through the wild and rugged land. Oldham (with John Rufus Alexander) was starving when he found a live animal. The two men wrestled it to the

ground and broke its neck. Afraid to start a fire, they ate raw meat. That animal was a big black bull.

To get to the cemetery (nothing remains of the old fortification) take FM 1362, south from Cook's Point for 2.4 miles; turn left on the road marked by a sign "Old Oldham Cemetery."

19. Fort Parker

(See colored pictures in the center section)

The gates were opened to allow a cool breeze to blow through the fort as a bright and hot early summer sun was burning down on May 19, 1836. No one had noticed Comanches, waving a truce flag, riding towards the fort until the Indians were almost inside. Ben Parker stepped out to meet the Indians as his father and the men of the fort were busy working in the nearby fields.

When Ben refused to give the Comanches any beef, the Indians became angry and killed young Parker then rode into the fort scalping any men and raping the women. Hearing the noise, men of the fort ran from the fields, firing their rifles, but it was too late. The Comanches had killed all men inside, raped most of the women, and then had ridden off taking two women, two young boys, and a young nine-year old girl. The girl, Cynthia Ann Parker, became famous.

Indians since prehistoric times had taken captives whose survival depended on the whims of their captors. Mature males were killed; captive white women were either used as concubines for braves, given menial roles, or given as slaves to the women of the tribe; often the worse fate. Young boys were frequently adopted by the tribe and taught the Indian ways. Children who lagged behind when the

attackers moved out, or babies who cried, were often brutally killed.

Sometimes, however, a young girl or woman would be treated with much respect. That is apparently what happened to young Cynthia Ann Parker. The leader of the raid, Peta Nocona, took the girl as his wife. She gave birth to Quanah Parker who became a great Comanche chief.

Of the other kidnap victims, Sam Houston later purchased one woman from Delaware Indians, and General Zachary Taylor ransomed two boys in 1842. Cynthia Ann Parker did not want to return home when she and her small daughter were later rescued. Neither Cynthia Ann nor her daughter was able to adjust to white culture and both died soon after being rescued.

Next to the Alamo and Presidio La Bahia, the Parker family fort may be the most famous in Texas history. Reconstructed Fort Parker is between Groesbeck and Mexia off Highway 14. There is a commemorative monument in the nearby Fort Parker cemetery for settlers killed there. The fort is open 9 a.m. to 5 p.m. (10 a.m. to 6 p.m. during the summer).

20. Fort Tenoxtitlan

After Mexican won its Independence from Spain, General Manuel de Mier y Teran built military garrisons on the frontier to promote Mexican expansion and check illegal immigration and smuggling. Teran's plan was to establish a fort halfway down the San Antonio Road (now Highway 21) where the road crosses the Brazos River en route to Nacogdoches.

In 1830, the famous Alamo de Parras Flying Company built Fort Tenoxtitlan under command of Lieutenant Colonel Jose Francisco Ruiz. The garrison's permanent site was on a bluff on the west bank of the Brazos 12 miles above the San Antonio crossing, opposite from where the present Brazos and Robertson county line meet the river. Fortifications themselves were made of logs available in the area. Teran envisioned Tenoxtitlan would be the future capital of Texas and had sent elaborate instructions from Matamoros for the design of the fort.

Despite the ban on American settlement, the nearby farming community included a number of American immigrants. In late October 1830, Major Sterling C. Robertson of the Texas (or Fort Nashville) Association, appeared at Tenoxtitlan requesting permission to select a settlement site for 50 American families accompanying him. Robertson carried a colonization contract that his group had made with the authorities. (The official invalidation of this contract would reach the fort a few months later). Colonel Ruiz, who was Texas-born and sympathetic to the settlers, did not follow orders to capture the colonists and turn them over to the authorities. (As Fort Nashville was built, Ruiz apparently did give his permission.)

In 1832, depressed in the failure of his plan to settle Mexicans in the Texas wilderness, Mier y Teran committed suicide, and a demoralized Colonel Ruiz abandoned Tenoxtitlan. He began evacuation of the fort and the entire Mexican settlement to San

Antonio in August 1832. A trading post and settlement continued in the vicinity for years, but it disappeared after 1860.

Duty at the fort may have been interesting, as one of the garrison's most important duties was to assist in the transportation of military funds from San Antonio to Nacogdoches. There is however no record of the soldiers that were transporting gold coins ever being attacked.

A commemorative marker was erected west of Cooks Point in a rest and picnic area off of State Highway 21 five miles east of Caldwell. There are two commemorative markers in the rest area. The one about Tenoxtitlan's is in the center of the turnaround. In Spanish, Tenoxtitlan means "Prickly Pear Place". It is also a name given to early Mexico City by the Aztecs.

21. Camp Chambers (Falls County)

A regular army post near the site of present-day Marlin in Falls County, Fort Chambers was established in May or June of 1840 on the east bank of the Brazos River, two miles north of the present-day Highway 7 crossing. Captain John Holiday's Company D, 1st Infantry Regiment that joined with Colonel William Gordon Cooke's First garrisoned it. Both were part of forces established for the Texas Military Road.

In December 1839, the Congress of the Republic of Texas passed a law directing the military to cut a road between Austin and Fort Inglish (now Bonham). The road was intended to connect a series of forts to be erected from San Patricio northward to a point on the Red River.

Colonel William Gordon Cooke was in charge of the expedition. In the fall of 1840, they began a road on the Texas side of the Red River in what is now northwest Red River County and which terminated at the Brazos. They angled towards the east from near present-day Abbott and followed a route close to that of present-day Interstate Highway 35.

A drought, loss of supplies, bitter cold, and a scarcity of game delayed the effort to construct the forts. Cooke camped north of Fort Inglish and after establishing Fort Johnston, southwest of Coffee's trading post, he chose not to terminate the road there because of the western settlements that would be left unprotected. Instead, he led a westward search for hostile Indians, north of the Red River, past the North Fork and over the Pease River before returning to Austin in 1841. Interest in the Military Road diminished when Houston temporarily became the capital in 1842. However, the road that developed along Cooke's passage became an early day thoroughfare for the immigrants. It became knows as the Shawnee Trail, the route of the first great southwest cattle drive trail.

A detachment under Captain Adam Clendenin replaced Holiday's troops at Camp Chambers. His detachment moved to Waco in December, but returned in January 1841. There they remained until March, when they moved to Austin for discharge. Nothing remains.

22. Fort Milam (And Fort Burleson)

The tiny village of Sarahville de Viesca, now Viesca, near present-day Marlin, was built on a bluff overlooking the Brazos River. It was the location of Fort Milam and at the location of an Indian battleground in the early days when Indians continually harassed the settlers. The fort was in the line of forts established to protect against raiding Kiowas and Comanche Indians during 1837–1838. Other forts built at that time were Little River Fort, Fort Colorado and Fort Houston. In 1839, a second Fort Milam was built 2 miles south from present-day Marlin on the east bank of the Brazos a few miles east of the old Fort Milam. Lieutenant Colonel William S. Fisher, on August 26, 1839, ordered the name of the post changed to Fort Burleson, in honor of Edward Burleson, commander of the Army of the Republic.

The new fort was a response to Indians attacking that winter. It was built and manned by the Milam Guards under Captain Joseph Daniels. Its fortification was 150 feet square, built from double-blanked cedar pickets and 11 feet high with bastions at each angle. The Milam Guards were a company of riflemen from Houston and the first recorded militia unit to form after Texas became independent from Mexico. The 75 men of the unit were required to provide their own tents, wagons, and camp equipment during active duty. They functioned as an escort unit, as a police force, and as frontier guards for the Republic of Texas during 1838 and 1839.

After Daniels' men departed the fort in mid-February, Lieutenant

William G. Evans marched 34 Houston volunteers, nicknamed the Travis Spies, into the fort on April 3. Captain John Bird raised an additional company that arrived at Fort Milam on May 6. There these two companies remained through the spring and summer. In 1842, the unit volunteered in the effort to repel the Mexican invasion, but had only reached Columbus when General Adrian Woll's retreat toward the Rio Grande prompted the government to order the Milam Guard to turn back.

The troops were later moved to nearby Camp Chambers. Fort Milam–Burleson passed into private hands and was maintained by local citizens until danger of Indian attacks had passed. Any remains of the old fort are not accessible. A state commemorative marker has disappeared.

23. Little River Fort (Also know as Fort Smith and Fort Griffin, and Fort Bryant)

This was one of a line of forts established to protect against raiding Indians. Other forts along the line were Fort Milam and Fort Colorado. These three forts were credited with making a significant contribution to the lull in the warfare during 1837–1838 between white settlers and the Kiowas and Comanche Indians. Texas Rangers Sergeant George B Erath, Lieutenant Charles Curtis, and Captain Daniel Monroe commanded this fort. It was first called Fort Smith (another Fort Smith was to be later built further north) after Major William H. Smith. It then received its official name from its proximity to the Little River settlement that it was built to protect. After 1841, the name was changed to Fort Griffin in honor of a local settler, Moses Griffin, who maintained the fort for two years after the government abandoned it.

The fort covered half an acre near the junction of the Leon and Lampasas rivers in what is now Bell County. Six or seven cabins stood against the north wall of a 9-foot-high stockade, and a 16-foot-square blockhouse provided additional defense. Fights between the garrison and the Comanches were fought during 1837. In 1839, Rangers on patrol fought with Indians who outnumbered them by

240 to 35. Indians who formed a battle-line commenced to yell from one end of the line to the other then attacked. The Rangers, from behind a hastily erected barricade, opened fire causing the Indians to retreat. Under cover of darkness the Rangers safely escaped.

As the frontier moved west, Little River Fort went unoccupied for nearly two years after the Rangers withdrew to bolster the defenses of Forts Colorado and Milam and the fort at the town of Nashville. After that, the fort saw only sporadic use, serving as a stop for the ill-fated Santa Fe Expedition in June 1841, and then used as a shelter for a Ranger company during 1846.

A story of treasure hidden in the area around Little River Fort still survives. A German settler by the name of Karl Steinheimer had joined the filibuster Louis Aury's efforts to make his private kingdom of Texas. Steinheimer later moved to Mexico where he struck it rich in mining. He then returned to Texas with a treasure of loads of silver and gold that he was taking to Saint Louis to seek the hand of a lady in marriage, but Texas was in an uproar at the time. The Texans considered him a Mexican so he traveled on the back roads. Steinheimer made his way north to where three streams combine into one (where the Little River is formed) and it was there that he decided to bury most of the treasure, keeping only a small sum of gold for his journey. Karl, according to the legend, then marked the location by driving a large brass spike into an oak tree.

While he continued his journey, Indians attacked Steinheimer. Though he was wounded and dying, he made his way further north where he met up with others traveling north and told them his story. Giving them a letter that contained a map of where the treasure was buried, he asked that they have the letter delivered to his lady in Saint Louis. According to the story, they did. After fighting in Texas subdued, friends of the lady came to find where the ten mule-loads of gold and silver were buried, but they, like everyone since, found nothing.

The Texas Historical Commission in 1936 marked the site of Little River Fort with a commemorative marker on the north side of FM 436 five miles southeast of Belton at the city limits of Little River-Academy. There are no visible ruins of the fort.

Nearby was Fort Bryant. It was Colonel Ben Bryant's family

fort built in 1841 with a blockhouse for defense against Indians. Bryant had moved from Fort Tenoxtitlan with his and several other families. It was along the Little River in Bell County near the Milam County line. The settlement grew into a town, Bryant's Station, then it disappeared in the 1880s.

24. Black's Fort

William Black moved to a site on the South San Gabriel River in eastern Burnet County with his wife, their five daughters, and three sons in 1851. The house was built from native stone. It was a thick-walled, two-room structure with a springhouse as a storage place for supplies and ammunition. A surrounding stockade was built with cedar logs to protect local settlers and the Black family. Guns and ammunition were available at the fort for public use.

A formidable structure, Black's Fort saw little service, as most raids occurred in other parts of the county, but the home served as a fortress until 1868. Thereafter, it continued to be used as a residence. In 1936, the Texas Centennial Commission placed a marker on the site. The reported ruins are on private land east of Highway 1174 off of a county road near the marker for a Strickland settlement. Strickland is no longer there but the marker is north of Bertram, just south of the intersection of FM 1174 with Highway 963. A cemetery remains near the road.

25. Fort Croghan (Also known as McCulloch's Station, Camp Croghan and Camp Hamilton)

A United States military post was established in 1849 at McCulloch's Station, on Hamilton Creek 3 miles south of present-day Burnet. Henry E. McCulloch and his Texas Rangers were stationed there when the Commander of Company A of the Second Dragoons, Lieutenant C. H. Tyler, chose the site for a fort. A new location was chosen on October 12 and the fort was built 3 miles above the first site. This post known as Camp Croghan, then Camp Hamilton was finally named Fort Croghan, in honor of Colonel George Croghan.

Buildings were made of oak covered with shingles. Officers'

quarters were 4 log houses, each with 2 rooms separated by a hall. The hospital was a four-room log house. In 1852, the fort became headquarters of the Second Dragoons, but the government started removing its troops in 1853. A small guard remained when orders were issued to abandon the fort in 1855.

Burnet County's Historical Society have moved buildings that had been built at the time of the fort from original locations to a site on Highway 29 west of the Highway 281 intersection. Descendants of the settlers contributed nineteenth century articles to furnish the buildings. April to November, it is open to the public on Thursday through Saturday between 10 a.m. and 5 p.m.

Burnet might have become the home of another fort had Sam Houston had his way. In 1860 when Sam Houston returned from being U. S. Senator to again become Governor of Texas he sent word to 23 frontier counties to form companies and establish a camp in which to train. To arm the new companies he requested all Texas counties to return to Austin all of the arms and ammunition that the state had loaned to them. He also asked the U. S. Secretary of War for arms to equip 3,000 men, and he proposed that he would recruit 5,000 men for service on the Texas frontier. At this same time, he wrote the Secretary of the Interior requesting all of the Indians of the Southwest be settled in Texas, under control of a Texas agency, which he would establish.

What grand scheme did Houston envision? Whatever his plan was, the government in Washington turned down his requests, and the Civil War intervened. Historian have built a case that he had plans to again mount his horse and lead Texans to battle. Armed by the equipment he requested, Houston envisioned a force of Texas Rangers allied with the Indians in a campaign to "liberate" the Mexican people and bring that country into the United States. Of course, this also would have brought fame and glory to Sam Houston, which was part of the plan. Letters by Houston to financiers in London for support give some credence to this story. Burnet, like the other counties, never received a new fort and Houston never became the President of the U. S.

26. Fort Tumlinson (Also known as Tumlinson's blockhouse)

In 1836, Captain John Jackson Tumlinson, Jr., of the Rangers charged with patrolling and protecting the new Anglo settlements along the Colorado River north of Austin, built this fort on Brushy Creek in present-day Williamson County. Tumlinson had traveled to Texas with his parents in 1821. When Indians killed his father 2 years later, John and his brother Joseph and other settlers tracked and killed the guilty parties. In 1835, when a Lieutenant in Robert M. Coleman's command John Jr., participated in the Battle of Gonzales and the Siege of Bexar.

Under government orders to defend settlers from Indian raids he organized a company of Rangers who defended what became known as the Tumlinson Blockhouse. Hearing the news that Santa Anna had invaded, Tumlinson left to go fight the Mexicans. After the revolution he served as a Texas Ranger.

The area around the fort was also the site of an Indian attack in 1838. Near Brushy Creek between the North and South Forks of the San Gabriel River, near present-day Leander, Indians attacked a group of 13 families that were enroute to build a settlement in west Texas. Led by John Webster, the men circled their wagons to form a defense but to no avail. All of the men were killed. Mrs Webster and her two children were taken captive. She with her daughter later escaped from the Indians when the Indians went to the Council in San Antonio. Her son was ransomed two years later. A commemorative marker was placed at the burial site of the men who were killed in what was to be named "the Webster Massacre".

There is a state historical marker on Highway 183 near present-day Leander noting the location of Fort Tumlinson.

27. Camp Cazneau (Also know as Camp Caldwell, and one of the several Camp Cooke)

Located adjacent to Kenny Fort, east of present-day Round Rock, Camp Cazneau was on Brushy Creek at the Double File Trail Crossing created by Indians passing through the area. It was used in 1840 by the Travis Guards and Rifles under the command of George W. Bonnell when he led raids against the Comanches in May and June of that year. This was probably the site of Camp Caldwell, which was a regular Texas army camp in 1839-1840. Camp Cazneau was named for William L. Cazneau, a merchant, soldier and commissary general of the Republic.

In 1841, the site was one of the assembly points for volunteers for the Texan Santa Fe Expedition. This expedition was sent to Santa Fe by President Mirabeau B. Lamar in an effort to divert to Texas at least a part of the trade carried over the Santa Fe Trail. Texas needed trade and Lamar also wanted to offer the New Mexicans a chance to be annexed by Texas.

Without Texas Congressional approval, President Lamar authorized the expedition and a call for volunteers was issued. Merchants were invited to ship goods with a promise of a military force to provide protection for their goods and teamsters. The total number of participants was 321 with 21 wagons carrying supplies, as well as the merchandise valued at $200,000.

On June 19 1841, the party officially designated the Santa Fe Pioneers, set out from Kenney's Fort. By August, they had been harassed by Indians, lacked sufficient provisions and suffered from a scarcity of water. Then their Mexican guide deserted them. The Texans had expected to be welcomed by the citizens of New Mexico and certainly did not anticipate armed resistance. Nevertheless, the Governor of New Mexico, learning of the expedition, sent troops to wait for the Texans' arrival. A member of the first delegation to reach New Mexico turned traitor and persuaded others in the expedition to lay down their guns. The Mexicans defeated the Texans, reduced in number by the journey and broken in health and spirit, without the firing of a single shot, and the goods from the expedition passed into Mexican hands. The Texans were then beaten and marched as prisoners to Mexico City where they later participated in the black bean drawing with the survivors of the ill-fated Mier Expedition of 1842. In New Mexico the Santa Fe expedition is noted in history as the Texas invasion of 1843.

East of Round Rock is a commemorative marker for Kenney Fort. Camp Cazneau on Brushy Creek was adjacent to that fort. Another camp named Cazneau was located on Onion Creek southeast of Austin. The Texas First Infantry Regiment moved to this camp from Camp Caldwell, and then in 1840 it was moved to San Antonio.

Camp Cooke, built on the Colorado River near the mouth of Waller Creek near present-day Austin, was also one of the assembly sites in 1841 for volunteers for the Texas Santa Fe Expedition. The camp was named for William Gordon Cooke, a civilian commissioner on the expedition. This camp was closed after the expedition was assembled.

28. Kenney Fort

In the summer of 1839, Dr. Thomas Kenney, who served during the Texas Revolution as the surgeon with the Mina Volunteers, built Kenney Fort for his wife and family east of present-day Round Rock. Other settlers joined in relocating to the fort. The fort was built by placing picket fences between the settlers' cabins to form a gated, rectangular fortification.

Life at the fort was not dull as it had its share of Indian raids. It was a place where the Texan Santa Fe Expedition of 1841 stopped. (See Camp Cazneau) Kenny's Fort was also the site of the March 1842 "Archives War." This was an argument over possession of the territory's official records and land grants. When the Mexican army under General Rafael Vasquez in 1842 appeared at San Antonio demanding the surrender of the town, President Sam Houston directed that the Texas archive be removed from Austin and taken to the city of Houston. Citizens of Austin, fearing that the president wanted to make Houston the capital (which he did), formed a vigilante committee and warned that an attempt to move state papers would face resistance.

President Houston called the Seventh Congress into session at Washington-on-the-Brazos and in late December 1842 sent Texas Rangers under Colonel Thomas I. Smith and Captain Eli Chandler to Austin with orders to remove the archives, but not to resort to bloodshed. Vigilantes in Austin were not prepared for the raid. The Rangers loaded the archives in wagons and drove away. On January 1, 1843, a vigilante committee, under Captain Mark B. Lewis, with a cannon from the arsenal overtook the wagons at Kenney Fort on Brushy Creek. Only a few shots were fired before the Rangers, in order to avoid bloodshed, gave up the papers. The archives were returned to Austin where they still remain. Austin became the capital again in 1844.

A Kenny Fort commemorative marker is located on Highway 79 east of Round Rock. Another marker located at the Texas State Library in Austin tells of the Archives War, and a third marker on Highway 79 tells of Kenney Fort and a Double File Trail made by Indians.

29. Camp Austin

In 1846, during the Mexican War, a detachment of the 2nd Dragoons of the U. S. Army was moved from Indian Territory to Austin. Their camp, like many other holding camps at the time had no name. Two years later, the camp was named Camp Austin and was more involved with paperwork than patrols. It included temporary shanties of cedar posts, weatherboard and shingles. A member of the garrison stationed in Austin was Albert Sidney Johnston, who later became famous as a general for the Confederacy. As the paymaster at Camp Austin, Johnston became a legend by keeping the funds of the garrison in gold and silver. He made a bimonthly trip to every other camp, carrying the coins in a small, iron chest. He was never robbed.

Picket fences surrounded the camp, which consisted of 7 buildings including a hospital, officers' quarters, kitchen and mess hall, facilities for the quartermaster, a blacksmith shop, stables, and a lot where animals could be tied. Enlisted men lived outside the stockade fence.

When the Civil War broke out, the camp's arsenal manufactured cannons and cartridges. Following the Civil War, 26 regiments of Federal infantry and cavalry were stationed here to restore order in Texas. Camp Austin at this time consisted mostly of tents with a mess hall, kitchen, bakery, and quarters. In August of 1875, the camp's garrison was closed and troops were moved to the frontier.

30. Fort Colorado (Also known as Coleman's Fort, Fort Coleman and Fort Houston, and a nearby Bastrop County fortification named Reuben Hornsby's Fort)

After Texas gained its independence, Sam Houston authorized the formation of Texas Rangers and the establishment of blockhouses to protect settlers from Indian attacks. Two facilities were near Austin in 1836. The Texas Rangers established Camp Coleman, or Fort Colorado as it would later be called. It was on high ground above the north bank of the Colorado River just west of Walnut Creek and 6 miles southeast of Austin in present-day Travis County.

Blockhouses were frequently an enlargement of a family structure. Sometimes they were built in connection with a community which settlers had already started. Reuben Hornsby's fort was such a blockhouse and was built, ten miles south of Austin, on Walnut Creek.

Fort Colorado's fortification consisted of 2 two-story blockhouses and a number of cabins enclosed within a high stockade wall. Built during 1836 by Colonel Robert M. Coleman, it was first garrisoned by two companies of his battalion. Lieutenant William H. Moore was the last commander of the fort when it was abandoned in April 1838. Settlers in the area, pleased to have a source of dressed logs, lumber, and hardware, soon stripped the fort, and today the site, two and one half miles northeast of the Montopolis Bridge in Austin, is marked only by a state historical marker. Noah Smithwick, a Ranger stationed at Fort Colorado, left a description of life in a frontier fort in his interesting book, Evolution of a State.

Life at a camp or a fort was far from glamorous, frequently boring, and most often risky. In 1836, Rangers had just arrived at Reuben Hornsby's Fort (also called Hornsby's Station) when a young white woman, her clothing hanging in shreds from her bleeding body came into the Rangers' camp. Her name was Mrs. Hibbons, and she had walked from near the Guadalupe River where Comanches had attacked her, her husband, a brother and two children. Her men had been killed and she and the children kidnapped. After watching one of her children killed by the Indians simply because the scared child would not stop crying, the woman had later, while the Indians slept, escaped by crawling and walking to Hornsby's camp, hoping to find help so she could go back after the other child.

The Rangers quickly mounted their horses, taking the Hibbons woman along, and started in the direction that she had described. The Ranger came upon the Indians' trail and tracked it to their campfire. By mid-morning they found the Indians' camp. The Rangers charged and killed several Indians and scattered the others. The Hibbons little boy was still alive. He had been left behind when the Indians escaped and was happily reunited with his mother.

Early in 1839, Rangers from this troop attacked a small party of Indians near the point where the San Gabriel and Little River meet. The skirmish was insignificant except for what the Rangers found on the body of one of the men with the Indians, Manuel Flores, a Mexican. He was carrying documents that revealed a plan by Mexico to invade Texas and to involve the Cherokee and other Indians.

There are no remains of the blockhouses, abandoned as the frontier moved westward.

31. Camp Mabry

One of the latest camps added during this period, Camp Mabry is located in northwest Austin. It was built in the 1890s as a summer camp for the Texas Volunteer Guards (which are now the National Guard for Texas). Most activities of the camp did not develop until after 1900.

The camp is still active and the post is the Texas Military Forces Museum built in 1992.

32. Mission San Ildefonso
(And Mission Nuestra Senora de La
Candelaria)

The two missions were part of three missions originally located on the San Gabriel River north of present-day Thorndale. Candelaria was unsuccessful at that location due in a large part to its own David and Bathsheba type of affair. The commander of the presidio was a Captain Felipe de Rabago y Teran, whose name will be found in records of many of the early East Texas missions to missions on the Rio Grande. When Teran became involved with the wife of a soldier named Juan Jose Ceballos, Ceballos fled to the nearby mission for asylum. Teran came to the mission for Ceballos and returned him to the presidio. Strong protests from the mission priest, Father Pinilla, caused Teran to allow Ceballos to return to the mission.

Relations between Teran and Pinilla deteriorated as reports about other lewd behavior among the Spanish troops spread to the mission. After consulting with the other missionaries, Pinilla excommunicated the garrison, only lifting the order after each soldier requested penance. One day while another priest and Ceballos were dining with Father Pinilla, unknown assailants attacked them. Ceballos died from a gunshot wound, Father Pinilla survived, but the other priest

took an arrow through the heart. Captain Teran blamed the murders on Indians, but subsequent events suggested Captain Teran had plotted the murder.

This incident did much to destroy the morale of both the missionaries and the soldiers of the San Xavier missions (as the missions in this area were called). In 1756, mission property was transferred to Mission Santa Cruz de San Saba that was established to serve Lipan Apaches. Mission Candelaria and Ildefonso were moved to present-day Aquarena Springs and merged.

The Aquarena Springs, located off of Interstate 35 in San Marcos, is part of a cluster of 200 springs originating 16 miles to the north forming the headwaters of the San Marcos River. Tonakawa Indians, finding the warm springs to their liking, frequently made camp there. The springs were an important stop on the Old San Antonio Road, which ran between Mexico and Nacogdoches. They later served as a stopping place on the Chisholm Trail. Missions Candelaria and San Ildefonso were later moved southwest in 1762 to near Montell to Christianize Apaches.

Today, a reconstructed chapel sits on a hillside overlooking the Aquarena Springs Inn.

33. Presidio San Marcos de Neve (Also referred to as Presidio San Juan Xavier, and Camp Clark)

One of the last Spanish attempts at colonization in Texas was the establishment of a chain of defensive settlements stretching from Bexar to Nacogdoches. The Spanish Governor of Texas, Manuel Antonio Cordero y Bustamante, personally funded this project.

Presidio San Marcos de Neve was founded in the early nineteenth century four miles below present-day San Marcos, where the Old San Antonio Road crossed the San Marcos River. This was near where the mission of San Xavier had been temporarily relocated 50 years earlier. Colonists were recruited from south of the Rio Grande rather than from Bexar and Louisiana. The first group of colonists set out from Refugio (now Matamoros) in December 1807 and by February 1808 had settled near the San Marcos crossing. Estimates of the village's size vary from about 50 to 80 people, and included perhaps a dozen families, servants, and as many as 1,700 cattle, horses, and mules. A central plaza was laid out and titles issued to 13 town lots then a flood in June of 1808 nearly wiped out the community. The colony held on for several years, but harassment by Comanche and Tonkawa Indians forced settlers to abandon it in 1812.

Archeologists recently have discovered ruins, which are probably of the presidio and community. The location of these ruins is still being kept a secret.

Presidio San Marcus de Neve was originally named Presidio San Francisco Xavier de Gigedo when the Spanish built it in 1751 on the south bank of the San Gabriel River to protect the San Xavier missions. Gigedo was located five miles from present-day Rockdale where the garrison remained until 1755. Archeological testing on private property in 1983 at a probable site for the living quarters of this presidio recovered Spanish ceramics, horse trappings, ceramics, and sun-dried mud plaster. This presidio was relocated to the San Marcus area and renamed.

On the south side of the San Marcos River about 7 miles from present-day San Marcos, Governor Edward Clark established Camp Clark in 1861 as a facility for volunteers training to go to active duty in the Civil War. The Fourth Texas Regiment, which became a part of Hood's Texas Brigade, trained here along with Colonel Peter C. Wood's 36th Texas Cavalry, which was composed of many Hays County settlers. The 32nd Texas Cavalry from Camp Clark later served in the 1864 Red River Campaign. A cotton farm was built on the site in 1996, and nothing of the fort remains.

34. Mission San Francisco Xavier Los Horcasitas (Known earlier as Mission Nuestra Senora de Los Dolores Del Rio de San Xavier and subsequently as Mission San Francisco Xavier del Rio Guadalupe)

San Francisco Xavier de Horcasitas was the first of three San Xavier missions, located on the San Gabriel River (then known as the San Xavier River) about five miles from present-day Rockdale. The beginning for the mission came in June 1745 when a group of Indians, including members of the Yojuane, Deadose, Mayeye, and

Ervipiame groups, came to San Antonio asking for a mission to be built in their territory. During the winter of 1745 a temporary mission, known as Nuestra Senora de Los Dolores Del Rio de San Xavier, was built. Later in 1748, a permanent mission was established on the south bank to serve those tribes.

The mission suffered from attacks from Apaches, drought, and epidemic. It was moved to the San Marcos River in August 1755 and shortly thereafter more than 1,000 Lipan Apaches joined the missionaries. The San Marcos site, however, could not support the large gathering, and in 1756 the Indians from Mission San Francisco Xavier de Horcasitas were sent to the San Antonio missions. The Mayeyes persuaded the missionaries to build them a separate mission on the Guadalupe River in the vicinity of present-day New Braunfels. It lasted only two more years.

The new mission was named San Francisco Xavier del Rio Guadalupe. This location had ample water, excellent timber, and good land for pasture and cultivation, but its success or failure was tied to plans for a major missionary effort among the Lipan Apaches. The Guadalupe site was only 15 leagues from San Antonio and the friars there were jealous of the new mission. When the mission Santa Cruz de San Saba was destroyed, fear that the Indians would direct their hostilities against San Francisco Xavier caused the site to be abandoned in March 1758.

Archeologists working in an area near the original site of the mission found indications of walls and burials, Spanish ceramics and glass, and Indian pottery and projectile points.

35. Fort Wilbarger

The book *Indian Depredations in Texas* that was published in 1889 by John Wesley Wilbarger was said to be "the cost complete accounts of Indian warfare in nineteenth-century Texas." Wilbarger was a Methodist preacher who came to Texas from Kentucky in 1806 at the urging of his brother, Josiah. John Wilbarger's book contains more than 250 accounts of Indian-settler conflicts, but the most amazing story is the one about his brother Josiah.

Josiah had join Stephen F. Austin's colony in 1828 and received a Mexican land grant in present-day Bastrop County where he settled in the community of Utley near the Colorado River. He and his wife, Margaret, had seven children. Their five boys became Texas Rangers and four of them died before reaching age 18. (Josiah Wilbarger and his eldest son are buried along with their friend Stephen F. Austin in the State Memorial Cemetery in Austin.) The Wilbarger's home consisted of a cabin and a stockade that may have been a family fort. He also prepared a cave in the banks of the Colorado River for shelter in case of Indian attack. Little else is known about the fort.

The story for which Josiah Wilbarger is famous concerns the time he was attacked by Indians, scalped, and left for dead. A friend, Reuben Hornsby lived nearby, and Mrs. Hornsby dreamed three times that Josiah needed help. She convinced her husband to go look for him, and legend says she told her husband exactly where Wilbarger could be found. Josiah Wilbarger was rescued and lived many years after the attack, despite having been scalped.

At one time there was a commemorative marker at the site of Wilbarger Bend in the Colorado. If the marker still exists, it is now on private property.

36. Wood's Fort

Zadock Woods was one of the settlers Stephen F. Austin recruited to come to Texas, and he and his family moved to Austin's colony in 1824. His fortified home was used as a place of refuge from Indian attacks in Fayette County. It was named Woods' Fort (and Woods' Prairie).

Zadock volunteered in 1835 under Captain Michael Goheen and Colonel John H. Moore to fight in the Battle of Gonzales, the Battle of Concepcion, and at the Grass Fight near San Antonio. He returned home to find a house full of a company of Tennessee volunteers on their way to the Alamo (names are omitted from history, but Davy Crockett could have been there).

In 1842, Woods and his sons Norman and Henry G. were recruited by Captain Nicholas M. Dawson to fight with Matthew Caldwell's forces against the Mexican General Woll at Salado Creek. On their way to engage Wall, they were ambushed. Mexican soldiers, though superior in number, elected not to fight a rifle battle. Instead they surrounded the Texans. Staying out of rifle range the Mexicans blasted them with artillery fire until Texan's Captain Dawson raised the white flag of surrender. Woll continued the bombardment killing all but 15 Texas, among the dead was Zadock Woods. Zadock's son Henry escaped unharmed, but his son Norman was captured and taken to prison. (Another son, Leander, was killed in the 1832 Battle of Velasco.)

Zadock Woods was the oldest man to die at Dawson Creek. He was first buried in a mass grave near Salado Creek but was later reburied at the Monument Hill Historic Site in La Grange. Historical markers in West Point commemorate Woods as being a significant early settler.

37. Moore's Fort

(See colored pictures in the center section)

In 1826, John Henry Moore built two blockhouses within what are now the city limits of La Grange. Area settlers were also allowed to use this shelter as a defense against the Indians.

Moore was one of the Old Three Hundred who were the first settlers in Austin's original colony. In 1834, he led an expedition against the Waco and Tawakoni Indians on the upper Brazos River, and in July 1835, he organized four companies of volunteers to attack Tawakonis in Limestone County. In September of 1835, he was so outspoken in favor of independence that he was ordered arrested by the Mexican General Martin Perfecto de Cos. September 25, 1835, Moore took command of the Texans in the Battle of Gonzales. He reportedly designed the "Come and Take It" banner displayed in Gonzales when Mexicans demanded the town surrender its cannon.

Henry Moore fought in the Texas Revolution and after that in the war against the Indians. Buildings from Moore's Fort have been rebuilt in the nearby community of Round Top.

38. Camp Felder

Camp Felder was a Confederate camp for Union prisoners of war. It was located near present-day Chappell Hill in Washington County, and Colonel Clayton C. Gillespie was its commander. It was named for Gabriel Felder, owner of the Brazos River bottomland where the camp was established. A guard of Confederate cavalry, and their horses, stayed in sheds on the hill above. In September 1864, the Union prisoners were moved to avoid a fever epidemic. Reports say that the death rates of the prisoners at this camp were high. After the epidemic had passed, the prisoners were moved to Camp Groce.

39. Camp Waul

"It was one hundred and twenty-six years ago that 2,000 men assembled here on New Year's Creek under the leadership of General T. N. Waul. They were to fight many skirmishes before surrendering at Vicksburg. They had carried with them a spirit of Texas; a spirit of independent action and forthright courage. That is the tradition of Texas and its people. Ill equipped, clothed and under fed they were still willing to give their lives for those ideals they believed. Like their forefathers who fought for the freedom of America some eighty-five years earlier, they were men of courage. Even before that the colonists exhibited that same courage and faith.

They started by thanking God for their bountiful crops."

Quotation from the dedication speech at the placement of the commemorative marker for Waul's Texas Legion campsite along New Year's Creek.

Camp Waul was a Confederate training camp seven miles north of Brenham. New Year's Creek ran through this camp that was named for Thomas Neville Waul. Waul's Texas Legion was organized on May 13, 1862 and ordered out of state in August that year. During the training a severe measles epidemic resulted in the illness of six hundred cases among the soldiers, but not many died. Soldiers at the camp had plenty of food, but suffered shortages of arms and supplies.

40. Washington-on-the-Brazos

(See pictures on the back cover)

A dozen small cabins stood in the town of Washington when

elected delegates from each settlement in Texas arrived there in 1836. They established a tent camp from which they used pen and ink as their powder and balls. Their muskets were only sheets of paper, but the action that took place at Washington-on-the-Brazos on the second day of March in 1836 caused as many camps to be built in Texas as would any Indian uprising, or any war with Mexico or Spain.

It was here that Texans fired a shot that had an effect on the future of the continent, if not on the entire world. The delegates met while soldiers of General Santa Anna marched towards San Antonio and the Alamo. In a small building now called "Independence Hall" they fired not a musket but wrote a constitution and the declaration of independence for a new country, the Republic of Texas. It was indeed a shot that had long range and far-reaching impacts.

Washington-on-the-Brazos Historical Park is located in Washington County, 21 miles northeast of Brenham on Highway 105. Texas' Parks and Wildlife Department manages the park that includes Independence Hall (see back cover) where the documents were signed. It also includes a visitor complex and a conference center, the Barrington Living History Farm, which was the home of the last President of the Republic, and the Star of the Republic Museum, a must-see if interested in Texas history. It is open daily until 5 p.m. except on holidays.

41. Camp Millican

Texas' northern most terminal of the Houston and Texas Central Railroad was the settlement of Millican. It became the site of Camp Millican during the Civil War. Enlistees arrived by train to this camp that was nothing more than a gathering site. Sometimes recruits were trained here before marching for duty in Arkansas and Louisiana but some went to nearby camps to train: Camp Speight, Camp Racquet to the south, Camp Carter near Hempstead, or Camp Killough on Cedar Creek. Then they would be sent by rail to the Gulf coast where they were stationed near Houston, or they were placed on ships transporting them to the Confederate fortifications built along the coastline.

New recruits were obligated to furnish their own weapons and hunting rifles were the most common weapons, with double-barreled shotguns running a close second. These might have worked for shooting a bear, but they were not made for battle. At one time the weapons were such a problem that George W. Carter, a Methodist clergyman in charge of the camp, had lances made in nearby Chappell Hill.

The railroad station at Millican was also a shipping point for cotton sent by rail to the end of the line and then on to Brownsville by carts and wagon. In Brownsville, cotton was shipped on to Matamoros, Mexico where it was sent by ship to Europe. Cotton exports were a sorely needed source of revenue for the Confederates. Return shipments, along the same route, brought supplies and merchandise to be distributed throughout central Texas.

Legend has it that Texas has so many mesquite trees because the Mexican supply train drivers fed mesquite beans to their mules as they pulled the carts carrying cotton across Texas.

A marker for Camp Millican is across from the Millican Post Office on Highway 159.

42. Camp Groce (Also known as Camp Liendo)

Colonel Leonard W. Groce's Liendo plantation stood on Clear Creek two miles east of present-day Hempstead in Waller County. Camp Groce, or Camp Liendo as it was frequently referred to, was probably established in 1862 to house Union soldiers captured by Confederate forces at the Battle of Galveston (see region four). The camp had four rows of barracks and a permanent militia guard of seventy men. Most of the Federal prisoners remained at Liendo only temporarily while en route to a larger prisoner of war camp at Camp Ford near Tyler.

Camp Groce served as a recruiting station for the Confederate Army and a refugee center for women and children fleeing southern states. In December of 1864, all of the prisoners at Camp Groce were paroled and the camp was permanently abandoned as a military prison as nearly 500 prisoners were taken to the port of Galveston where they were turned over to Union forces. The 29th Texas Cavalry regiments disbanded at this camp during March and April of 1865. After the end of the war, Confederate veterans used the camp as a place to meet again.

Region Three

The area around San Antonio was the center for most activities during the development of Texas. In San Antonio, or nearby, Spaniards fought Spaniards, Mexicans fought Spaniards, and Mexicans fought Mexicans with Texans fighting on both sides in these conflicts. Later the Texans fought Mexicans here to gain their independence. The Spanish, Mexicans and Texans all fought the Indians. The United States also became involved and they too fought the Mexicans.

During the colonization period, San Antonio served as the shipping terminal for supplies headed for Nacogdoches and La Bahia. Early missions, for which San Antonio is now world famous, were established in the 1700s. In the 1800s, missions became battlegrounds. In 1813, the Republican Army of the North marched towards San Antonio where nearby the Battle of Rosillo was fought on March 29. That battle resulted in the Republican Army of the North capturing Bexar (San Antonio) and established a "Republic of Texas," for the first time.

Only five months later, the Battle of Medina, the bloodiest battle ever-fought on Texas soil, was fought between the Republican Army and a Spanish army under General Joaquin de Arredondo. Spanish Royalists crushed the Republican Army and Texas did not become a free Republic again until 1836. Arredondo's notable assistant was a Lieutenant Antonio Lopez de Santa Anna, who learned his lesson well. He returned to San Antonio twenty-three years later with another army to fight another battle. This time; against the Texans.

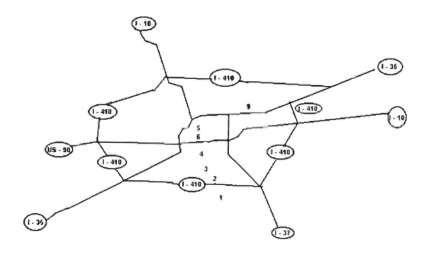

Region Three (San Antonio) Map

(Numbers are as the sites are listed in the text for this region)

Location	Region Three
1	Mission San Francisco de la Espada – on Mission Trail
2	Mission San Juan Capistrano – on Mission Trail
3	Mission San Jose y San Miguel de Aguayo – on Mission Trail
4	Mission Senora de la Purisima Concepcion de Acuna – on Mission Trail
5	Alamo (Mission San Antonio de Valero) – 300 block of Alamo Plaza
6	San Fernando Cathedral – Plaza de Armas
7	Camp Crockett – San Pedro Park
8	Cooke's Camp – there are no remains of this camp
9	Fort Sam Houston – north off of I-35. This is still an active Army fort.

1. Mission San Francisco de la Espada

(See colored pictures in the center section)

Mission Espada was established in 1731 in San Antonio when the Mission San Francisco de Los Tejas was moved from East Texas and its name changed. The community around Espada has the distinction of participating in the oldest continually operating irrigation system in the United States. Spanish Franciscan missionaries, pursuing their vision for God and country, taught farming, ranching, architecture, blacksmithing, weaving, and masonry to the Coahuiltecan Indians who gathered at the mission. The times became turbulent in the 1800s.

In 1813, the Republican Army of the North with an estimated 600 to 900 men, started on the road to San Antonio expecting to find food and use the quarters at Mission San Francisco de la Espada for the night. There was, however, a Spanish Royalist force of 950 to 1,500 men that had prepared an ambush along a ridge that borders the creeks near the mission. The ensuing battle was bloody and brief, lasting no more than an hour, but it resulted in the complete rout of the Royalists and the capture of most of their arms and ammunition, six cannons, and 1,500 horses and mules. The Royalist troop losses were estimated to be 100 to 330 men, while the Republicans only lost 6 men.

The defeated Royalists retreated to San Antonio, and a victorious Republican Army of the North spent the night at Mission Espada. The next day the Republic Army of the North took up quarters at the Mission Nuestra Senora de la Purisima Concepcion. On April 1, the army marched in battle formation to the gates of San Antonio, where they were met by a flag of truce. A declaration of independence was adopted on April 6, 1813, establishing the first Republic of Texas, and a constitution. That Republic of Texas came to an end after the disastrous Battle of Medina, August 18, 1813.

This mission was also the site of a skirmish with Mexican soldiers when on October 27, 1835, Stephen F. Austin ordered James Bowie and James W. Fannin, Jr., to lead 90 men from Espada to locate a protected position close to San Antonio. The four companies led by Andrew Briscoe, Robert M. Coleman, Valentine Bennet, and Michael Goheen engaged Mexican scouts before reaching Mission Concepcion, where the four officers decided to camp for the evening. The Texans occupied a bend in the San Antonio River protected by an embankment, and sent out pickets to warn of Mexican attack. A few cannon shots from the Mexicans in town failed to inflict any losses. The Siege of Bexar followed.

Mission San Francisco de la Espada is on the Mission Trail in San Antonio. It is partially in ruin, but its chapel and walkway are beautiful. All missions on the trail are open daily (9 a.m. to 5 p.m. except for National holidays). The first Sunday in August is the colorful "El Dia de las Misiones" (The Day of the Missions) annual salute to the historic structures.

2. Mission San Juan Capistrano

There is a story that before the Battle of the Alamo, Mexican president Santa Anna saw a lovely girl as he rode into San Antonio with his troops and had the girl brought to his quarters to make her a mistress. The girl's mother objected so Santa Anna married the girl, even though he already had a wife in Mexico. The wedding took

place in Mission San Juan Capistrano.

Originally named San Jose de Los Nazonis, this mission was once located north of Cushing in East Texas. In 1731, it was relocated to San Antonio and renamed San Juan Capistrano in honor of the friar Saint John of Capistrano, a saint who had carried a crucifix in battle at the Siege of Belgrade when Hungarians had defeated the army of Mohammed in 1683. Mission San Juan Capistrano is located on San Antonio's Mission Trail. A statue of Saint John (shown below) stands guard at the ruins outside the chapel (which contains a museum).

The site was filled with the sound of activities when more than 50 Indian families lived at the mission with their cattle, sheep, goats, and horses. The population soon diminished when the mission started being attacked by other Indians. Cabellos Colorados (Red Hair), a Lipan Apache chief, figured prominently in a raid on Mission San Juan Capistrano. His band kidnapped two citizens in a raid, stole horses from Mission Espada, and killed Indians at the Mission Concepcion. After numerous raids, Red Hair was captured on

December 11, 1737, and imprisoned at Bexar until 1738. When Apache raids were renewed, Chief Colorado was sent as a prisoner to Mexico, where he later died.

3. Mission San Jose y San Miguel de Aguayo

One of the most romantic stories involving Enchanted Rock, near Fredericksburg, is that of a young Spanish soldier, Don Jesus Navarro, and his rescue of the Indian maiden Rosa. In 1750, Don Jesus supposedly came from Monterey to the Mission San Jose y San Miguel de Aguayo where he met and fell in love with Rosa, the Christian daughter of the Indian Chief Tehuan. But Rosa was kidnapped by a band of Comanches bent on sacrificing her to the

spirits of the Enchanted Rock. Her daring lover, Don Jesus followed the Indians and managed to rescue her as she was about to be sacrificed and burned at the stake.

Mission San Jose was one of the missions that moved to San

Antonio from East Texas when the war between France and Spain caused unrest in that area. Numerous Indian groups came here as Apache raids prompted Indians to seek refuge among the Spaniards. In 1768, a stone wall and stone watchtowers were built to enclose the compound.

The Texas Historical Commission's archeological studies in 1968 - 1970 disclosed the remains of Indian quarters. By 1973, studies on San Jose by the National Park Service, and the Texas Parks and Wildlife Department, as well as the Texas Historical Commission had exposed the foundations of colonial walls. The mission is located on the Mission Trail in San Antonio.

4. Mission Senora de la Purisima Concepcion de Acuna

(Pictured on the front cover)

Mission Concepcion was first established as Mission Senora de la Purisima Concepcion de Los Hainai in East Texas in 1716. It was moved to its present site near San Antonio in 1731 after Spain and France went to war. (See the story of these earlier missions in Region Two.) The priest and Christianized Indians that moved from East

Texas were given the land of Mission San Francisco Xavier de Naxara and the name changed to Concepcion. Missionaries had the Indians build homes inside the walls, and tried to replace the traditional Indians rituals with Christian beliefs. Initial success was quickly overcome when other Indians raided. An Indian pictograph on the cliffs near the town of Paint Rock shows smoke coming from a burning church with two bell towers. Concepcion was the only mission in the state with two towers.

Indian attacks continued into the 19th century. Later, during the times before the Texas Revolution, this mission was a frequent meeting place for revolutionaries and it was the scene of a battle in the Siege of Bexar in 1835. During the Mexican War, Mission Concepcion was used as a barracks for Federal troops (see Camp Crockett – site 7 below).

Concepcion is well preserved and located on Missions Trail in San Antonio. Its church has never fallen into ruin and it is considered to be the oldest un-restored mission in the U. S.

5. The Alamo (Officially named Mission San Antonio de Valero and originally referred to as San Antonio de Padua)

(See colored pictures in the center section)

In 1718, Father Olivares moved a mission from the Rio Grande to San Antonio to become a way station on the road to the East Texas missions. Olivares had instantly fallen in love with the area around the San Antonio River. The mission he moved was named San Antonio de Valero (known as the Alamo). Its protector was Presidio San Antonio de Bexar.

In 1803, the mission served as a garrison for the Second Flying Company of San Carlos de Parras, a company of 100 Spanish lancers. This detachment of seasoned veterans provided increased protection from Indians, and reduced the theft of livestock and the smuggling of other goods. In place of the company's long name the name La

Compania del Alamo, or El Alamo, became used, and the Mission Valero soon came to be known as the Alamo. Then in 1809, when rumors of an invasion by the United States spread across the province, the La Compania del Alamo ordered materials to add to the existing walls of the mission's enclosure.

Even the early history of the Alamo included warfare. In 1813, forces of the Republican Army of the North occupied San Antonio. Facing a superior force and possible imprisonment, royalist troops from the Alamo and the Presidio San Antonio de Bexar surrendered without resistance. Many troops from the Alamo quickly joined the Americans. Alamo commandant, Lieutenant Vizente Tarin, abandoned his command to become a captain in the insurgent army and participated in the Battle of Medina. When the Royalists' troops under General Joaquin de Arredondo then entered Texas to retaliate, soldiers unresolved renewed their Spanish loyalties, and the Alamo was virtually abandoned leaving the city open to Indians.

In December 1835, the Alamo troops joined the army of General Martin Perfecto de Cos to defend San Antonio during the Siege of Bexar. With the defeat of his army, on December 11 Cos surrendered San Antonio and the Alamo to the Texan forces led by Stephen F. Austin. On March 6, 1836 in a battle remembered throughout the world by the cry, "Remember the Alamo", San Antonio was retaken by Mexican forces commanded by General Antonio Lopez de Santa Anna during the Battle of the Alamo. Texan defenders were killed.

After the subsequent defeat of Santa Anna's army at the Battle of San Jacinto, Texan forces reoccupied the city. In March 1842, six years after Texas had declared independence, Mexican General Rafael Vasquez briefly re-captured and occupied San Antonio. In September of that year, General Adrian Woll led another Mexican invasion force that temporarily seized the city and the Alamo before he was chased back to Mexico that same year.

The Alamo stands in Alamo Plaza in downtown San Antonio. The Alamo Museum is operated by the Daughters of the Republic of

Texas and located on the same grounds. Hours are 9 a.m. to 5 p.m.
Monday through Saturday.

6. San Fernando Cathedral (Originally the Presidio San Antonio de Bexar)

(See colored pictures in the center section)

The cathedral was built in 1783 on the Plaza De Armas on the
site once occupied by the Presidio San Antonio de Bexar in San
Antonio. A commemorative plaque outside states that within the
cathedral is a tomb containing the remains of those that fought and
died at the Alamo. It was from the San Fernando Cathedral's bell
tower that General Santa Anna flew a red flag in 1836 letting the
Texans defending at the Alamo know that "no quarter" would be
given to them.

Presidio San Antonio de Bexar, which once stood on the same
grounds as the church, was the center of Spanish defense in western
Texas. It was built here on the west side of the San Antonio River
near the area of Mission San Antonio de Valero, "The Alamo."

Then in 1722, Presidio Bexar was relocated across the river from
Mission Valero. It was an adobe building thatched with grass and
the soldiers lived in huts. Recommendations were made that
permanent fortifications should be erected, but no walls or stockades
were ever built even though the presidio was charged with the
protection of five missions and the settlement. Because it was close
to the Rio Grande and the better-organized missions in this vicinity,
Bexar did not suffer want and distress, as did many other Spanish
presidios in Texas. In 1726, there were 45 soldiers at San Antonio
de Bexar of which 25 were detached to a camp on Cibolo Creek
protecting the ranchers and settlers. Captains of the presidio served
as the Governor of the Province of Texas.

Presidio San Antonio de Bexar became the northernmost Texas
outpost of New Spain following the withdrawal of the presidios of
San Saba, San Agustin de Ahumada, and Nuestra Senora del Pilar de
Los Adaes (the latter was located in present-day Louisiana). In 1806,

soldiers were stationed to the east of the river near the Alamo, which by then had ceased to function as a mission and had became the headquarters building for the military. To the end of both Spanish and Mexican rule in Texas, the two central plazas served as a municipal defense, but the Alamo remained the city's military defense. The San Fernando Cathedral was partly rebuilt in 1868. The rear section of the church and its small dome are the only areas that now appear as they did in earlier days. The building is still a functioning church and visitors are asked to respect those saying prayers. Markers in the plaza and in front of the church commemorate the church's role in the early days of Texas.

7. Camp Crockett

Located on a spring three miles north of the Alamo, this camp was home to the troops of General John E. Wool in the Mexican War. This was another of the many holding camps for volunteers who had enlisted in the U. S. Army when war was declared. As at the other camps, sickness was a major problem. Sanitary conditions were poor and the food supplied through the quartermasters was of questionable quality and frequently lacking in quantity. Nevertheless, unlike the camps along the Gulf coast, this location had fresh spring water.

The primary past time for the troops was partying in the local cantinas though some found their amusement in visiting the old missions in the city. Visitors today can see a few of the pockmarks in the walls of the missions from the soldiers' gun practice. Supposedly there was a tunnel between Mission Concepcion and the Alamo (though that story seems incredible due to the distance) and troops assigned to cleaning the mission found some old stone steps that descended into a dark and gloomy room. There the soldiers' lights revealed hundreds if not thousands of bats hanging from the ceiling. Not knowing any better, a few soldiers fired rifles at the bats, creating a black windstorm as the bats took flight knocking down soldiers in their path. It was reported that it took two hours for all of the bats to leave the mission. The mission was to have been the quarters for the troops, but the subsequent stench made the area unlivable.

Fighting at the camp was limited to a duel between two doctors.

President of the U. S. routinely appointed the surgeon for the troops, but before that occurred the Governor of Illinois appointed an acting surgeon. When the presidential appointee arrived, the acting surgeon thought he had been wronged and hit the new arrival with a cane. A duel was scheduled for the next day. The presidential appointee's shot was a miss; the second, fired by the Governor's appointee hit his opponent in the abdomen. Pride interceded when the wounded presidential appointee made a self-analysis and declared that the body-piercing wound was not even serious.

For the welfare of the city, and the senoritas at the cantinas, the life of this camp thankfully was short. Beautiful San Pedro Park in San Antonio is now where Camp Crockett once stood.

8. Cooke's Camp

The story of Cooke's Camp that was in San Antonio is more a story of a man than of a place. William Gordon Cooke, for whom this camp was named, was one of the many unsung men of Texas who contributed much to its development.

He arrived in Texas at Fort Velasco with a group of volunteers called the New Orleans Greys in October of 1835, and was elected First Lieutenant the next day at Fort Quintana. He went to San Antonio that November, raised volunteers to storm the town, and led the party that forced the Mexicans to surrender. Cooke then volunteered for the Matamoros expedition of 1835-36 and as their captain he led the San Antonio Greys to Goliad. As were many Texans in 1836, William Cooke was motivated by the words of Sam Houston, "Remember the Alamo."

From Goliad he was sent with the San Antonio Greys to Refugio when the Mexican forces were reported to be enroute. Cooke was ordered to fall back to Goliad, where he arrived on February 12, 1836. Cooke was then sent with two Mexican prisoners to Washington-on-the-Brazos, where he joined Houston's staff as his assistant inspector general.

At the Battle of San Jacinto, Cooke was in charge of guarding the Mexican prisoners when Antonio Lopez de Santa Anna was captured. He prevented angry Texans from executing Santa Anna so that he could be brought before General Houston. While Sam Houston was recovering from the wounds he had received at San Jacinto, Cooke was given administrative duties. Cooke then retired from the army because of ill health. On June 9, 1837 he was made official signer of the President's name to promissory notes issued by the Republic of Texas. He was responsible for issuing stock certificates and certificates to fund the Texas public debt.

In March 1840, Mirabeau B. Lamar named him commissioner to sign treaties with the Comanches, and in this role he took part in the Council House fight. The same year he was appointed colonel of the First Regiment of Infantry, the unit that laid out the Military Road from the Little River to the Red River. Cooke declined an invitation to become the vice-president of Texas and instead accepted an appointment in April 1841 as senior commissioner on the ill-fated Santa Fe Expedition. He was imprisoned with the rest of the members of that expedition in Mexico. Santa Anna when learning of the capture of the Texan, who had saved his life at San Jacinto, ordered his release. After being released he ignored his pledge not to take arms against Mexico and joined General Edward Burleson in chasing Mexican General Woll back to Mexico from San Antonio.

Cooke fought with the Somervell Expedition, and helped organized the infamous Snively Expedition (see Fort Johnston in Region Five for further information). Still seeking the revenge for those he served with in the Mexican prison, Cooke joined Edwin Moore's expedition to the Yucatan hoping to capture Mexican prisoners to be exchanged for Texans in Mexican prisons.

Cooke's Camp, Cooke County, and Cooke Avenue in San Antonio were named for him.

9. Fort Sam Houston (Also Camp Sheridan and Camp Salado)

(See colored pictures in the center section)

"Geronimo," the paratroopers of World War II would cry as they jumped from their planes, but quiet was Geronimo as he jumped from the window of a cell at Fort Sam Houston where he was confined in 1886 while enroute to a reservation in Florida. The legend of the Apache chief caused his name to be associated with courage and bravery into the twentieth century.

As early as 1846, attempts had been made to secure a United States military installation in San Antonio. During the Mexican War, the U. S. Army established a depot at San Antonio, and in 1849, San Antonio was named headquarters of the United States Army Eighth Military District with forces barracked at Mission Concepcion. The Alamo was used for storage.

In February 16, 1861, when General David E. Twiggs, commander of the Federal Department of Texas, was headquartered in San Antonio, he surrendered all U. S. forces, arms, and equipment in Texas to secessionists backed by a large force of Texas Rangers. Although Bexar County escaped the destruction that devastated other parts of the South, the Civil War years were difficult for the citizens who were forced to deal with the lack of markets and the wild fluctuations in Confederate currency. With many of the men away fighting, the county and the surrounding region experienced an upsurge in cattle rustling and other crimes. A committee of vigilantes organized "necktie parties" for bandits, and cattle thieves and Union sympathizers.

A formal proposal made in 1870 for a permanent army post was met with opposition in Washington. Secretary of War W. W. Belknap illegally held up funding until 1875. He resigned in 1876 rather than face impeachment, which was threatened partly over his refusal to fund congressional appropriations for the San Antonio base.

On June 7, 1876, construction was finally begun on 93 acres of city-donated land known as Government Hill. Construction of the fort included a one-story north wall 624 feet long, east and west walls 499½ feet long, and a two-story south wall with the only entry gate. In 1879, the depot that had been occupying space in the Alamo moved to the new fort, and immediately thereafter expansion began with construction of officers' quarters. A 10,830-square-foot commander's home, named the Pershing House, was built along with a tent hospital, replaced by a permanent hospital in 1885. During 1885-1891 infantry facilities were added. In 1890 the base was designated Fort Sam Houston.

The fort and Fort Sam Houston museum are open (Wednesday – Sunday 10 a.m. to 5 p.m.) to the public and many of the early day structures remain. They are located off of I-10 in the northeast section of San Antonio and near the site of the Battle of Salado Creek (and of Camp Salado). Also once located in this area was a Camp Sheridan, established in 1866. Nothing else is known of it.

Mission Concepcion

Beautiful Fort Davis in Region One

Chapel of the Presidio San Elizario in Region One

Fort Leaton in Region One

Fortin El Cibolo in Region One

Mission Dolores in Region Two

Mission Tejas in Region Two

Fort Parker in Region Two

Moore's Fort in Region Two

Mission Espada in Region Three

Beyond this Plaza de Armas water fountain is the San Fernando
Cathedral in Region Three

The Alamo in Region Three on the last night of the 20th century.

Fort Sam Houston in Region Three. The Basis for the cry
"Geronimo" orginated here.

Presidio "La Bahia" in Region Four

Fort Travis in Region Four

Texans attacking at San Jacinto in a painting in the Museum at San Jacinto Monument (Region Four)

Mexican soldiers at San Jacinto in a painting in the Museum at San Jacinto Monument (Region Four)

Fort Fisher in Region Five

Fort Griffin in Region Five

Fort Inglish in Region Five

Fort Belknap in Region Five

Fort McKavett in Region Six

Presidio "San Saba" in Region Six

Fort Phantom Hill in Region Six

Fort Concho in Region Six

Region Four

Shortly after the Spanish sent soldiers and priests to East Texas to build missions, they did the same at the outlet of the Trinity River east of present-day Houston. Again the purpose was to settle the territory. In fear of the French and British taking Texas, the Spanish sent troops and priests to establish missions and to try to Christianize the Indians so they could be settlers of New Spain. For many reasons this did not work, and Spain had to turn elsewhere to find settlers. Indians were not reliable; Mexicans did not want the hard work, so Anglos became a last choice.

Spain enticed settlers from the United States, where economic conditions were bad and land was expensive. In Texas, however, a settler could buy on credit 4,428 acres for what 80 acres would cost in the U. S. Before the Anglo immigration began in earnest, Mexico gained its independence from Spain and received Texas in the bargain. The Anglos and the new Mexican government did not get along very well and after Santa Anna became the President of Mexico in 1834 the conflicts boiled over into revolution.

Santa Anna is coming! Santa Anna is coming, bury your treasures; flee to the woods! Santa Anna is coming. Run for

your life! General Santa Anna is coming!

Following victory at the Alamo, General Antonio Lopez de Santa Anna went on a march to put a final end to the Texan's dissension. Word spread of his coming and the settlers in this area did indeed bury their treasures and run for their lives.

The guide to this region starts on the route that Santa Anna then took, starting at Mission de Las Cabras, the San Antonio missions' ranch, where he changed horses then proceeded into the seat of the Texans unrest in the Anglo colonies along the coastline to stop the revolution.

Briefly the tour leaves that route and drops down to the coast where an early Spanish expedition found the beach littered with ships, and pieces of ships, washed ashore from storms.

The tour then returns to Santa Anna's route after which it goes to the land of pirates and filibusters around Galveston. After visiting the site of an early-day mission and presidio, the tour goes to the southeast tip of Texas at Sabine Pass, site of a state park located among construction of huge offshore drilling platforms, and then returns in the vicinity of Interstate 10 to Houston.

Region Four Map
(Numbers are as the sites are listed in the text for this region)

Location   Region Four

1	Mission De Las Cabras – in Wilson County
2	Presidio El Fuerte de Santa Cruz del Cibolo – Karnes County
3	DeWitt's Fort – in Gonzales
4	Fort Waul – in Gonzales
5	Presidio Nuestra Senora de Loreto La Bahia del Espiritu Santo – in Goliad
6	Mission Nuestra Senora del Espiritu Santo de Zuniga – in Goliad
7	Mission Nuestra Senora del Rosario – west of Goliad
8	Fort Casa Blanca – near Sandia
9	Fort Lipantitlan – a museum is in nearby San Patricio
10	Camp Corpus Christi – in Corpus Christi
11	Camp Marcy – in Corpus Christi
12	Camp Nueces (Nueces County) – in Corpus Christi
13	Mission Nuestra Senora del Refugio – in Refugio
14	Camp Semmes – San Jose Island
15	Camp Irwin – near Port Lavaca
16	Fort Esperanza – Matagorda Island
17	Fort Saint Louis – artifacts in a Victoria museum
18	Camp Chambers (Victoria County) – near Victoria
19	Camp Henry E. McCulloch – near Victoria
20	Round Top House – in Victoria
21	Camp Bowie – near Edna
22	Camp Crockett – in Jackson County
23	Camp Independence – near Edna
24	Camp Johnson - in Jackson County
25	Fort West Bernard Station – artifacts in Wharton
26	Fort Bend – near Richmond
27	Fort Quintana – near Quintana
28	Fort Velasco – near Surfside Beach
29	Fort Crockett – in Galveston
30	Maison Rogue – in Galveston
31	Fort de Bolivar – on Bolivar Peninsula

32   Fort Las Casas – on Bolivar Peninsula
33   Fort Travis – on Bolivar Peninsula
34   Fort Griffin – south of Port Arthur
35   Fort Grigsby – in Port Neches
36   Fort Manhassett – near Sabine Pass
37   Fort Sabine – in Sabine Pass
38   Fort Anahuac – in Anahuac
39   Fort Chambers – near Anahuac
40   Mission Nuestra Senora de la Luz – museum in Wallisville
41   Presidio San Agustin de Ahumada – museum in Wallisville
42   Champ d'Asile – vicinity of Moss Bluff near Liberty
43   Camp on the San Jacinto – off of I-10 along the San Jacinto River
44   Camp Bee - in Houston

1. Mission de Las Cabras

Rancho de Las Cabras State Historic Site off of State Highway 97 just southwest of Floresville in Wilson County includes the site of a ranching outpost (the Rancho de Las Cabras). This was a ranching outpost of the San Antonio Mission San Francisco de la Espada and Mission de Las Cabras. This was where the missionaries and their Indians raised livestock from 1731 to 1794 before it changed to private ownership. The site, which included fortifications and a chapel, has a few foundations remaining.

2. Presidio El Fuerte de Santa Cruz del Cibolo (Also called El Fuerte de Santa Cruz, El Fuerte del Zivolo, El Fuerte del Cibolo, Arroyo del Cíbolo, or simply El Cibolo)

This eighteenth-century Spanish fort existed from 1734 to 1737 and again from 1771 to 1782 to protect ranches between Bexar and La Bahia from raids by Apache Indians. El Fuerte del Cíbolo was a small stockade fort where nearby ranchers who wanted the shelter of a fort could bring horses. That site was along Cibolo Creek halfway between Bexar and La Bahia, at a place known by local residents as Carvajal Crossing (where present Farm Road 887 crosses Cibolo Creek in Karnes County). The fort continued to protect the ranches of the area for about ten years. Soldiers on patrols from this presidio had many fights with hostile Indians.

From the time when San Antonio was first established, the Indians, mainly Apaches or Comanches subjected presidios, missions, and settlers there to constant raids upon the livestock. In order to stop the raids, Governor Manuel de Sandoval decided to strengthen the fort with additional soldiers to protect the Presidio's horses, and moved them to a more defensible position near Arroyo del Cíbolo southeast of San Antonio. But the early attempt to establish this location failed after raids by Apaches in 1737.

The reopening in 1771 was a result of the adjustments made in Spain's colonial policy in New Spain after the Seven Years' War between Spain and France. The building of 15 presidios was authorized along a line from the Gulf of California to the Gulf of Mexico. This included the reopening of El Cibolo with a detachment of 21 men. The reopening was out of necessity when renewed Apache raids began forcing the abandonment of the farms and ranches of the missions.

This fort also played an important role in the American Revolution. Twenty soldiers at Cibolo on July 4, 1776 helped drive cattle and horses to the Spanish forces of General Bernardo de Galvez. Galvez was instrumental in the defeat of the British in Louisiana and Florida.

Presidio El Fuerte de Santa Cruz del Cibolo was destroyed in 1782 leaving no physical remains. On May 4, 1991, a Texas historical marker commemorating the old fort was placed in front of the Church of the Nativity of the Blessed Virgin Mary at Cestohowa, two and one-half miles south of the presidio location.

3. DeWitt's Fort

Empresario Green B. DeWitt received a grant from Mexico in 1825 that allowed him to bring 400 families into the territory embracing the present-day counties of DeWitt, Gonzales, Guadalupe, Caldwell, and parts of Comal, Lavaca, Fayette, and Victoria counties.

The first settlement was established on Kerr's Creek in 1826. Shortly after moving in, the settlers went to a dance on the Colorado River to celebrate the fourth of July. As they journeyed to the dance, Indians attacked, driving off their horses and leaving them to walk home. Upon their return they found their homes were burned and the town completely deserted except for one dead man. In January, DeWitt sent men to build an Indian fort, DeWitt's Fort, in Gonzales. A letter from DeWitt to Stephen F. Austin on April 3, 1827 mentions there were two blockhouses, but there is no mention of the additional second fortification in the history of the settlement.

A local story tells of a James Kerr who was an employee of DeWitt's. He moved to Gonzales and gave his daughter a scare that she long remembered. The two were riding on one horse in the country when unfriendly Indians let out wild whoops and gave them a chase. Riding a faster horse, Kerr, once out of sight, placed his daughter in thick bushes and told her to stay still and be quiet until he returned. Kerr rode to the nearest neighbors and enlisted their help. When the group returned to the bushes, Kerr's daughter was still there safe and undiscovered. She had not moved a muscle nor made a sound since he had left her.

Gonzales grew and had several other encounters with Indians and with the Mexicans. As the westernmost Anglo-American settlement and the closest town to San Antonio, Gonzales was in the center of much of the Texas revolutionary activity. October 2, 1835, Texans led by John H. Moore challenging the Mexicans to "come and take it" fought Mexican troops who were sent to capture the town's cannon. The Texans rallied around the gun and fought the Battle of Gonzales, the first fight of the Texas Revolution. October 11, Stephen F. Austin took command of the volunteer army that had concentrated at Gonzales and there made preparations for the Siege of Bexar. Then in February 1836, Gonzales volunteers rode to the aid of William Barret Travis's command at the Alamo, where 32 men from Gonzales perished.

A month later, on March 13, Susanna W. Dickinson, widow of one Alamo defender, and Joe, William Barret Travis' slave, arrived in Gonzales with news of the slaughter at the Alamo. Sam Houston, who was attempting to reorganize the Texas army, then had the town of Gonzales burned and ordered a retreat, starting the famous Runaway Scrape.

After the Battle of San Jacinto many Gonzales citizens remained in exile. But by the early 1840s rebuilding of the town was concentrated on the original site near the Guadalupe River. In 1840, Gonzales volunteers responding to the Comanche attack (known as the Linnville Raid) rushed to the Battle of Plum Creek and helped defeat the Comanches south of Luling.

A marker on St. Louis Street commemorates DeWitt's Fort, the "Indian Fort Site".

4. Fort Waul

At the intersection of Highway 90A and FM 794 in Gonzales is Fort Waul situated on Waldrip Hill. It was one of the few Confederate earthwork fortifications built in Texas. This fort was intended to be a supply depot for the Confederacy as well as a defensive post on the Guadalupe River. This site was chosen because of its location between Austin, San Antonio, Houston, and Victoria. In addition, it is at the confluence of the Guadalupe and San Marcos rivers, both of which could be used to transport goods and supplies. The construction of the fort was designed to have outside embankment walls 8 feet high, 4 to 6 feet thick at the top, and 12 feet thick at the bottom. There was to be a defensive trench, or moat, surrounding it. A large, square bastion for cannons was to be situated at each of the four corners. A blockhouse was designed to be underground in the center of the fort.

In December of 1863, Colonel Lea was instructed to use slave labor from the surrounding counties to aid in the construction, which continued throughout 1864. But as the threat of a Union invasion of Texas declined, so did the defensive need for the fort and its supply depot. Construction was never completed. The unfinished fort fell into decay, and the stones from the blockhouse were used to rebuild the Gonzales College dormitory. It was not until the late 1870s that the site was named Fort Waul, in honor of General Thomas N. Waul, who lived in the area.

The outer walls of the original fort and a portion of the defensive ditch along the west wall are still plainly visible from the parking lot for Pioneer Village, a collection of structures from the 1800s that have been assembled for public view. A commemorative marker for Fort Waul is on the north side of the Pioneer Village parking lot. The village is open Saturdays and Sundays, or by appointment.

5. Presidio Nuestra Senora de Loreto La Bahia del Espiritu Santo (Which Texans renamed Fort Defiance and Fort Goliad)

(See colored pictures in the center section)

The presidio was originally established in 1721, at the site of old Fort Saint Louis, the fort that Cavelier La Salle had built in his ill-fated expedition in 1682. The presidio was moved to Goliad in 1749 where it played an important role in the development of Texas.

In 1835, Texas and Mexico were both in a political mess. General Santa Anna had taken control of Mexico and his Centralist party refused to abide by the Constitution of 1824. The Federalist Party in Mexico opposed Santa Anna and sought to restore that constitution. Many Texans who were satisfied with that constitution openly supported the Federalists while some Texans saw this as an opportunity to break free of Mexican rule. Citizens of Goliad actually signed the "Goliad Declaration of Independence" in 1835. Following that action, and several battles that took place in the area between Mexican troops and Texans, Santa Anna sent troops north to end the uprising. A group of battles known as the "Goliad Campaign of 1835" followed.

Conflicts, which had been escalating for several years, came to a boil as many Texans, in anticipation of physical support from the Mexican Federalists, marched on Matamoros. Fights between the Texans and Mexican Centralists near San Patricio were defeats for the Texans, who did not receive any meaningful military support from the Federalists. Santa Anna was reportedly in route to San Antonio (Texans had captured the town and presidio a year earlier during the Siege of Bexar) and Mexican General Jose de Urrea marched in route to La Bahia (Goliad).

Colonel James W. Fannin was the senior Texas officer in the field, and upon learning that Santa Anna was marching to the Alamo, Fannin moved his headquarters to La Bahia; a tragic mistake. His decision was based on his "conviction of its importance, as being advantageously located for a depot of reinforcements, clothing, provisions and military stores. It commands the sea coast, particularly Aransas and Matagorda Bays, and consequently the only convenient landings for vessels of any tonnage."

In early February, William B. Travis, commander at the Alamo, sent James Bonham, who was Fannin's long-time friend, to ask Fannin for help. Fannin considered the idea of moving his headquarters to San Antonio to reinforce the Alamo, but he stayed at Goliad to rebuild the presidio. Work was still unfinished when another of Travis's calls for help arrived on February 25. On March 11, General Sam Houston, learning that the Alamo had fallen, sent Fannin word ordering Fannin to fall back to Victoria "as soon as practicable . . . with your command, and such artillery as can be brought with expedition. The remainder to be sunk in the river." Fannin received this order either on March 13 or 14; the day is a matter of considerable historical dispute, since he was later charged with disobeying Houston's command.

Fannin now had his orders to retreat. Retreat started at midmorning during a heavy fog on March 19, but General Urrea had skillfully stalked his foe, overtook the Texans on the open prairie. Surrounded without food or water, Fannin's men fought throughout the long and bloody afternoon of March 19. The men, unwilling to leave the wounded, chose not to escape under a cover of darkness. They were aroused on the following morning by fire from Urrea's artillery.

Fannin was convinced of the futility of the fight and the necessity of seeking surrender terms, especially since his men were huddled helplessly in trenches and their many wounded were suffering. By order of Santa Anna, however, Urrea could offer no terms other than an unconditional surrender. The Texans accepted those terms and surrendered their arms.

Despite Urrea's plea to Santa Anna to treat Fannin's command as prisoners of war, the Mexican president ordered the Texans to be executed. Urrea carried out the execution order on Palm Sunday, March 27, 1836. More than 400 men were marched out of the presidio to be shot. A few escaped, but 342 were killed. "Remember Goliad!" along with "Remember the Alamo" now became battle cries when word of the execution reached other Texans.

Presidio La Bahia is the best-reconstructed presidio in the United States. As you walk behind its thick stone walls it is easy to imagine the battles that took place here. Also visit its museum. It is open daily 9 a.m. to 5 p.m. except Good Friday and Christmas

Texans shot that Palm Sunday in 1836 were buried at a site now marked by a monument at the nearby Fannin Battleground State Historical Park, 9 miles east of Goliad.

6. Mission Nuestra Senora del Espiritu Santo de Zuniga (Often referred to as Mission La Bahia)

This mission is named in Spanish records as La Bahia del Espiritu Santo de Zuniga. The name is in reference to its original location on La Bahia del Espiritu Santo (the Bay of the Holy Spirit, now referred to as Matagorda Bay and Lavaca Bay). Established in 1722, the mission was connected with the Presidio Nuestra Senora de Loreto.

Spanish efforts to keep possession of the territory north of the Rio Grande had led the government to authorize an expedition to evaluate ways to halt the encroachment of the English and French. It recommended moving La Bahia presidio and mission inland to the San Antonio River to protect the main road from Mexico to Bexar and East Texas. The area was also suited to crop and stock raising, and timber, stone, lime, and other building materials were plentiful.

But, before the mission was moved, it is credited with giving birth to the Texas cattle industry. The mission's main industry had been livestock raising, and exporting the cattle and horses that grazed on the prairies bordered by the Guadalupe, Lavaca, and San Antonio rivers. When the mission did move, the cattle were left to run wild, and as they later multiplied in the rich grassy region they became a foundation for many Texans to later accumulate fortunes.

In 1749, they moved. Temporary structures were rebuilt in 1758 from stone and mortar, though the mission's Indians were still living in huts. The missionary work focused on Aranama, Tamique, Tawakoni, and Tonkawa Indians and had some success, though many deserted. By the early 1760s Apaches began preying upon cattle, though the mission still prospered. Estimates are that 40,000 cattle and horses belonged to the mission and the settlers of La Bahia in 1778. Later, Indian cowhands drove the herds to East Texas and Louisiana and exchanged them for corn and needed supplies in what may have been the first cattle drive in Texas.

On March 24, 1931, the City of Goliad and Goliad County transferred ownership of the current site of the mission to the State of Texas, which agreed to preserve it as a historical park. By 1987, the reconstructed mission appeared as it did in 1749. Located across San Antonio River from the presidio, it is open to the public and decorated at Christmas with many lights.

The original mission site (known as the Keeran Archeological

Site) was on Garcitas Creek near present-day Inez in Victoria County. The site wasn't rediscovered until the early twentieth century. It was excavated in 1950 and again in 1973. Though on private property, it did receive a Centennial marker in 1936, and was listed in the National Register of Historic Places in 1971. (See Fort Saint Louis in this region for the latest news of excavation progress.)

7. Mission Nuestra Senora del Rosario

This mission was located west of present-day Goliad and was under protection of nearby Presidio La Bahia. It was begun in an attempt to make peace with various Karankawan tribes, which did not get along with the other Indians at the existing missions. Also the Spanish did not want the French gaining a foothold in the area by making the Indians their allies. So in 1754, nine presidio soldiers assisted in constructing buildings made of timber and whitewashed clay. Stone and mortar were used later. By 1768, the mission owned a ranch with 5,000 cattle, 400 milk cows, and 700 sheep and goats. The cattle herd grew to 50,000 cows by 1789, nevertheless the mission still failed in its goals with Christianizing the Indians.

In 1778, the Karankawas massacred a group of Spanish sailors and fled. Authorities pardoned them, except for the leaders of the assault. Troublemakers proceeded to cause further trouble at the mission by abducting other Indians and setting fires. The mission was virtually abandoned and the Indians argued for a mission to be built closer to their homes. As a result Mission Nuestra Senora del Refugio was established in 1792. In 1807, mission Rosario was formally combined with the mission in Refugio.

The Texas State Historical Society has an archeological dig for this mission south of Highway 59 between Beeville and Goliad, 0.5 miles west of the San Antonio River. The large-scale archeological work was commenced in 1940-41 under the National Park Service. Some artifacts from the excavation are stored at the Texas Archeological Research Laboratory at Texas University in Austin. In 1972-73 the Texas Parks and Wildlife Department sponsored additional excavations and found evidence of four phases of building, and grave outlines were recorded. These diggings may be seen from the highway, but it is illegal to take or disturb any artifacts.

8. Fort Casa Blanca (Also known as Camp Merrill or Camp Casa Blanca)

This fort was erected in the1850s as a family fortification on the Nueces River. During the Civil War it was a shelter for wagon trains carrying cotton to Mexico and a rendezvous point for Confederate boats hauling out bales of cotton after delivering guns, ammunition, medicine, and other supplies. The boats had to out-maneuver the Union ships blocking Nueces Bay.

Walls of 2 to 3 feet thickness made the fort almost impregnable. The gate was made of heavy cypress and wide enough for a two-wheel cart to enter. The fort was designed with corner parapets and loopholes to give defenders extra protection.

Though the fort has disappeared, legends persist of treasures hidden in its walls. The site of the Fort Casa Blanca, north of Sandia, is now on private property, inaccessible to the public. Camp Merrill (its history is brief) may have been a sub camp of Fort Merrill in Live Oak County.

9. Fort Lipantitlan (Also Camp San Patricio)

Fort Lipantitlan was one of a string of forts Mexico built in 1831 as a part of its efforts to enforce immigration laws in Texas. In 1728, the site had once been a Spanish fort with the same name, Lipantitlan, meaning "Lipan land" (the history of the earlier fort has disappeared). The location was the early camping grounds of the Lipan Apache Indians on the Nueces River bank. The site is 3 miles upstream from San Patricio, and 3.7-miles south of Sandia on Highway 70. Turn right off highway 70 at the T and go for 1.5 miles to an unmarked road to the left. There is a 1936 commemorative marker about Fort Lipantitlan. San Patricio has a museum of artifacts since the 1830's – call San Patricio Trading Co. (361-547-5507) for the museum hours and days.

Across the river, while the Mexicans were watching for illegal aliens, Empresarios were given the land concession for San Patricio under the condition that all new immigrants could not be citizens of the United States. Saving the cost of going to Europe to find settlers, Empresarios James McGloin and John McMullen went to New York City where they found new arrivals from Ireland (technically not U. S. citizens) and talked them into founding San Patricio.

In 1835–36, Fort Lipantitlan and Camp San Patricio played important roles in the Texas Revolution. Texans came from Goliad crossing the Nueces by canoe and captured the fort after Goliad's Declaration of Independence in 1835. In the Battle of Lipantitlan, fought in a heavy thunderstorm and a "blue norther", Texans destroyed most of the earthworks and burned the buildings. Cannons from the fort were pushed into the river. After their victory, the Texans let the Mexicans retreat to Matamoros. The loss of Fort Lipantitlan cut off the supply route for the troops of General Coz whose Mexican army was under siege in San Antonio. General Santa Anna then sent additional troop north to suppress the revolution in Goliad in late 1835.

It was at the Battle of San Patricio in 1836 that General Santa Anna's troops killed 16 and captured 30 Texans who were enroute to invade Mexico. Mexican troops then defeated another Texan force at the Battle of Aqua Dulce Creek. San Patricio became a ghost town as colonists fled to Victoria and other refuges, leaving their homes and livestock unprotected.

Nothing remains of the early embankment fortification of Fort Lipantitlan. When it was built it was lined by fence-rails to hold the dirt in place. Four parapets were designed for one cannon each and log barracks were built inside the embankment. The site is on private property.

After the Texas Revolution, wild gangs composed of former Mexican soldiers and cattle rustlers controlled the area. In 1841, the San Patricio Minutemen were formed to protect the people of San

Patricio with a Camp San Patricio established 2 miles outside of San Patricio on the road leading to McGloin Bluff on Ingleside Cove. At the time, Texas rules for Minuteman provided that county companies could have only a total of four months' service a year. However, in September 1841, the Texas War Department granted the San Patricio Minutemen sanction after a Mexican raid on Refugio illustrated the lack of area security.

In March 1842, when a Mexican army raided Goliad and Refugio they sent troops to destroy the San Patricio Minutemen, which they did in the ensuing fight on March 7. Nothing remains of Camp San Patricio but a commemorative marker located in the center of the town.

10. Camp Corpus Christi

In November of 1850, Camp Corpus Christi was established in Corpus Christi for two companies of the Fifth Infantry. The camp was moved the following April, when Commander, Major G. R. Paul, moved his troops 30 miles inland to a location that was also given the name Camp Corpus Christi. Regardless of a lack of good drinking water, and there not being any permanent building materials, the camp stayed at this location for four years.

Two companies of the Seventh Infantry manned Camp Corpus Christi and in 1852 it became the headquarters for General Persifor F. Smith until he moved his headquarters to San Antonio in 1855. There are no remains of Camp Corpus Christi.

11. Camp Marcy

Sailing from New Orleans on the steamship Alabama, General Zachary Taylor and his troops landed off San Jose Island near Aransas Pass on July 25, 1845, and there planted a U. S. flag on Texas soil for the first time. While waiting for the entire company of troops to land, Taylor selected a site for an encampment on a strip of the coast north of a settlement called Kenney's Ranch. The camp was strongly fortified with a surrounding wall that had slots cut for rifle firing and two cannons mounted for defense. The camp was called Camp Marcy.

While Taylor's troops were camped there the United States was negotiating to avoid war. Mexico had never conceded that Texas won its independence, and had warned the U. S. that the annexation of Texas meant war. Nevertheless, Texas was annexed, and the Mexican War began.

As the troops waited for action, Kenney's Ranch changed into the town of Corpus Christi. Houses sprung up like flowers. Stores opened, and gamblers appeared overnight, looking for easy marks. Soldiers enjoyed the activity but they did not enjoy the Texas weather.

The camp was hit by a thunderstorm that August, the likes of which none of the soldiers had ever experienced. The thunder roared so loud that it was heard 50 miles off, and the rain poured and poured. Then in November, a "blue norther" dropped temperatures 50 degrees in a single day when the bone-chilling winds from the arctic blew through the soldiers' tents, clothing and skin. Then January brought a "wet norther" with freezing rain covering everything with a coat of solid ice. Some of tents collected so much ice that the troops were imprisoned in their tents. A few soldiers had left a flap open enough to crawl out and they rescued the others.

Artesian Park in Corpus Christi has a monument and marker to honor Zachary Taylor, otherwise there is no way to know that 3,000 troops once camped in what is now downtown.

12. Camp Nueces (Nueces County) (And Kenney's Camp, Camp Williams and Camp Everitt)

This Camp Nueces was established in 1842 in the Corpus Christi Bay area near another camp called Kenney's Fort. The two camps as well as nearby Camps Williams and Everitt were probably built in response to a fear in the 1830-40s that Mexico might invade Texas by the sea.

A settlement grew up near where Camp Nueces had stood. This settlement was the victim of an attack called the Nuecestown raid of 1875 (also known as the Corpus Christi Raid).

Juan N. Cortina, Mexican outlaw and later Mexican general, was probably an instigator of the raid. In late March 1875, a number of men left Mexico and began stealing horses. Then the raiders robbed a home and took a woman hostage. Then 18 of the raiders robbed a store taking all valuables as well as supplying themselves with horses and saddles. Eleven of the Anglos and Hispanic women and children were taken captive. A Hispanic Texan was killed when he refused to join the raiders.

The raiders and their captives then headed to Nuecestown, 13 miles from Corpus Christi.

There they tried to rob another store, but the Anglo owner managed to shoot one of the raiders and scared the others off. The owner escaped through a door in the floor to a trench that had been dug for this purpose. The store property was destroyed. An Anglo man nearby was shot and killed, and raiders set the building on fire. The raiders freed their female captives and left.

Word of the raiding reached Corpus Christi and two vigilante companies formed to pursue the raiders. One posse caught up with the raiders but retreated when they ran out of ammunition. One man of their group was killed. The raiders now released the male prisoners.

Another posse caught a wounded raider and a mob hanged him a few days later.

The Mexican raiders then turned to the border sending two escorted wagons of plunder ahead. As they passed by Piedras, they shot and killed a man for his horse. On April 2, they surrounded the town of Roma, intending to rob the customs house. They were stopped there by U. S. troops. Later, in Mexico, some of the raiders were identified and arrested, but Cortina himself avoided trial.

Anglo residents plotted retaliation and bands of volunteers organized "minute companies" in every county from the Nueces to the Rio Grande. The avengers not only hunted down the Mexican outlaws, they went after peaceful rancheros, and plain merchants. They looted property and burned homes. They killed Mexicans with new saddles figuring they were stolen, and they killed all of the adult males at a Mexican-owned ranch in present-day Kenedy County. Finally the sheriff in Corpus Christi requested assistance of Texas Rangers, who disbanded the militia. Rangers stopped further militia violence, but the raids from across the Rio Grande continued.

13. Mission Nuestra Senora del Refugio

This was the last mission the Spanish established in Texas. Founded February 4, 1793, it was part of a plan by Spanish priests to convert all the Indian tribes living along the Texas coast. Missionaries earlier had attempted to settle and convert the Karankawa at Nuestra Senora del Rosario and Nuestra Senora del Espiritu Santo, but the Indians had deserted. They promised to come to another mission if one was established for them nearer the Gulf coast.

Indians helped choose the mission site in an area known as El Paraje del Refugio "Place of Refuge." This new mission was named Nuestra Senora del Refugio. In January 1795, the mission moved to its final location at the site of the present-day town of Refugio. Despite difficulties, the construction of the mission was nearly completed by 1799. Many buildings were constructed with thatched roofs. Only the church and the shop for the blacksmith were made from stone. The church roof was wooden and its floor was tile. A stockade fence provided protection from Indian attacks.

Like its early predecessors, this mission became a focus of attack by Comanches raiding for livestock. It was these continuing attacks by Indians, combined with an unstable source of supplies that led to the mission's abandonment on January 7, 1830. It was left to ruin. When Irish settlers moved into the area during the 1830s, they named their town for the mission.

In 1836, the mission played a role in Texas' fight for independence when Mexican forces were advancing north, Colonel Fannin of the Texas forces in Goliad sent Amon King to warn the area. King stumbled upon General Urrea's advancing patrols at a ranch. Pursued by a force of about 50 or 60 men, King retreated with the ranch families to Mission Refugio and then sent a messenger to Fannin for help. Fannin sent William Ward and a group of volunteers in relief.

Meanwhile, Mexican General Urrea had been advised that the Texans had stopped at Refugio and sent cavalry units made of local ranchers to hold the Texans until the Mexican army could arrive. Ward and his men, like King's, were eager for a fight. Instead of returning to Goliad, the Texans sent out scouting parties. King wanted to seek out and punish the ranchers who had helped Urrea, and killed eight local Mexicans that he assumed were spies. A group of Texans under Warren J. Mitchell returning to the mission from a scouting party met Urrea's army of some 1,500 men. Urrea launched a vigorous assault, which the Texans withstood with only minor casualties. As King's forces returned to the mission as well, they stumbled upon the rear of Urrea's army and were attacked. King and his men took position in woods on the bank of the river and resisted all efforts to be dislodged, but they exhausted most of their ammunition and provisions. The Texans then tried to cross the river, but got their gunpowder wet. Overtaken the next day by Mexican ranchers, they were unable to resist and were captured.

Most of King's men were shot in Urrea's obedience to the Mexican decree of December 30, 1835, which commanded death to armed rebels. Ward made it to Victoria where he ran into Urrea's soldiers again. After a brief fight, ten of Ward's men ultimately escaped to safety.

Traces of the ruins of the mission are found under the structure of Our Lady of Refuge Catholic Church in Refugio. King Memorial State Park in Refugio is in honor of King's men who died in the Battle of Refugio. Both King and William Ward escaped only to return to Goliad where they were included in the troops that surrendered and were then shot.

14. Camp Semmes

Camp Semmes was built on San Jose Island in the Gulf of Mexico in Aransas County as a Confederate post for storing cotton. It was captured by the Union forces in 1863 and then recaptured by the Confederacy. It was then retaken once again as the Union fought to gain control of the cotton grown in Texas. These continuing fights destroyed the only town on the island, Aransas, and it was never re-built. Earlier, in 1845, the island was the camp (without a name) where General Zachary Taylor first landed in route to build Fort Polk at Point Isabel and Fort Brown at Brownsville. It was a short lived camp as troops almost immediately moved to Corpus Christi and made a camp there. An early visitor to San Jose Island was a Lieutenant and future General, Ulysses S. Grant.

15. Camp Irwin

Twelve miles inland from Port Lavaca, the Second Illinois Volunteers of Brigadier-General John E. Wool established Camp Irwin on August 1, 1846, as a holding camp until their supplies arrived. Mumps, measles and scarlet fever broke out among the soldiers, and the number of doctors and hospital tents was inadequate. Taking soldiers that could walk, General Wool marched his troops to San Antonio, a distance of 70 miles. It took 13 days for the trek through the low, marshy land covered with water and grass that grew 3 feet high. Nothing remains of Camp Irwin, except a place in history.

Near the site of Camp Irwin was the community of Linnville. Linnville was a wealthy port on the Gulf, and many items from New Orleans were unloaded there for transport to San Antonio. The town of Linnville was utterly destroyed in the most terrifying of all Comanche raids in southeast Texas when in 1840, Chief Buffalo Hump launched an attack down the Guadalupe valley with as many as 1,000 braves. The raid was motivated by the earlier "Council House Fight" in San Antonio that was supposed to have been a council of peace between Texans and the Indians. The Indians had agreed to bring all of their white captives to the meeting as a sign of friendship, but they brought only one.   Texans attempted to hold the Indians prisoners until the remaining captives were surrendered. A fight started and many Indian chiefs killed.

The Indians surrounded Linnville and began raiding stores and houses. Twenty-three people were killed before the surprised people of Linnville could flee to the water. Remaining aboard boats and a schooner out in the Gulf saved them, while they watched the destruction of their town. During the entire day the Comanches plundered and burned buildings. They herded large numbers of cattle into pens and senselessly slaughtered them. They looted goods valued at $300,000 that were stored in Linnville at the time. Then after loading their plunder onto pack mules, the Comanche raiders left, taking 3,000 horses and many people as their captives.

The Comanches were defeated at the Battle of Plum Creek near Luling on August 12.

16. Fort Esperanza (Also known as Fort DeBray, and Fort Washington)

Fort Esperanza was a Civil War earthwork fortification on the east shore of Matagorda Island constructed to guard Cavallo Pass, the entry to Matagorda Bay. It was built in1861 when it was determined that Fort Washington, a small fort near the lighthouse on Matagorda Island was too exposed. (Nothing else is recorded about Fort Washington.)

Esperanza had nine guns including eight 24-pound cannons and one 28-pounder. The fort was out of range of the guns of large Union vessels in the Gulf but had the same command of the channel as Fort Washington must have had. The Confederates thought the shallow water (10 feet deep) on the bar would prevent vessels larger than gunboats from entering the bay, but the Union navy still managed to get through. On October 25, 1862, soon after having captured Galveston, William B. Renshaw, Captain of the USS Westfield, sailed past the fort. Impressed by the Union's guns, defenders of the fort retreated to Indianola. The Union forces then seized Indianola after a brief battle. Port Lavaca was bombarded, but a Confederate battery of two guns put up a good resistance. In early November, the Union fleet withdrew from Matagorda Bay, and since they had no ground forces to leave behind, Confederates reoccupied Indianola and Fort Esperanza.

After the Union defeat at the Battle of Sabine Pass in September 1863, Union invasion plans for Texas shifted further south. The Rio Grande valley was invaded in early November, Corpus Christi and Aransas Pass fell, and Union troops advancing to San Jose Island crossed to Matagorda Island. The Confederates failed to stop them at a battle at Cedar Bayou in November of 1863. Union forces under General T. E. G. Ransom assaulted Fort Esperanza on November 27. On the night of November 29, the Confederates, outnumbered and outflanked, evacuated the fort after spiking the guns, burning their supplies, and blowing up their ammunition. The fort was occupied and repaired by Union forces using it as a base of operations for other campaigns in the area. In the spring of 1864, Union troops withdrew from Matagorda Bay to participate in the proposed invasion of Texas from northeast Louisiana.

Fort Esperanza was then reoccupied by the Confederates and held until the end of the war. Eastern walls of the fort were destroyed as the shoreline was eroded by a storm in 1868. By 1878 the rest of the 9-foot-high, 20-foot-thick, turf-covered walls had eroded away. Outlying emplacements and rifle pits can still be traced in some areas. Nothing else remains.

17. Fort Saint Louis

There have been few times when such a misfortune as occurred at Fort Saint Louis had such a positive effect on the world. When the ships of Rene Robert Cavelier Sieur de La Salle, whether due to faulty navigation or bad maps, landed on the coast of Texas instead of the mouth of the Mississippi, the mistake hastened the development of Texas.

Although Texas was claimed by Spain, the Spanish had ignored this new possession after the expeditions of Coronado found no gold to enrich the King's treasury. The United States had not yet separated from the British, and the French owned land along the coast line between what would become the United States and the province of New Spain, as the Spanish named this land.

La Salle brought nothing of value to Texas and his fort was a failure, but by establishing a French presence in Spanish territory, Spain was spurred to begin colonization efforts in Texas. After part of his fleet had been lost at sea and another ship sunk upon entering the harbor, La Salle landed near present-day Lavaca Bay and built a fort. It was a crude construction using lumber from the ship, cannons were taken ashore, but many supplies were lost and Indians attacked almost immediately. An alligator ate one of the settlers and another man lost a leg to amputation after being struck by a rattlesnake. The Indians also sent word to the Spanish in Mexico that white men were building a fort on the coast.

That was the news that caused the Spanish to send troops and priests to build settlements in Texas. It was the news that changed the future of not only Texas, but the United States also. No one can predict what would have been the history of North American had not the Spanish rushed to settle Texas. "If" is really a big word when applied to questions like "if" the Texas territory was claimed by France, "if" it was claimed by the English, or "if "Texas was left undeveloped for another 100 years? What then?" These were questions that did not have to be answered due to La Salle's misfortune.

Fort Saint Louis has not been forgotten. The Texas Historical Society has recovered one of La Salle's ships, "La Belle," which was sunk off Lavaca Bay, and started an archaeological dig at the fort site in 1999 on private land (not open to the public). Artifacts that were discovered in 1999 – 2001 include the cannons from the French ship, and bones believed to be those of the members of the expedition who were killed during an Indian raid. The artifacts are being taken to a small museum in Victoria for public display. The archaeological dig is also now uncovering the original site of the Presidio La Bahia, which the Spanish later built nearby.

18. Camp Chambers (Victoria County)

This was the last camp established along the Lavaca and Navidad rivers by the army of the Republic of Texas. It was occupied from August through October in 1837 under command of Colonel Edwin Morehouse, and was named for Major-General Thomas Jefferson Chambers who had recruited hundreds of volunteers for Texas from the United States to fight in the revolution. Promise of land for services had brought most of the volunteers. Many were undisciplined. The camp was located on Arenosa Creek near the road from Texana to Victoria.

In 1847, John Sutherland began a stage run from Houston to Victoria via Richmond, Egypt, and Texana along this road. The road also connected to Gulf coast ports, where supplies and settlers from the eastern United States and Europe were steadily arriving. Thus, by 1848 bimonthly service between San Antonio and Corpus Christi had commenced. In December 1849, the company of Harrison and Brown began weekly service between San Antonio and Lavaca via Seguin, Gonzales, Cuero, and Victoria. In 1851, James L. Allen ran stages between San Antonio and Indianola by a similar route, with an extra stop at New Braunfels.

Stagecoach travel was filled with danger from bandits and hostile Indians. This was especially true in the frontier areas such as in the country around San Antonio and Austin. Stage owners reported that Indian raiding parties stole mules and supplies, destroyed way stations, and murdered drivers, guards, and passengers. Even so, new stage lines were added every year as the growth in the population resulted in the frontier's expansion and in new towns being built.

19. Camp Henry E. McCulloch

Located four miles north of Victoria, Camp McCulloch served as a Confederate camp from September of 1861 through May 1862 for training volunteers from Calhoun, Victoria, Bell, Matagorda, Bexar, Gonzales, DeWitt, Travis, and Guadalupe counties for the Sixth Texas Infantry. The camp was named in honor of General Henry Eustace McCulloch. The first troops there were the Lavaca Guards from Calhoun County who reported one week after the first shot was fired at Fort Sumter in South Carolina. The recruits were drilled under the watchful eye of Colonel Robert R. Garland until they became adept at marching with a military precision.

In addition to infantry companies, two cavalry companies were also stationed at the camp, and in December of 1861 units were ordered to Indianola and Saluria to help defend the regions against an anticipated Union attack. When the attack did not materialize, troops were returned to the camp. In May 1862, the troops were moved out to the Arkansas Post where the majority died from exposure. Fewer than 100 men of the regiment survived the war.

In 1862 the camp was closed. There are no remains.

20. Round Top House

One of the earliest settlers in the area of present-day Victoria was a Mexican named Placido Benavides, who around 1833 built the Round Top House as a family fort for the defense of Victoria against Indian raids. He later fought with the Texans in the liberation of Goliad in 1835 and helped train Texan troops at Gonzales. In 1835, he marched against the Mexicans in the Siege of Bexar, and a year later he warned Texans of Santa Anna's plans.

In August 1840, Victoria County was the target of one of the most terrifying Comanche raids in southeast Texas. (See "Fort Irwin" for more information on the Linnville Raid). The raiding Comanches killed a number of slaves working in fields as well as whites who were unable to reach Victoria. When Buffalo Hump appeared near Victoria, the Comanches were mistaken for friendly Lipans. "We of Victoria were startled by the apparitions presented by the sudden appearance of hundreds of mounted Comanches in the outskirts of the village," wrote John J. Linn in 1883 of this attack.

The Indians captured over 1,500 horses belonging to area residents and to Mexican horse traders that had arrived with a large herd. The Indians surrounded Victoria, but the settlers' defensive efforts apparently prevented their sacking the town itself. The Round Top House served Victoria as a fortress against the Indian's attack.

The Comanches then left Victoria with their spoils and thundered toward the coast. They camped the night of August 7 on Placido Creek on Benavides' ranch, where two wagoneers were intercepted. One escaped and the other was killed. Then the raiders found and killed two men cutting hay. The next morning, Comanches surprised the town of Linnville. The Victoria-Linnville raid is commemorated by a State Historical Society marker in downtown Victoria on De Leon Plaza near the site of the Round Top House (of which nothing now remains).

Also in the area is the second location of Mission Nuestra Senora del Espiritu Santo de Zuniga. It is near present-day Mission Valley in Victoria County on private property. The site of the mission's associated *visita* or *rancheria* (now called the Tonkawa Bank Archeological Site) is located near the Guadalupe River in Victoria's Riverside Park. The site was listed in the National Register of Historic Places in the early 1980s.

21. Camp Bowie (And Camp Preston)

The principal encampment of the army of the Republic of Texas from April 22 through the middle of June 1837, was Camp Bowie located on the east side of the Navidad River at Red Bluff, 8 miles southeast of the community of Edna. The camp's first commander was General Albert Sidney Johnston who was also the commanding General of the Army.

The army had first been stationed in December 1836 at Camp Independence on the Lavaca River. This was after the victory at San Jacinto, and since that fight numerous volunteers from the United States had been joining the army. These men came to fight, but most of the fighting was over. Their restlessness bred discontent and in 1837 the men mutinied while General Johnston was recovering from a dueling wound and was not in camp (for information of the duel, see "Camp Independence" in this region).

The army was supposed to move to Camp Preston, also on the Lavaca River a short distance from present-day Lolita. But after the mutiny, the men were moved to Camp Bowie. Colonel Joseph H. D. Rogers of the First Regiment succeeded Johnston at this camp.

Camp Bowie, named for Alamo defended James Bowie was the

site of the murder of Colonel Henry Teal on the night of May 5, 1837. This incident caused President Sam Houston to issue indefinite furloughs to almost all of the men of this undisciplined army. In the latter part of May, Secretary of War William S. Fisher issued furloughs and travel orders to 1,200 troops, two-thirds of the Permanent Volunteers of the Republic of Texas Army.   By the third week in June the 200 men remaining at Camp Bowie were transferred to Camp Crockett, and Camp Bowie was abandoned (nothing remains).

22. Camp Crockett (Jackson County) (And Fort Settlement)

Named for Alamo defender David Crockett, the camp became the main encampment and headquarters of the army of the Republic of Texas after Camp Bowie was closed in June 1837. Camp Crockett was somewhere in central Jackson County, probably on the Navidad River near Camp Bowie and just to the south or southwest of the site of present-day Edna. Colonel H. R. A. Wiggington, of the Second Regiment of Permanent Volunteers commanded the camp until it was abandoned in July.   The troops were then transferred to Camp Chambers.

Near this camp was a Fort Settlement on which the history is very thin.

When troops or Rangers chased Indians, local settlers frequently joined in the chase. The journal of one settler from Jackson County provides an idea of what the life on a raid might have been like when it became time to eat. "We were told to get what potatoes we wanted, to kill a hog and rob a bee tree. Some of us were detailed to dig potatoes, some to kill a hog, and others to get wood and make the fire. The potatoes were not cleaned, a good deal of hair was left on the hog, and our salt was spilled in the sand. However, the dirty potatoes, the hairy hog, and salt and sand were put into a large wash kettle to cook. After the pork and potatoes were done, which was some time during the night, we would go and eat as we felt like it, and occasionally on through the night one or another would get up to eat. But when daylight came, all that was necessary to satisfy our appetite was to look into the kettle, and see what we had eaten! What a mess." For this life, the men volunteered; they were creating their future.

23. Camp Independence (And Camp Red Bank)

This was the main camp of the Republic of Texas' army until March 1837. It was established east of the Lavaca River 5 miles from the old community of Texana (there is an interesting Texana museum near the library in Edna) in Jackson County in December 1836. The camp's history is filled with conflicts, not with the enemy, but from within the Texans ranks.

General Felix Huston commanded the army stationed at the camp. Felix Huston was a swashbuckling Mississippi planter, slave trader, and soldier of fortune that had been appointed junior Brigadier-General of the army. He held command only briefly until General Albert Sidney Johnston arrived to replace him on February 4, 1837. As Huston considered Johnston's appointment an attempt "to ruin my reputation and inflict a stigma on my character", he issued a challenge to the new commander. The duelers met the following day on the Lavaca River.

Huston, by reputation was "a most expert marksman," and Johnston "made no pretension at all in that line." After three exchanges of fire, Johnston was seriously wounded when a ball passed through his hips. He lingered near death for several days then recovered after months of suffering. General Johnston never resented Huston's challenge, or his wound, as he considered their meeting "a public duty" and believed he could never have commanded the respect of the army if he had "shown the least hesitation in meeting General Huston's challenge." General Johnston maintained his headquarters at Camp Independence until the army was transferred.

Three months later on May 5, Captain Henry Teal was assassinated near the camp, as he lay in his tent asleep. Someone fired from outside the tent placing the muzzle of the gun almost in contact with the target. Teal was an adventurer who had been captured by the Mexicans as a political prisoner but had later escaped. At the camp, he was not an ideal leader. He reportedly had no tact and was not liked by the underfed, under clothed and underpaid troops in the Texas army. The assassin, or the motive, was never determined though there was speculation that Teal had caused hard feelings among the troops by parading around in his fancy full dress uniform.

In 1936 the Texas Centennial Committee placed a marker at a

site, 4 and 1/2 miles southwest of Edna. Take County Road 306 south from Edna to FM 1822.

Nearby, on the Lavaca River in 1831-32, was a Mexican army camp by the name of El Banco Colorado, or the Red Bank. There the Mexicans used convict labor to manufacture bricks and then shipped them back by boat to a port in Mexico. Anglos, which Mexicans thought were illegal immigrants, may have been used as convicts. A small part of the brick kiln remains.

There is a buried treasure story from around this area. During the war with Mexico (which one is not noted), a Mexican ship loaded with gold was pursued by a Texan boat that chased it up the Navidad River. The Mexicans scuttled their ship and ran up the hill to bury the gold (somewhere near Red Bluff). While many of the Mexicans fired at the Texans from behind trees, the other Mexicans buried the gold. Treasure hunters have dug many holes at the site, but no one has ever admitted finding any of the gold.

24. Camp Johnson (Jackson County) (And Camp Lavaca)

One of the many camps established in counties along the Gulf coast during the Texas Revolution, Camp Johnson was the headquarters for the Texans army around September 1836. The camp was probably named for Francis W. Johnson who had fought at the Siege of Bexar in 1835. His troop was one of the first to meet Santa Anna's forces (at the Battle of San Patricio in February 1836 when all but Johnson and four of his men were killed).

Texan generals Thomas J. Rusk and Felix Huston made the camp their headquarters. It was located near the Lavaca River five miles from the Dimmit Landing and four miles south-southeast of present-day Vanderbilt. Also in this area at the same time was a Camp Lavaca (frequently spelled as La Baca or Labacca) which was a camp of the Republic of Texas under General Rusk. This camp may have been moved to Camp Johnson because it was too close to the bay, causing the water to be brackish.

Panic followed as news of General Santa Anna's victory at the Alamo spread through the settlements. Families buried their belonging and took off in a mad dash to escape the advancing Mexican armies. A woman in Texana in a letter to her sister dated June 5,

1836 describes the turmoil: "There were a lot of scared folks in the runaway crowd. Some were on sleds, some on contrivances made with cart wheels, some on wagons, some on horseback, some on foot; anyway that they could run. At the Sabine, people were all mixed up and confused. Children were crying, women praying, and the men cursing. I tell you it was a serious time. The settlement of Texana was abandoned; all in flight. Where they were going, no one knows. Not a sole was left in all of Jackson County."

25. Fort West Bernard Station (Also called Post West Bernard Station, and Spanish Camp)

The Republic of Texas established West Bernard Station in 1837 on West Bernard Creek, a location that is now off FM 1161 between Hungerford and Spanish Camp in Wharton County. This strategically located major ordnance post fulfilled the needs for the Republic of Texas military before the completion of an arsenal in Houston in 1838. As late as May in 1839, wagoneers still transported ordnance between Houston and Post West Bernard. Ordnance department records indicated that most of the serviceable heavy ordnance was transported to Houston, but the Texans continued to operate this repair facility at West Bernard.

The post was not an easy place to live, according to Thomas P. Anderson, the medical officer for the garrison of five men. In his resignation letter he complained that he was "five or six miles away from human habitation, having to carry his own wood and water and cook his own meals, and being forced to eat and sleep in the open air without shelter from weather."

An archeological dig is now being conducted under the direction of Joe Hudgins, a descendant of early settlers in Wharton County. Artifacts are on display at the Wharton Junior College library and the Wharton County Museum.

In the early days of Stephen F. Austin's Colony another camp was established in northeastern Wharton County on a mail route from Glen Flora. The community was called Spanish Camp and is now located at the junction of FM 640 and 1161. It was later named for the Mexican forces who camped at the nearby springs on Peach Creek. According to legend the Mexicans were carrying a large payroll of gold coins. They then hastily buried the gold upon receiving news of their country's loss at the Battle of San Jacinto.

The campsite became a landmark. If anyone ever found treasure, they kept it a secret, but then they might have struck oil and accepted that more valuable treasure for their efforts.

26. Fort Bend

Located near Richmond, the original settlement was an 1821 blockhouse that the "Old Three Hundred" of Stephen F. Austin's Colony made at a river bend on the Brazos. This was also where Santa Anna crossed the river with his army on the way to his fateful meeting with the Texan army at San Jacinto. The site was one of the more favorable crossings along the Brazos and when Santa Anna approached, a Texan rear guard detachment led by Wiley Martin briefly tried to defend it. After Martin was maneuvered out of his position, Santa Anna transported part of his Mexican army across the Brazos. (See #43, Camp on the San Jacinto)

After Santa Anna's defeat at the Battle of San Jacinto, the Fort Bend site was used briefly by the Texas army. Troops of Thomas Jefferson Green, in pursuit of retreating Mexican forces led by General Vicente Filisola, stopped at the fort in mid-May of 1836.

In 1936, the Texas Centennial Commission erected a monument to commemorating Fort Bend's role in the Texas Revolution. Fort Bend Historical Museum (open daily except Mondays) includes artifacts of the early 1800s. Buried in the Richmond cemetery are Texans Mirabeau Lamar and Mrs. James Long, frequently called the "Mother of Texas" (see "Fort Las Casas").

27. Fort Quintana (And Fort Terrell)

Shipwrecked by a storm in the Gulf of Mexico that had sunk their ship a few days earlier, the Spanish survivors were drifting in a small boat, sun burnt, hungry, and dying of thirst when they discovered a current of fresh water. Following the current they came to the inlet of a river where they found food and water to drink. They named this river Los Brazos de Dios (Brazos), meaning "the Arms of God."

In 1821, Mexico, newly freed from Spain, established a fortification at that fresh water inlet naming it Fort Quintana after General Andreas Quintana, the Mexican deputy minister of foreign and internal affairs. Records indicate the site of the fort became a Civil War stronghold for the Confederacy. This might have been so, or perhaps soldiers called their fort (known as Fort Terrell) by the older fort's name, or perhaps they were just referring to the community of Quintana, which had preceded the Mexican fort. A December 6, 1931, issue of the Houston <u>Post Dispatch</u> refers, however, to there having been two forts in the vicinity of Quintana. Whichever number is correct, hurricanes in 1867, 1875, 1899 and the big one in 1900 probably destroyed whatever fortifications were still remaining.

Quintana was bombarded near the end of the Civil War by a Union warship that was also shelling the nearby fort. Houses and civilians were hit. Cannon balls were still found years later.

A Fort Terrell near Quintana was also mentioned during the Civil War. Its may have never been completed. A report in 1865 stated that the workers were being withdrawn to Fort Velasco. Fort Terrell was named for Alexander Watkins Terrell, commander of Terrell's Texas Cavalry Regiment. On an 1878 map the site was marked with the name of "Old Fort." It is possible the details in written descriptions of the fort are taken from the plans, and the fort did not actually exist. Terrell was one of the many fortifications the Confederacy in 1861 decided to build along this area of the coast. Sites designated were Sabine Pass, Beaumont, on Galveston Island, Mud Island, and at the inlet to the Brazos and San Bernard rivers, as well as on the bays at Caney Creek, Corpus Christi, and near Brownsville. Not all plans were carried out.

A marker was placed by the state at the location of the old village of Quintana.

28. Fort Velasco

"As soon as our company opened fire on the fort it seemed to ignite and flame like a volcano, until the battle ended. The fort seemed to emit one continual blaze of fire directed to all points. Laying down on the grass directly in a range between the fort and our schooner; the shots passed immediately over our heads. The stillness of the night, the flash and report of the gun, and the peculiar noise of the ball, caused thoughts to hurry through the mind, the pulse to vibrate, and the blood with an unusual flow to thrill briskly through our veins. Our vessel soon got to her moorings and opened her battery. The sight was truly sublime and the effect thrilling."

This description comes from Henry Smith, a Texan, who fought at the Battle of Velasco in 1832. The battle was waged at Fort Velasco, near the present-day community of Surfside Beach, close to Freeport. Fort Velasco was built in two circular rows of wooden pickets 10 feet high with the area within the pickets filled with sand. Logs were placed on top of the sand as a platform for a nine-pound cannon. The cannon could swivel to guard both the mouth of the Brazos River and the coastline. It was a formidable coastal defense.

The battle was the result of simmering hostilities between the Mexicans and the Texans. The Texans were upset at the commander of Fort Anahuac for throwing Texan William B. Travis (of future Alamo fame) in jail. Texans planned to free Travis but they did not want the Mexican commander at Fort Velasco, Domingo de Ugartechea, to interfere. The Texans sailed a schooner, loaded with cannons, down the river past the fort for the planned attack at Anahuac. As they attempted to sail past Fort Velasco, shots from the fort killed the schooner captain. John Austin, commander of the Texans, then attacked Fort Velasco. The Texans succeeded in capturing the fort and the Mexicans were put on a sailing ship bound for Mexico.

As the conflict between the two sides heated up, a group of Texas Rangers was stationed along the coast in 1835 to watch for a Mexicans invasion. They sighted a ship before dawn one morning, and signaled for the ship to send a small boat ashore. Once it arrived, the Rangers captured it and rowed back to the ship, which they also captured. The ship's captain was then ordered to signal the other two ships in the fleet to send their captains aboard for a meeting. Upon the Captains arrival, the Rangers captured those Captains and obtained control of their ships. All three Mexican ships were taken into the port at Velasco, and the Mexican cargo of supplies was turned over to the Texan Army. Those early-day Rangers were nicknamed the "horse marines".

In 1836, Santa Anna signed the Treaty of Velasco at Fort Velasco giving Texans the independence they won at San Jacinto. Fort Velasco is no longer around, but a historical marker in Surfside Beach commemorates the site of the battle between the Texans and the Mexicans.

Many installations were built all along the Texas coastline at the time of the Civil War. (Not all records give the names of those forts, but they are probably mentioned here as research found many forts and camps of that era.) Also in the area were several unnamed Confederate forts: one a mile above Quintana, one near Velasco, and another lying on the east bank of the river at a draw bridge across the canal connecting the Brazos with West Galveston Bay.

29. Fort Crockett (Also Fort San Jacinto, Fort Point, and others)

Fort Crockett was first established in Galveston around 1834. It was rebuilt in 1897 in the vicinity of present-day 45th Street at Seawall Boulevard. It was not manned until 1898, then destroyed by the hurricane of 1900. A new Fort Crockett was subsequently built in the twentieth century for a training facility for artillerymen. The buildings are being used by the National Oceanic and Atmospheric Administration, Texas A&M University, and also Galveston College.

Galveston Island had more than its share of old forts. In 1830, there was an unnamed Mexican garrison on the island. In 1836, the Republic of Texas built a fort on the island, Fort San Jacinto, to fight pirates and Mexicans who were threatening an invasion. Later, in 1839, Texas built Fort Point. During the Civil War, the Confederacy built Forts Bankhead, Jackson, Magruder, Moore, and Travis in 1861. In 1865, Forts Scurry, Hebert, Green (now Fort Travis on Bolivar Peninsula), and Nelson were built as was Eagle Grove Fort and South Fort. The 1900 hurricane destroyed them all.

An interesting story of Galveston during the Civil War tells that Confederate troops at Virginia Point under Colonel Joseph J. Cook used a steam ship made to look like a man-o-war with cannons (many of which were wooden) to keep the Union forces from landing while the Confederates recaptured Galveston. Once the fake was known the Union landed reinforcements and recaptured the island. Galveston changed hands several times during that war.

30. Maison Rouge (The Red House)

"My treasures is buried at Three Palms," shouted Jean Laffite as his ship pulled out of the port, leaving Galveston Island (at the insistence of the United States Navy). Followers of the pirate then dug below the three palms, which were a popular landmark, and jumped with joy when their shovels struck the metal of a chest. Within the chest they did find Laffite's treasure; the body of his wife who had recently died. No other treasures of the pirate were ever found.

Pirate Jean Laffite, and his brother Pierre, established their headquarters on Galveston Island in 1817 after having fought for the United States with Andrew Jackson in the Battle of New Orleans in 1815. Their stay on Galveston Island brought them in contact with Louis Aury who wanted to use the island as a base for invading Mexico, and later Doctor James Long, who wanted Texas as his own personal property. But the Laffites found their fame and fortune in pirating, and "Maison Rouge" was their fortress.

Maison Rouge, at the present-day site of Saint Mary's Infirmary, was a block long and it was armed with 36-pound cannons inside and a battery of 42–pounders outside. Frenchmen, escaping from Champ d'Asile came to Galveston in 1818 in time for the hurricane that struck that year and flooded the entire island. Laffite gave the French women and children shelter, as Maison Rouge was the strongest building on the island. Men from Champ d'Asile took shelter wherever they could find it; under barricades, in buildings and under boats turned upside down. The storm destroyed the water supply, food and stores of Laffite, but it took no lives.

At the insistence of the United States government, Laffite left Galveston after disclosing the location of his loved one. He established another buccaneer safe-harbor in the Yucatan off of Mexico where he practiced his love for piracy until he died there, not from gunshot or a blade, but from an illness. A museum in Galveston is dedicated to the history of the legendary Laffites. Maison Rouge was destroyed by one of the hurricanes that ripped Galveston in the 1800s.

The Pier 21 Theatre in Galveston shows an interesting 30-minute video about Jean Laffite's colorful life. Galveston County's Historical Museum has information on the early history of the island, its forts and those located on Bolivar Peninsula. To get to Point Bolivar, where the remains of Fort Travis are located, take the 24-hour, free-of-charge ferry service from Galveston across the bay. It is a 20-minute trip in each direction, and then return to Galveston, or drive east across the peninsula towards Beaumont (the way this guide proceeds).

31. Fort de Bolivar

Serving as a rendezvous place for Indians, pirates, freebooters, privateers, filibusters, explorers, and settlers, the peninsula of Point Bolivar found its place in the history of Texas. Francisco Xavier Mina (whose story is told in the entry on "Fort Travis" in this region) built an earthwork fortification there in 1816 and after Mina's defeat by Mexico, the French pirate, Pierre Laffite (whose brother made Galveston his home base) recruited Mina's troops. Pierre made a base, Fort de Bolivar, on the peninsula. There is evidence that both Laffite brothers may have been in conspiracy with French settlers at Champ d'Asile in what was later revealed to be a Napoleonic plot to invade Mexico. (For this story see the entry "Camp d'Asile" in this region).

Confederates troops destroyed the Point Bolivar lighthouse to avoid assisting the enemy.

32. Fort Las Casas (Also known as Long's Fort)

The peninsula of Bolivar served as a base to a variety of people, few of whom were admirable. The first to establish a headquarters on the peninsula may have been the French general Jean Amable Humbert who arrived in advance of the French settlers at Champ d'Asile. Later filibusters Warren Hall and Henry Perry in 1815 planned their invasion of Texas from here. The plans were abandoned after their army of volunteers was shipwrecked off the coast.

In 1818, Dr. James Long came to Texas with 300 troops to liberate the land. In 1819, he established his headquarters, Fort Las Casas, on the bay side of Bolivar Peninsula at the present site of Fort Travis. Las Casas was made of the only material available; mud and sticks.

Dr. Long's efforts were seen as a menace to the ambitions of the United States so every time any of his "troops" were found on U. S. soil, they were arrested and their arms seized. Long had a recruitment ploy that was very effective. He promised all new comers good land at a fair price. The offer made the headlines in many newspapers and it helped to build a large force. Interference of the U. S. caused Long problems and he turned to the pirate Jean Laffite for help.

While Mexico was busy seeking independence from Spain, James Long went so far as to prepare a declaration of independence for his Republic of Texas. Troops under Long attacked, captured and held Nacogdoches and La Bahia. When tricked at La Bahia by Mexican Colonel Perez into believing that Perez was supportive of his cause, Long and his troops were captured and taken to Mexico where Long was killed in an incident that could have been an accident. He was reaching into his coat pocket for his papers when a guard thought he was reaching for a gun.

His wife, Jane Long, who later was given the name the "Mother of Texas," spent the winter of 1821-22 at Fort Las Casas, where she was attacked by Indians. With only a servant and young daughter, Jane Long, while waving her petticoats like a flag, used an empty cannon to bluff Indians, who were coming across the bay, into retreating. Her diary tells of Galveston Bay being frozen so solid one winter that she saw a large black bear walking across the ice towards the fort. The day she gave birth to a child, it snowed so hard the accumulation broke her tent.

Dr. James Long was the last of the so-called filibusters. Jane became a legend in her own right. There are several books written of her life, before and after her marriage to Doctor Long.

33. Fort Travis (Once known as Fort Green)

(See colored pictures in the center section)

In the Civil War, Confederate officer Colonel Valery Sulakowski of the Galveston Military District used slave labor to erect a sand and log fortification known as Fort Green to protect the bay, but no trace remains of it today. Anglo settlers later established the community of Port Bolivar in the same area. Before then, the peninsula was active when Francisco Xavier Mina, Spanish revolutionist and filibuster made it his headquarters. With encouragement from General Winfield Scott of the United States and Father Jose Servando Teresa de Mier Noriega y Guerra, an ardent

Mexican liberal, Mina had set sail for Galveston with four vessels. There, Mina joined with Louis Michel Aury, who was also planning an invasion of Mexico. On March 16, in 1816, the 100-man force of Colonel Henry Perry, another filibuster, also joined him.

An arrangement was made whereby Aury was to be naval commander of the expedition, while Mina was to have command of the military. The invasion point of Mexico was to be Soto la Marina, Tamaulipas. The expedition left on April 7 with a force of eight ships and 235 men. The troops disembarked on April 15 capturing Soto la Marina without difficulty then marched inland. After several small victories over the Spanish, Mina's forces was defeated and captured at Venadito on October 27. He was taken to Mexico City, tried, and at the age of 28, Mina was executed with 25 of his companions on November 11, 1817.

In 1898, when the U. S. government began to develop Galveston as a port, it established the second Fort Travis to serve as an outpost for Fort Crockett on Galveston Island. The fortification consisted of several batteries (remains may be seen and the tunnels were frequently used for shelter in times of hurricanes). The 1900 hurricane did extensive damage to the fort.

The state runs ferries 24 hours a day between Point Bolivar and Galveston. The entrance to Fort Travis is 0.2 miles past the first traffic light after you drive off of the ferry. Turn right just before the Fort Travis historic marker that is located along the roadside.

34. Fort Griffin (Jefferson County)

Jefferson County's Fort Griffin was a Confederate fort located in the southeastern part of Jefferson County on FM 3322, fifteen miles south of Port Arthur. General John B. Magruder had dispatched Major Julius Kellersberg to build the fort at Sabine Pass in March 1863 to block Union threats to the upper Texas Gulf coast. Using 30 engineers and 500 slaves, Kellersberg constructed a triangular fort overlooking the Sabine River. The installation housed six gun emplacements. Bombproof rooms built into a sawtooth front, timber, and railroad iron reinforced the earthwork position. The fort was named for the commander of the Twenty-first Texas Battalion, Colonel William H. Griffin.

The story of Fort Griffin is incomplete without mention of the heroics of an Irish settler, Dick Dowling, who with a company of 42 Irish patriots on September 8, 1863 defeated a Union fleet. Four Union gunboats carrying 1,500 men were leading an amphibious invasion force up the river. They were to meet troops marching overland from the Red River to advance on Texas when they saw Fort Griffin. Two gunboats moved to launch an attack. As they moved towards the fortification there was no return fire. When the boats were within a thousand yards, Dowling ordered the fort's cannon to answer the fire, crippling two gunboats and causing the other two to retreat. Dowling's men, without losing a single man, captured two gunboats and 350 prisoners.

In anticipation of another possible Federal assault, Fort Griffin was strengthened with captured Parrott rifles and temporarily reinforced. By January 1, 1864, the garrison, one of the last coastal positions remaining in the Confederate hands, was reduced to 268 men. Confederate troops then spiked the five remaining cannons and abandoned Fort Griffin by May 24, 1865.

Erosion and the channelization of Sabine Pass removed evidence of Fort Griffin's exact location. However, a statue and a plaque at Sabine Pass Battleground State Historical Park at the end of State Highway 67 on the Gulf of Mexico marks what is thought to have been the fort site.

35. Fort Grigsby

It could "blow anything out of the water" with its two 24-pound cannons overlooking a bend in the Neches River. That was one description of Fort Grigsby when it was first built. Grigsby was located at the site of present-day Port Neches, southeast of Beaumont, as part of the defense to block any Union advance after the fall of Fort Sabine. A bar across the river to add to the defenses was made by sinking shell-laden ships downstream in the Sabine River. Fort Grigsby itself consisted of embankments of mud and clamshells reinforced by upright, pointed logs. It was occupied from October to December in 1862, then was no longer necessary after the construction of Fort Manhassett. Fort Grigsby seems to have been abandoned after July 1863.

36. Fort Manhassett

This fort was located six miles west of Sabine Pass near Highway 87 in southeastern Jefferson County. After the Battle of Sabine Pass, Confederates feared another Union attack on the upper Texas coast. To block this threat, a series of five earthen fortifications were built on the ridges west of the city. They were to prevent either a Union attack on the rear of Fort Griffin or a flanking movement aimed at capturing nearby Beaumont. These fortifications were named Fort Manhassett after a Union schooner, *Manhassett*, which was beached nearby during a storm on September 29, 1863. Seven companies held Fort Manhassett in October 1863; that force had been reduced to 266 men by January 1, 1864. As late as March in 1865 the post still had 6 heavy guns and 2 field pieces. Forts Griffin and Manhassett were both abandoned shortly before 1865.

Subsequent excavations revealed the Confederates buried their shells and gunpowder before they evacuated. A commemorative plaque now marks the location.

37. Fort Sabine

Citizens of Sabine Pass in the southeast corner of the state, fearing a Union invasion during the Civil War, built a fort to protect their town. Residents, including slaves, constructed a dirt and timber earthworks fort overlooking the Sabine River. September 24, 1862, the fort was shelled by Union gunboats and severely damaged.Following construction of a new fort (Griffin) the 32-pound cannons were then moved and installed there.

Located off FM 3322 and State Highway 87 one mile south of present-day Sabine Pass is the Battleground State Historical Park where the local militia, the Sabine Pass Guard, and later troops of the Sixth Texas Infantry Battalion were posted. When a yellow fever epidemic broke, the commandant, Major Joseph S. Irvine ordered the remaining Confederate guns to be disabled. The park contains commemorative markers to the fort and the heroics there.

An interesting legend of the Sabine Pass area tells of a rancher, Mr. McGaffey, who was visited one evening by a stranger that introduced himself as Josie Carlton. He asked for food and lodging for the night. At daybreak, Carlton offered to pay for the hospitality, then left. The following evening he returned again, and the following evening after that he again returned. Upset at the stranger's demands on his hospitality, McGaffey confronted Carlton telling him he was wearing McGaffey's welcome. Carlton then confessed that he had once been a pirate and had hidden a treasure chest of gold near McGaffey's ranch. It was a treasure that he was now searching to find, and offered half to McGaffey if he would help him find it. They searched for weeks without luck. Months later, after Carlton had gone away, so says the legend, McGaffey accidentally found the buried treasure.

38. Fort Anahuac

This fort was the site of the first skirmish (or possibly the first battle) between Texans and Mexicans prior to the beginning of the Texas Revolution. It is located south of Interstate 10 on Highway 63 near Anahuac. Mexicans established the fort under the orders of General Manuel de Mier y Teran to keep people from entering Texas from the United States. It was one of six forts built for this purpose.

In November 1830, Colonel Juan Davis Bradburn chose the site for the fort on a bluff, called Perry's Point, which overlooked the entrance to the Trinity River. Convict laborers made bricks for the walls and buildings. The fort's exterior walls were 100 by 70 feet long enclosing two redoubts diagonally opposite on the southwest and northeast corners. Inside the walls was a reinforced-brick building of about 50 by 35 feet. A maximum of 50 men manned the southwest redoubt. A passage connected the enclosure to a powder magazine on the east redoubt, where two bulwarks each with a cannon, guarded the compound.

Colonel Bradburn was a renegade Anglo who had been run out of Tennessee, had evaded a posse from Alabama, and left Mississippi one step ahead of the hangman. At Fort Anahuac, he had placed William B. Travis (who later was to lead the Texans in the Alamo) and other Texans in the jail at the fort for arguing with his laws.

When a negotiating team, led by John Austin, went to meet with Bradburn to obtain the Texans release, they met and captured a Mexican patrol taking a siesta in the woods. The Texans then used the captured patrol as their bargaining tool. Bradburn agreed to release the Texans, but Austin's group was attacked while leaving the fort. Two of the Mexicans were killed and two were injured. Austin withdrew to Fort Velasco.

This incident led to the Battle of Velasco at Fort Velasco. By the time that battle was over, the Mexican commandant from Nacogdoches had arrived at Fort Anahuac, dismissed Bradburn from command, and released Travis and all of the others. According to this version of history the Battle for Anahuac never took place. A conflicting story tells of Texan insurgents under Colonel Francis White Johnson attacking the fort on June 10-12, 1832, to rescue Travis. Johnson's men dismantled the fort when they left in July of 1832.

In 1835, forty Mexican troops arrived at the site to reopen Fort Anahuac, but when their lumber arrived, the Texans burned it. Mexicans, without artillery fire power, fled to the woods. Commemorative markers are found in Fort Anahuac Park, one mile south of Anahuac.

39. Fort Chambers

This was a mud fortification built during the Civil War by the Confederacy in late 1862. It was located halfway between the site of Fort Anahuac and the town of Anahuac in Chambers County. The small fort included two cannons, a 24-pounder and a 32-pounder, that were later mounted outside the doors of Galveston's Artillery Hall. Nothing else remains.

40. Mission Nuestra Senora de la Luz

Nuestra Senora de la Luz was established in 1756 east of the Trinity River near present-day Wallisville at a swampy, unhealthy site where a French trader, Joseph Blancpain, occupied a cabin. This mission and its presidio are known collectively as El Orcoquisac. They were an attempt by the Spanish to prevent French and Anglo contacts with the Orcoquiza and Bidai Indians.

By November 1759, the mission occupied a strategic site in the area. A temporary building had been replaced by a more substantial structure built of wood and clay, and the Orcoquiza Indians were cooperating with the missionaries when in 1766, a hurricane leveled both the mission and presidio. A new presidio was built slightly to the east of its previous site, and the new mission covered with shingles and plastered mortar, was about 33 feet long and 19 feet wide. The mission had a sacristy, choir, pulpit, raised altar, confessional, and baptistery, a cemetery, and a courtyard about 48 feet wide.

The acquisition of Louisiana in 1763 by the Spanish and that removal of a French threat left little reason to minister to the small numbers of Indians. Although they begged the mission to stay, it closed as part of a general pullback to the San Antonio-La Bahia area.

The site is near Lake Miller (on private land) where there have been archeological digs.

41. Presidio San Agustin de Ahumada

Established in 1756-1766, this presidio was built to provide protection for the Mission Nuestra Senora de La Luz and the Orcoquiza Indian rancheria associated with the mission, and to stop illegal smuggling from French Louisiana into east and south Texas. The presidio and two historic sites make up the El Orcoquizac Archeological District listed in the National Register.

Presidio San Agustin de Ahumada was located on the east bank of the Trinity River near the site of present-day Wallisville in northern Chambers County, 40 miles west of Beaumont.

In May 1754, a French trader along with several families arrived from New Orleans establishing a trading post near the mouth of the Trinity River. The post was named Village de Atakapas. The Spanish soon detected it, arrested the French trader, and destroyed the village. Presidio San Agustin de Ahumada and Mission Nuestra Senora de La Luz were then established near the site of the village. A 1766 hurricane damaged the mission and destroyed the presidio.

Life at the presidio was difficult for troops, as their captain, Pacheco, was mean. He cheated the soldiers in pay and charged excessive prices for goods they bought through the presidio. Those that complained were knocked to the ground or placed in irons where they were defenseless against bites of mosquitoes and flies. When word of his conduct reached Mexico, a replacement was sent, but when he arrived, Pacheco refused to surrender his authority locking himself in his house where he fired his musket at the replacement. Troops then set fire to Pacheco's house, but when it had burnt to the ground, Pacheco's body was not found among the ashes. Pacheco had slipped out by a trap door under the floor; he was later seen walking towards the presidio at La Bahia.

In 1771, the presidio was abandoned when the troops were called to aid against Apaches.

Smuggling continued after the troops withdrew. In 1798, the adventurer, filibuster, and horse thief, Philip Nolan captured almost 2,500 wild horses in Texas and smuggled them through this area to Louisiana and the United States, without paying any taxes to the Spanish government.

During the 1960s (after John Clay, an amateur historian, recognized a map of Presidio Ahumada as matching the topography of the south shore of Lake Miller near Wallisville) more than 200 aboriginal sites described as Rangia shell middens were located and reported within the Wallisville Reservoir area. Archeologists believe excavation of the El Orcoquizac Archeological District will be valuable in understanding the earliest day aborigine settlers to this part of the United States. Though many of prehistoric sites have been investigated and reported, very little research had been conducted concerning area sites built in the early French and Spanish period.

Near the museum at Wallisville is a historical marker for the mission and the presidio.

The road the Spanish created from El Orcoquizac north to the missions at Nacogdoches is still accessible to the public. The route is north by today's Highway 563, then east on Highway 190, and north on Highway 67. This route passes near Moss Bluff, location of Champ d'Asile.

42. Champ d'Asile

Did Napoleon Bonaparte have dreams of becoming the dictator of Mexico? Did the United State of America want to help Napoleon realize this goal? The answers to these questions are still a mystery.

Another mystery, nearer to Texas, involves a group of Frenchmen and their fort, Champ d'Asile ("Mother Country"). Did peaceful French farmers build this fort in Texas, or were they too, part of a plot by Napoleon to invade Mexico?

The Frenchmen arrived in Galveston in 1818, led by French General Charles Lallemand whom the British refused to accompany Napoleon into exile. The group claimed to be exiles from France and only wanted to settle in Texas and establish a new life. They built their fortification along the Trinity River near the Liberty-to-Nacogdoches Trail. One source reports the camp was in the vicinity of Moss Bluff, north of Wallisville, in Liberty County. While another source, a book published in Paris in 1819, says the location was near Liberty. A third source reports there were two forts built (at undisclosed locations) along the river.

The 1819 Paris book reported that the settlement had more than 400 persons, including Germans and Spaniards, and contained four forts with 8 artillery pieces. Another report describes it as being a five-sided fort containing 28 wooden houses, each a miniature fort in itself. Despite these reports of it large size, archeologists today have found no ruins or artifacts.

Despite the claims of the leaders of Champ d'Asile, the Spaniards suspected that their intentions were not honorable. A letter to the Spanish consul at New Orleans reported:

"As soon as you receive this letter you will inform the viceroy of New Spain and the commandants of all of the military post of the frontier that there is not a moment to be lost, but that the territory must be placed in a state of defense against a general attack under the leadership of a certain French General which seeks for his object the proclaiming of Joseph Bonaparte as King of Mexico. This is not simple conjecture, but is a most positive proof of the conspiracy that is to be carried out as a prearranged insurrection of the Western States with the secret objective known only to its leaders of making Bonaparte a claimant to the throne of Spain and the Indies."

Also, Spaniards who had joined the Frenchmen in Philadelphia before arriving in Galveston were captured by the Spanish officials and questioned. According to their report, "the French intruders numbered seventy-five, were supplied with arms, ammunition, and men, and erected a fort. The colony was constantly receiving recruits, and they sent representatives to many different European ports and to different States recruiting additional men."

The Spanish expelled the settlers and destroyed the fort. The survivors of the raid went to Galveston when the hurricane of 1818 hit. Their women and children were sheltered at the Maison Rouge of Jean Laffite (see the entry for "Maison Rouge" in this region). After the storm the women and children sailed to New Orleans, while the men had to walk there. Thus was the end of Champ d'Asile and the termination of one of Napoleons schemes to rule Mexico.

43. Camp on the San Jacinto
(See colored pictures in the center section)

The Alamo had fallen. Texans who surrendered at Goliad had been executed. Families were running for safety. Santa Anna had split his troops into three forces and directed them to march to the east to put down the uprising in Texas. Then Santa Anna made a mistake when he further divided the army he was personally leading. That force was only slightly larger than the group of volunteer Texans that had camped nearby along the San Jacinto River. Sam Houston, when learning of Santa Anna's maneuver, decided his 900 Texans

had an advantage over 1,300 Mexicans and moved his forces to a site where he was on higher ground then the Mexicans.

The events developed with General Santa Anna having the objective of taking possession of the Texas coast and seaports. Then on April 11-14, Santa Anna led his men towards the coast. At Harrisburg, he burned that town, then headed toward the area of present-day Houston. He crossed the San Jacinto River at a bridge over Vince's Bayou, not knowing his troops would have to cross the same bridge to return. Recognizing that fact, General Sam Houston ordered for the bridge to be burnt, but Mexican General Cos crossed before it could be burnt leading another Mexican army to reinforce Santa Anna's. With the bridge burnt, neither the Texans nor the Mexicans could retreat in that direction. General Houston and his army camped and waited.

Sam Houston reminded his men of the fall of Goliad and the Alamo before forming their battle lines the following morning. Edward Burleson's regiment was stationed in the center; Sidney Sherman's forces were on the left wing and artillery under George Hockley was on Burleson's right. Infantry troops under Henry Millard were to the right of the artillery, and the mounted cavalry under Mirabeau Lamar was stationed to the extreme right. The forces under Sherman ran forward as the battle began, crying, "Remember the Alamo! Remember Goliad!"

San Jacinto Battleground State Historical Park, the site of the Battle of San Jacinto, is located along the San Jacinto River off of I-10 east of Houston. There is a short (free) ferryboat ride to the park. The museum has an interesting 35-minute film about Texas in 1836. Hours for the museum are 9 a.m. to 6 p.m. daily except on December 24 and 25.

Nine of the 910 Texans were killed. Mexicans killed numbered 630 with another 730 captured. Santa Anna was later found hiding in tall grass. He was dirty, wet and in disguise, dressed as only a common soldier. He then conceded that Texas had won its independence.

44. Camp Bee

The Second Texas Infantry, a Confederate regiment organized in Galveston in 1861, was moved to Camp Bee in the Houston area for training. Little is known of Camp Bee. It remained in existence only until after the war. There is no history of the camp after that era.

Region Five

The tour of the forts in this region is in a circle that begins in Waco and heads west, then north, then east along the Red River, and finally south and west back near the beginning. Along this route were the fortifications of the early French traders, the small family fortifications of early settlers, and the beginning of the large ranches and the forts that were built to protect them.

Early settlements began here along the Red River before the Texas Revolution. The first Anglos are believed to have settled the area about 1815. Settlers in this area were not sure if they were subject to the laws of Mexico or if they lived in a lawless territory. In 1836, these settlers did send representative to Washington-on-the-Brazos where Texans met and declared their independence from Mexico. After the revolution, more settlers moved into the area, and the Indians (that had earlier had been pushed out of the United States) now found themselves being pushed further from their native lands. This, of course, led to conflicts.

Before the Civil War, stagecoach lines were formed and after the war was over, cattle drives began to pass through the area on their way to the northern markets. In 1869, President Ulysses S. Grant signed the Quaker Peace Policy, which placed Indian reservations under that civilian control and prohibited military movements into the reservations. This led to the Indian raids increasing because the Indians knew soldiers could not follow them to the reservations.

This was an area not only of stagecoaches, cattle drives, and buffalo hunts, it also was an area of bloody and brutal conflicts between the displaced Indians and settlers advancing west.

Region Five Map
(Numbers are as the sites are listed in the text for this region)

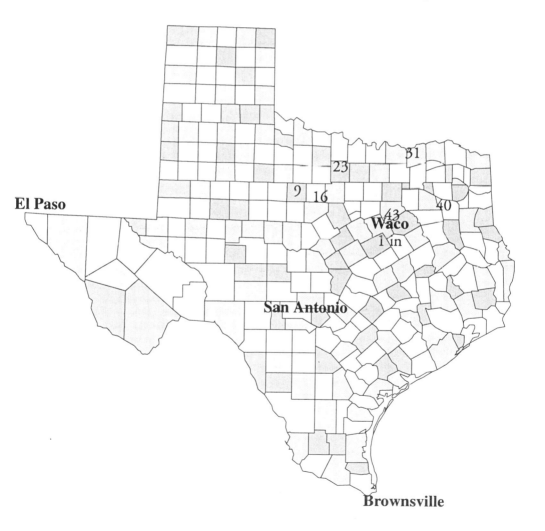

Location   Region Five

1	Fort Fisher – in Waco
2	Fort Gates – near Gatesville
3	Fort Colorado – in Mills County
4	John Duncan's Fort – near Richland Springs
5	Camp Collier – in Brown County
6	Blair's Fort – in Eastland County
7	Camp Pecan – in Callahan County
8	Camp Salmon - in Callahan County
9	Fort Griffin – in Shackelford County
10	Camp Cooper – in Throckmorton County
11	Camp Kenney – in Stephens County
12	Camp Reynolds – near Fort Griffin
13	Camp Breckenridge – in Stephens County
14	Camp Runnels – in Stephens County
15	Fort Davis –in Stephens County
16	Fort Belknap – near Newcastle
17	Camp Van Camp – near Newcastle
18	Camp Cureton – near Archer City
19	Fort Murrah – near Olney
20	Camp Eureka – in Archer County
21	Camp Nowlin – in Archer City
22	Camp Radziminski – in Wichita County
23	Fort Richardson – near Jacksboro
24	Fort Buffalo Springs - near Jacksboro
25	Fort Rowland – in Montague County
26	Spanish Fort – in Montague County
27	Fort Fitzhugh – in Cooke County
28	Fort Coffee – in Grayson County
29	Fort Preston – in Grayson County
30	Fort Johnston (or Johnson) – in Grayson County
31	Fort Inglish – near Bonham
32	Fort Warren – in Fannin County
33	Fort Lyday – in Fannin County
34	Camp Rusk – in Delta County
35	Fort Saint Louis de Carloretta – in Lamar County
36	Le Poste des Cadodaquious – in Bowie County

37   Fort Sherman – in Titus County
38   Fort Crawford – near Hallsville
39   Fort LeDout – in Wood County
40   Camp Ford – near Tyler
41   Fort Houston – near Palestine
42   King's Fort – now Kaufman
43   Fort Smith – in Hill County
44   Fort Graham – near Lake Whitney
45   Fort Worth – still Fort Worth
46   Bird's Fort – now Birdsville

1. Fort Fisher (Originally known as Camp Fisher)

(See colored pictures in the center section)

"Waco was in the possession of buffalo, and only a short time before had been vacated by the Waco Indians," so said one soldier assigned to the area. Camp Fisher was built in February 1837 near the big spring on the Brazos River near the town of Waco. A battalion of Rangers under Captain Thomas H. Barron built the camp and named it for the Texas Secretary of War, William S. Fisher, who later achieved notoriety as a commander with the Mier Expedition. (See the "Mier Expedition" in Region One.) Camp Fisher was abandoned in June 1837.

In 1968 the camp was reconstructed and made into a museum. Now called Fort Fisher, it is the headquarters for a company of active Texas Rangers. Located on the east side of I-35 in Waco, the museum displays interesting memorabilia and is home to a collection of firearms. Among the weapons on display is the Colt revolver, which Rangers helped to develop. The task of loading and firing a musket while riding fast after someone or escaping from a band of Indians was impossible. A young inventor in the East had developed a repeater revolver, but it had three parts to handle, and it was still not too easily loaded on a horse galloping at full speed. Rangers suggested changes eliminating the difficulties and soon the Colt revolver became the standard Texas Rangers side arm. The weapon led to the defeat of many Indians.

Probably the first fight where the Rangers used the Colt revolver was the Battle of Walkers Creek, and a Comanche later complained that the Rangers "had a shot for every finger on the hand." This fight pitted 200 Indian warriors against 14 men of a Ranger company who were scouting the hills for a Comanche war party led by Yellow Wolf. The Rangers had camped on the Guadalupe River in present-day Kendall County and had begun to fell a bee tree when one Ranger yelled from atop the tree, "Jerusalem, Captain, yonder comes a thousand Indians!"

Rangers quickly mounted their horses while the Comanches fell back into a thicket from which they hoped to spring an ambush. The Indians left a single horse as "bait" to draw the Rangers. The Ranger advanced to within a few hundred yards of the hidden Indians when some 20 warriors sprang out of hiding asking for a fight. The rest of the war party remained concealed in the woods. When the Rangers refused to fall into the trap, the entire Indian force rode forward in a line of battle to draw the Rangers attack. As the Rangers advanced, the Indians again fell back, this time to a hillside behind rocks and trees where they taunted the Rangers, hoping to provoke an assault. However, the Ranger commander, Colonel Jack Hayes, led his men around the hill and attacked the Indians from the rear. The fight for the hill soon turned into hand-to-hand combat. The Rangers withstood two counterattacks, after which the Indians fled the field and were pursued for three miles under heavy fire from the Rangers' new Colt revolvers. "Crowd them! Powder-burn them!" were Hays' orders. At the end of the hour-long battle, the Indians' casualties were estimated at more than 50 killed and wounded, with Yellow Wolf among the dead. The Rangers had one killed and four wounded.

The Texas Rangers were started before Texas even became a Republic; they still fight for Texas today. Fort Fisher is a show place with a fine museum that is open daily 9 a.m. to 5 p.m.

2. Fort Gates (Originally Camp Gates)

Captain William R. Montgomery established Fort Gates on October 26, 1849, as a stockaded camp on the bank of the Leon River above Coryell Creek, about five miles east of the site of present-day Gatesville. The fort was named for Brevet Major Collinson Reed Gates, who during the Mexican War won distinction at the Battle of

Palo Alto and Resaca de la Palma.

The fort's territory lay in the northern part of Tonakawa country and was visited by the Waco, Comanche, and Lipan Apache Indians. It was the last of a series of posts established to protect settlers in central Texas from Indians. There were eighteen buildings: four were built for officers' quarters, two for company quarters, three for laundresses, one for muleteers and employees, and one each for a hospital, a stable, a forage house, storehouses, a guardhouse, a bakehouse, and the blacksmith shop. Quarters for a third company were half completed before orders for the construction were canceled in 1850. The fort only had enough soldiers to protect the immediate settlements. It needed at least two companies to operate within a radius of 60 or 70 miles as the nature of the country was such that the Indians could move in all directions.

By 1852 the frontier had moved further west and this Federal fort was abandoned on March 1852. It was the first of the line of posts to be evacuated. For the period after the removal of the garrison, settlers used the fort as a refuge from occasional Indian raids. The buildings soon disintegrated, however, until only the rocks from the fireplaces remained.

A commemorative marker is on private property southeast of Gatesville.

3. Fort Colorado (Possibly also referred to as Camp Colorado)

This Federal camp was first established along Mukewater Creek on the route between Fort Mason and Fort Belknap near the present-day community of Ebony in Mills County. Then it was moved in 1857 to a site along Jim Ned Creek. The buildings were constructed from adobe with shingled roofs and pine floors. Ox teams from East Texas hauled the lumber for the doors and the windows. The camp had communications by telegraph lines to San Antonio, and those lines became one of the primary properties the troops were assigned to protect.

The camp became the main settlement in Coleman County as settlers moved near the camp's waterholes. When the Civil War started, by order of General David E. Twigg, Camp Colorado, along with all of the other Federal forts in Texas was abandoned. Many men stationed at the camp joined the Confederacy under the command of Captain W. Pitts and Captain James Monroe Holmsley. Texas Rangers under Captain J.J. Callan occupied the camp in 1862–1864. After that, a Texan volunteer force occupied it in order to patrol the area as a defense against Indian raids. When the Civil War was over, the Union troops never reoccupied the camp.

Fourteen years later, H.H. Sackett purchased the land and built a ranch using stone from the camp, and attached his home to the guardhouse. A stone fence remains, on private property.

4. John Duncan's Fort (And Camp McMillan)

A private fort, Fort Duncan, was established near Richland Springs in the late 1850s when Indian trouble started on the frontier. The fort was located off of Highway 190 fifteen miles northwest of San Saba in northwestern San Saba County. Nothing remains of the old fort.

Texas Rangers established a Camp McMillan nearby around San Saba in 1862. It was named for the Frontier Regiment's Captain N.D. McMillan. Rangers scouted the territory for Indians until regiments stations were consolidated in 1864. Nothing remains of that camp either.

5. Camp Collier

After the Union Army left the Texas frontier at the beginning of the Civil War, James M. Norris was appointed a Colonel of the Frontier Regiment (a Texas regiment of soldiers formed to protect the Texas settlers during the war). The Frontier Regiment had 1,089 men and officers and 1,347 horses scattered at camps no more than a day's ride from each other on a line from the Red River to the Rio Grande. Each camp was manned by about half a company assigned to patrol the area and to cover the entire line on horseback at least every other day. The Texas Legislature had intended for the regiment to be part of the Confederate Army, but Governor Francis R. Lubbock would only consent to the transfer with the condition that men not be removed from Texas. The regiment was transferred to the Confederate States as the Forty-sixth Texas Cavalry and garrisoned at Fort Belknap until the regiments consolidated in March 1864.

Camp Collier was established on March 23, 1862 near Vaughn's Springs on Clear Creek in southwestern Brown County, 13 miles from Brownwood. Captain Thomas N. Collier was in command. Volunteers stationed here saw none of the war, only the frontiers' hardship. They were sheltered by only tents, the food was frequently in short supply, and they had to supply their own weapons and horses. Due to the poor conditions, illnesses were frequent and many disciplinary problems occurred.

In 1863, two area citizens who had taken bacon to the camp were attacked by Indians and killed. Men from the camp found the scalped bodies and buried both men in the same grave.

Without any permanent structures, the camp was then quickly dismantled in 1865 when the Frontier Regiment was consolidated due to a shortage of men. No trace of the camp remains.

A commemorative marker was placed by the State in 1936 on the Brown County courthouse lawn in appreciation for the troops who brought a degree of safety to area settlers.

6. Blair's Fort

Considered the largest family fort in the west, Blair's Fort was located in Eastland County. Accounts reveal that Comanches and Tonkawas raided the Blair ranch between 1857 and 1862 when the Indians were very active along the frontier. Though their objective was to steal horses, they killed and burned residences on the slightest provocation.

During this era and until after the Civil War settlers in many areas along the frontier were forced to come together for mutual protection and fortified ranches were established. At Blair's Fort, a dozen log cabins were built; tents were stretched around a square area, and a ten-foot high fence enclosed it all. During the time the fort was used, eight families found protection there.

Blair's Fort was a frequent stop for patrolling Texas Rangers. The commemorative marker at the site is only accessible to the public with the ranch owner's permission.

Nearby, during this era, was another civilian fortress (not given a name). Allen's Ranch (possibly a fortification) in the northeastern part of Eastland County protected that ranch family and the surrounding neighbors during Indian raids. There are no visible ruins of either.

7. Camp Pecan

Camp Pecan on Pecan Bayou in Callahan County on March 23, 1862, was established as a Ranger post of the Frontier Regiment under Captain T. M. Collier. It was on the road between Camp Cooper and Fort Colorado. Indians, especially Tonakawas and Comanches, gathered the nuts for which the stream was named as well as red cactus fruit, wild plums, and acorns. The creeks were also known for their abundant fish and mussels, and Pecan Bayou was a famous fishing stream during the frontier era. It received favorable comment from travelers and soldiers for beauty, sweetness of drinking water, presumed richness of soil, and pecan and oak timber.

Many military expeditions and explorations before the Civil War, including those of Robert S. Neighbors in 1849, R. B. Marcy in 1851, and A. S. Johnston in 1855-56 passed this area. As early as 1851,General W. G. Belknap had recommended establishing a camp in the Pecan Bayou area and planned an expedition to begin this work, but his proposal was vetoed.

Camp Pecan may not have been established because of the veto. If it was built, it was then abandoned in 1864. Records do not disclose the exact location or existence of the camp.

8. Camp Salmon

Colonel James M. Norris also established Camp Salmon for the Frontier Regiment in March 1862 on a branch of Hubbard Creek near Sloan's Ranch in northeast Callahan County. Norris placed half a company under the command of Captain John Salmon near the site of present-day Breckenridge (at Camp Breckenridge) in Stephens County and the other half at Camp Salmon. Troops initially lived in the open, as huts were not built until 1862.

The principal mission for the soldiers was protecting the Ledbetter Salt Works in southwestern Shackelford County against Indian attacks. At Ledbetter's, the salt was extracted from a nearby saline spring. The extraction process was to fill barrels with the salty brine, allow the water to settle, and then boil it in pots until the water boiled away leaving the valuable salt. Salt was precious in those days as it was the only way to cure meat, and Indians needed it as much as the settlers did. Raids there became so frequent that soldiers at Fort Griffin loaned Ledbetter a cannon to use for protection. A legend is that during one Indian raid, Ledbetter ran out of ammunition so he used parts of his wagon as projectiles and fired them from the cannon at the attacking Indians that then retreated. Ledbetter's Salt Works were abandoned in 1880 when the railroad bypassed the area in favor of larger salt deposits elsewhere along the tracks.

A marker commemorating the salt works stands on the courthouse square in Albany.

9. Fort Griffin (Shackelford County) (First named Camp Wilson)

(See colored pictures in the center section)

Fort Griffin was a strategic unit of the string of outposts built to defend Texas settlers against hostile Indians and outlaws. Established in 1867, it was located on the Clear Fork of the Brazos River in Shackelford County by Lieutenant Colonel Samuel D. Sturgis who led four companies of the Sixth United States Cavalry there on July 31. In June 1868, companies of the Seventeenth Infantry under Lieutenant Colonel S. B. Hayman joined the garrison. The original picket, log, and frame structures, were replaced by stone structures but the soldiers' quarters, stables, and even the hospital were always temporary, some mere canvas-covered shelters.

Forts Belknap, Phantom Hill, and Chadbourne became subposts of the new Fort Griffin, which supplied garrisons for the first two. These subposts furnished escorts for stagecoaches, wagon trains, and surveying parties. Griffin became the center of the border-defense line from Fort Richardson to the Big Bend country. Law enforcement at Fort Griffin was strengthened in 1877 by the arrival of over two dozen Rangers who were commanded by Lieutenant George W. Arrington, whose Indian-fighting talents were preferred by townspeople over those of the Army.

The prosperous days were from 1874 to 1879 when the town of Fort Griffin was built around the fort. The town grew up on the level bottomland between the military fort and the Clear Fork of the Brazos River. The fort stood on a hill, so the townsite was frequently called the Bottom or the Flat. The community served as a major supply source for buffalo hunters, especially during the busy seasons from 1874 to 1876-77. The town grew and quickly gained a reputation of as a lawless outpost that attracted such lawmen as Pat F. Garrett, Doc Holiday, and Wyatt Earp, and outlaws like John Wesley Hardin. By 1874, lawlessness in the community had become so extreme that the commander of the fort placed the town under government control and forced a number of undesirable residents to leave. This situation

lasted until a sheriff was appointed after the organization of Shackelford County later in the year.

Fort Griffin had the best known and probably the most active vigilante committees in Texas. On the night of April 9, 1876, those groups caught a man stealing a horse and hanged him, leaving below the swinging body a pick and shovel for anyone who wished to remove the spectacle. In a few months, Fort Griffin's vigilantes shot 2 horse thieves and hanged 6.

The Butterfield Overland Mail route passed near the town at Clear

Fork Crossing, and herds of cattle on the Western Trail passed in route to Kansas. By 1879, the nearby buffalo herd was depleted, and the fort and its outposts were considered to be within a settled area. On May 31, 1881, Captain J. B. Irvine closed Fort Griffin and sent Company A of the Twenty-Second Infantry southward to Fort Clark on the Rio Grande. When the fort closed, the town's end came.

Ruins of the fort may be seen in Fort Griffin State Park, 15 miles north of Albany on U. S. Highway 283. Restoration of the fort is ongoing. A visitors' center is open daily.

10. Camp Cooper

Established by the Texas legislature in January 1856 it was named for Adjutant General Samuel Cooper of the United States Army. Located on the Clear Fork of the Brazos River in Throckmorton County, it was seven miles north of the site of present-day Fort Griffin. Its mission was to protect the frontier and monitor the Comanche Indian reservations. Sketches of the camp showed stone and picket buildings for the officers' quarters, hospital, and commissary. Enlisted men and the band were quartered in barracks with shingle roofs and mud bricks walls.

The post, founded by Colonel Albert Sidney Johnston, became headquarters for four companies of the Second United States Cavalry under the command of Lieutenant Colonel Robert E. Lee. This was Lee's first fort command. He remained in charge until July 22, 1857. While Lee was at the fort, each company was composed of men from the same state and each company's horses were of the same color. A company of Alabama troops rode grays, the Ohio company rode roans, and the company of troops from Kentucky rode bay horses.

Before leaving Cooper in 1857, Lee wrote to General Winfield Scott that the troops on the front were insufficient to keep out Indians. As if to reinforce Lee's statement, Indians shortly thereafter raided the camp and stole 70 troop horses, from the fort.

The soldiers participated in many campaigns against Indians, including the pursuit of Peta Nocona's Comanches. In that campaign, Peta Nocona was killed and his wife, Cynthia Ann Parker was rescued. She had been kidnapped 20 years before and when soldiers found her, she considered herself Comanche. She was not happy to be have been "rescued." Her son with Nocona was the famous Comanche chief, Quanah Parker.

The Battle of Blanco Canyon was fought between Quanah Parker and Colonel Ranald S. Mackenzie in September 1871. Mackenzie's 10 companies and a group of 20 Tonakawa scouts set out from Camp Cooper hoping to find the Indian village and the warriors led by Quanah. The troops were camping in Blanco Canyon near the headwaters of the Freshwater Fork when late the next evening Parker and a Comanche force stampeded through the cavalry camp, driving off 66 troop horses. The following morning as troopers went off down the canyon chasing a small group of Indians that were driving several horses, they topped a hill and were confronted with a much larger party of Indians, waiting in ambush. Lieutenant Robert Goldthwaite Carter and five men held off the Comanches while the rest of the troops retreated, an action for which Carter would be awarded the Medal of Honor. Timely arrival of the main column saved the troops from annihilation and forced the warriors to withdraw. The Comanches, sniping at troopers, retreated up the canyon before disappearing.

Mackenzie continued pursuing the Indians, forcing them to abandon their lodge poles, tools, and many possessions and finally caught up with them on the afternoon of October 12. An unseasonable blue norther accompanied by blinding snow and sleet halted the cavalry and prevented an attack, forcing the troops to camp for the night. The next morning Mackenzie continued the pursuit. In a skirmish that followed on October 15, two Comanches were killed, and Mackenzie and a soldier were wounded. The weather worsened. With the horses and men exhausted, Mackenzie ended the expedition, regarding the campaign as less than a success. He and his troops had marched 509 miles with the loss of one man and many horses but they had done little more than to frighten one Comanche band. Nevertheless, they had penetrated into a unexplored area of the plains, and had become more knowledgeable about Indian warfare. They had demonstrated that never again would the vast plains provide a refuge for Comanches.

The site of Camp Cooper is now on private land. Any ruins are not accessible.

11. Camp Kenney

The Texas Legislature in 1874 authorized the formation of the Frontier Battalion (not to be confused with the Frontier Regiment of the 1850s). Six Texas Ranger camps were established under Major John B. Jones to protect the frontier. In the first seventeen months, the battalion had 21 fights with the Indians. Camp Kenney was one of the Frontier Battalion camps.

The camp was established at the head of Gonzales Creek in southern Stephens County in October 1874. Patrols were sent out to scout at irregular intervals but the Indians quickly learned how to evade the soldiers by sweeping in behind the troops and raiding the settlements. Nevertheless, Indians attacks in the county stopped after 1875 and the camp was closed.

The Frontier Battalion remained in existence until 1900 when a Federal court order ruled that only commissioned officers could make arrests. This ruling diminished the effectiveness of the battalion and its responsibilities were then given to the present-day Texas Rangers.

12. Camp Reynolds (Also known as Rath City)

The brainchild of a buffalo hide dealer from Dodge City, Camp Reynolds was built to compete with Fort Griffin for the commercial business in the area. In 1876, Charles Rath sent a wagon caravan with carpenters, lumber, nails and tools to build Rath City, and the camp. Rath also sent a second caravan of 50 wagons carrying supplies and merchandise to stock his store.

This was the era of the great buffalo hunt, or slaughter. It was estimated that there were more than 1,500 hunters, including skinners and others, on the range west of Fort Griffin. (With the hunting camps, the number possibly increased to 5,000 men.) The number of buffalo killed was in the tens of thousands, or even greater, for each camp. Three years previous, a herd of buffalo had been reported covering the Texas plain as far as the eye can see.

General Philip Sheridan, who was under orders to "punish the Indians wherever they may be found" encouraged the slaughter. He told hunters to "destroy the Indians' commissary." The Indians were terrified when they saw this source of food disappearing, and retaliated. A party of 75 attacked Camp Reynolds one day at dawn. Their war cries echoed off the walls of the village as they raced their horses through the town. When the Indians rode away, they stampeded all of the hunters' horses in from of them.

The Sharps Buffalo Rifle was the firearm used to eliminate the buffalo. This rifle had a breech mechanism strong enough to handle the large cartridges needed for killing buffaloes from a long range. The 12-to-18 pound gun fired a .50-caliber lead slug from brass shells containing 110 grains of powder. It was said that a competent marksman could kill bison from incredible distances using this rifle. The Sharps dramatically altered the Great Plains. In the mid-1880s buffalo were estimated to number in excess of twenty million. Scarcely a specimen remained of the four great herds twenty years later. The purpose of the buffalo "harvest" was to supply meat to railroad workers, and many herds were found near rail activity. A development of a method for tanning the hide into leather brought a new reason to slaughter the buffalo. Almost overnight an army of hide hunters descended on the herds, which roamed from near Dodge City, Kansas, to the Colorado River north of Austin. A slaughter began with the hunters and camps protected by the troops at Fort Griffin, Fort McKavett, and Fort Phantom Hill.

In less than five years, the buffalo were gone and the Indians lost their food source. The plains of Texas opened to white men for raising cattle and farming. Camp Reynolds vanished.

13. Camp Breckenridge

Colonel James M. Norris and 50 of Captain John Salmon's Frontier Regiment established Camp Breckenridge on March 21, 1862. It was located on Gonzales Creek 6 miles above where it joins Hubbard Creek in northern Stephens County. Half of Salmon's company of 100 men maintained Camp Salmon, while the other half maintained Breckenridge as Indian defenses.

Captain R. Whiteside, who commanded Camp Breckenridge in 1863, stated that the only service satisfactorily rendered was to carry the mail, because "the patrol keeps our horses poor and when we find Indians they can outrun us." With inadequate supplies and low morale, the camps gave little protection against the Indians. A roll-call in 1863 found only 26 out of 54 men who should have been in camp: one had been killed, 4 were absent without leave, the remainder were either sick, on patrol, or hunting for their lost horses. The entire Frontier Regiment was mustered into regular Confederate service in the last year of the Civil War. Area settlers who then took refuge at the camp against Indian raids again used the camp during Reconstruction for protection against a new danger, the outlaw gangs that entered the area after the war.

A marker on the courthouse lawn in Breckenridge commemorates the camp's history.

14. Camp Runnels

"Tonkawa and Comanches put on a demonstration of yelling and taunting of each other, from a distance, that it reminded me of stories of the middle ages when competing forces would taunt each other, out of range of any arrow, lance, or sword. Both Indian tribes carried on this way for half an hour. Only stopping when a group of my Texas Rangers joined their taunting." This was Captain Rip Ford's memory of when his company of regular Rangers, militia and the Tonkawa Indian scouts from the reservation caught up with the Comanche after leaving Camp Runnels in the Spring of 1858.

Ford had received the following orders from Governor Hardin R. Runnels. "Follow any and all trails of hostile or suspected hostile Indians you may discover, and if possible, overtake and chastise them, if unfriendly." With 102 men and the 113 volunteer Tonkawa braves, Ford moved north across the Red River (leaving Texas) to where Comanches, who had been raiding south of the river, were camping. Tonkawa braves welcomed an opportunity for revenge on their old enemies and led the attack on the Comanches' camp. In the battle, Chief Iron Jacket (named so because he wore armor that had probably been taken from an earlier Spaniard) was killed.

When Ford's company returned to Camp Runnels, they had captured over 300 horses, killed 76 Comanches and captured 18 prisoners. The importance of this raid was that the Rangers demonstrated that the Indians could be followed into their own country and defeated.

Camp Runnels was near an Indian reservation by the Brazos,

probably in northern Stephens County. There are no longer any ruins to be seen.

15. Fort Davis (Stephen County)

In 1861, the Civil War was starting and soldiers were leaving the frontier. The Union soldiers withdrew and the state's troops were needed by the Confederacy. This left the settlers vulnerable, and they expected attacks from the Indians to begin anytime. Many settlers left their ranches and moved to the larger communities or returned to other areas. Even though Texas tried to provide Rangers to protect the frontier, it had no more than 1,000 men to protect the land from the Red River to the Rio Grande. Settlers electing to stay on the frontier had to protect themselves from Indian attack, and renegade outlaw gangs avoiding the war.

When Camp Cooper closed in 1861, several white families remained along the Clear Fork of the Brazos River between Fort Belknap and Fort Phantom Hill in Stephens County. After the Comanches' Elm Creek Raid of October 1864, in which several settlers were killed and three were kidnapped, several families decided to gather in one location for protection against the Indians. In October 1864, they established a stronghold called Fort Davis.

It was only one of several such "forts" along the frontier. The post was located on the east side of the Clear Fork about fifteen miles down river from Camp Cooper. It measured about 300 by 325 feet, with a street running through it from east to west. About 20 picket-style houses with dirt roofs formed a loose stockade. A picket stockade fence enclosing the entire fort was begun, but it was never completed. A large stone house that had been built earlier anchored one corner of the fort providing protection for women and children during any attack. Supplies for the inhabitants were hauled in by wagon from Weatherford, a journey of some days over poor roads. Although an attack did not materialized the settlers had several fights with Indians.

Other fortress built in Stephens County included Fort Owl Head and Fort Clark. The Picketville settlement also built a large stockade fence for protection. Frontier life was rough. Susan Newcomb, whose husband, Sam had designed the layout of Fort Davis, wrote in her diary in 1867, "Such a country as this I almost wish I had never seen. If I had wings to fly, I would abandon it forever. It surely is the last place on earth for a woman to live, or any one else. I don't believe it was ever intended for civilized people; it was made for the wild Indians."

Fort Davis was abandoned in 1867 when Federal troops returned and established Fort Griffin on the Clear Fork about ten miles upriver. The site of Fort Davis is privately owned, and the stone structure has been restored as a hunting lodge.

16. Fort Belknap

(See colored pictures in the center section)

Near a triple bend of the Brazos River stood Fort Belknap. Many famed and infamous figures served at the fort. Explorers, settlers, California bound gold hunters, and more than a few renegades passed though on the way to destiny or death. It was organized in 1851 by Lieutenant Colonel William Belknap of the Fifth U. S. Infantry to serve as protection for travelers on a route across Texas to Santa Fe. It would later guard two Indian reservations; one that was established nearby and one built further west. Fort Belknap is credited with launching the legal expulsion of Indians from Texas in 1859, when the court ordered 2,000 Indians to be marched to reservations in present-day Oklahoma. Indian raids, however, did not stop with this exodus.

Fort Belknap was a four-company post. The first buildings were built by covering walls made of wooden stakes with mud. The roofs were usually poles laid across the top and covered with long grass. Several buildings were later replaced with stone. Stationed there during its existence were companies of the Fifth United States Infantry, the Second Dragoons, the Seventh Infantry, the Second Cavalry, and the Sixth Cavalry. Belknap was built as a post without any defensive works. It was the anchor of a chain of forts founded to protect the Texas frontier from the Red River to the Rio Grande, and its troops pursued raiding bands of Indians. On occasion its mounted expeditions carried the war to the enemy as far north as Kansas. The fort gave confidence to citizens, who came in such numbers that surrounding counties were organized.

In early 1861, believing that war was imminent, General David E. Twiggs ordered Colonel William H. Emory to gather all Federal troops and move them to Fort Leavenworth in Kansas. Then on February 9, 1861, General Twiggs, from his headquarters in San Antonio, surrendered all of the United States forts and military equipment in Texas to the Confederacy. As with many forts of this era, Fort Belknap was at one time the home to many men who would later become generals in the Civil War.

After the Civil War, troops of the Sixth United States Cavalry reoccupied Fort Belknap. When Fort Griffin was founded in Shackelford County, Belknap was abandoned in September 1867. After it was abandoned, the fort was occupied from time to time by troops of the Texas Frontier Regiment under Colonel James M. Norris.

Near Belknap was a rolling, timbered prairie named the Salt Creek Prairie that extended nine miles on either side of Salt Creek from the fort to Rock Creek. This became known as the most dangerous prairie in Texas in the 1860s-1870s, as it was a favorite area for Comanche and Kiowa war parties striking south from the reservation in Indian Territory to raid travelers and attack settlers. On May 16, 1869, a dozen cowboys were attacked by Comanches northwest of what is now Jean. They held off the attackers for an entire day until the Indians withdrew under the cover of darkness. In July 1870, Kiowa raiders led by Kicking Bird robbed the mail stage at Rock Creek Station. Graves were dug on the prairie for 21 victims of Indian attacks in the early 1870s, including graves for the county sheriff, W. F. (State) Cox, and for Second Lieutenant William R. Peveler, both victims of Indian attacks. Rangers camped for two months on nearby Flat Top Mountain, chasing Kiowa and Comanche raiding parties in July and August of 1874.

Now restored in a picturesque area frequently used as a site for local entertainment and family meetings, the fort's commissary serves as an interesting museum and offers a collection of weapons, clothing, and archives of the 1800s. It is open 9 a.m. till 5 p.m. daily except on

Wednesdays. From Graham follow Highway 380 northwest towards Newcastle. Highway markers will guide you the last 3 miles from there to the fort site.

17. Camp Van Camp

Camp Van Camp, a subpost of Fort Belkap, was located near the site of present-day Newcastle in Young County. It was established on April 30, 1859, and named in memory of Lieutenant Cornelius Van Camp. Van Camp was killed in a battle at Wichita Village in 1858. (See "Camp Radziminski" in this region for the story of that fight). The camp was abandoned in 1859 and a Texas commemorative was placed a marker at the site, now on private property.

18. Camp Cureton

Camp Cureton was established on March 17, 1862, where the Gainesville-Fort Belknap road crossed the West Fork of the Trinity River southeast of Archer City. It was one of the posts set up to restrict Indian raids after the Federal troops withdrew. One hundred and twelve men of the Frontier Regiment under Captain J. J. (Jack) Cureton, for whom it was named, manned the camp. It had long buildings for the Rangers' quarters and a rock-fence corral for the horses. The first hardship encountered at the camp was an epidemic of measles.

This location was near the site of the Battle of Stone Houses fought in November of 1837, when Texas Rangers chasing a band of 200 Keeci Indians found the entire tribe waiting, ready to fight. Rangers found some protection in a six-foot ravine; though every time they raised a hat it was shot. Impatient, the Indians set fire to the prairie grass to burn the Rangers from their protection. Smoke from the fire, however, provided the Rangers with the opportunity to escape. Running through the smoke, they passed the Indians and reached a wooded section where the Indians did not follow. The fight lasted for two hours; the Rangers walk to safety took 17 days, as they constantly watched over their shoulders for the Indians.

Camp Cureton closed by March 1864, when the regiment was moved to Fort Belknap.

19. Fort Murrah (And Fort Bragg and Fort Growl)

A lookout stockade fort named Fort Murrah was built on the Brazos River ten miles southwest of present-day Olney during the Civil War. Families gathered here for protection from Indians after the soldiers had withdrawn from the area in 1861. Murrah was near the site of perhaps what was the largest Indian raid in North Texas. Chief Little Buffalo of the Comanches recruited Kiowas to join him in the raid to gain horses, wealth, and prestige. He wanted to make his name famous as a Comanche leader. As many as 1,000 Indians may have been in the raid.

Crossing the Red River with extra horses near present-day Burkburnett the Indians reached Elm Creek and commenced their looting and butchery. One morning, smoke drifting over the hills gave settlers evidence of a large attack. Before many settlers could reach the safety of Fort Murrah, they were slain or taken captive in their fields or in their homes. One family sought shelter in a cave, only to be tricked by an Indian yelling at the family in good English that he had come to help them. Their dog, tricked into leaving the cave, was met with deadly arrows.

Rangers patrolling the area came at the sound of shots and put up a resistance that turned the Indians towards the fort. During the night, settlers in the fort could see the Indians dancing around their campfires. When dawn brought light, the settlers were surprised to see that the Indians were gone, taking their loot of horses and a dozen women and children with them.

Other settlements heard of the attack and started strengthening their settlements. Fort Hubbard was established along Hubbard Creek near present-day Albany. Further to the south Mugginsville, in Shackelford County, was a fortress with an 8-foot tall stockade enclosing five acres, and a schoolhouse. Fort Bragg, on Elm Creek, and a Fort Growl, located at the junction of Fish Creek and the Brazos River were both established in present-day Young County.

Fort Murrah was located in the vicinity of where Highway 79 crosses the Brazos River today. The site is now on private property.

20. Camp Eureka

The history of Camp Eureka is mostly lost, although it is known that it was established as a station on the Butterfield Mail route in norther Archer County somewhere near Ranger Lake and the Wichita River. It may have been in the middle of what is present-day Wichita Falls.

The camp was established in the territory of the Wichita Indians, that were part of a confederation of language related tribes from the north (including Tawakoni, Taovaya, Iscani, Wichitas, and Toweash), that had moved south in the early 1700s to escape the more powerful French armed Osages. The Wichitas lived on both sides of the Red River, where they profited by trading surplus crops for horses with the Comanches on the west and trading horses for supplies with French and Caddo Indians on the east. This French-Caddo-Wichita-Comanches trade lasted until the early years of the Anglos settlement of northern Texas.

Although the Wichitas tried to establish trade with the Spanish, the Spanish could not compete with the trade the Wichitas had with the French. Also, the Spanish had sided with the Lipan Apaches, a tribe the Wichitas considered their deadly enemies. In fact, when the Spanish established Mission Santa Cruz de San Saba for the Lipans, the Wichitas were among the 2,000 Indian warriors who attacked and destroyed the mission in 1758. (See "Mission Santa Cruz de San Saba" in Region Six for the story of that attack.)

After the Seven-Year's War between France and Spain, France cut back on its trading with the Indians and Wichitas made peace with the Spanish. Eventually, however, the influx of the Anglo settlers in the 1800s pushed the Wichitas completely out of Texas.

21. Camp Nowlin

This temporary camp near the Little Wichita River lasted only three weeks. Captain John H. Brown had established it in August 1859 as part of the operation for escorting Indians from the reservations on the Brazos to Indian Territory in present-day Oklahoma. Once the Indians were moved, the camp was closed. There was an outbreak of disease that contributed to the camp closing quickly. The site is now probably somewhere under present-day Archer City.

22. Camp Radziminski

This camp began as a picket stockade along Otter Creek for a detachment of troops sent to find and punish a Comanche band that had been plundering Anglo settlements in north central Texas. Brevet Major Earl Van Dorn of the U. S. Second Cavalry led troops north from Fort Belkap to a site near present-day Wichita Falls. There they established Camp Radziminski.

For more than a year 200-300 soldiers were stationed there. The camp was moved at least twice in order to find grazing for horses. One move put the camp southeast of Radziminski Mountain, which is two miles north and two miles west of Mountain Park, Oklahoma. More permanent structures were built there, though only the ruins of the camp's chimneys now remain. (They are on private property inaccessible to the public.)

After establishing the camp, Van Horn moved his troops against the Indians camped at Wichita Village at the head of Rush Creek, 20-miles south of present-day Chickasha, Oklahoma. This was a fight in which both sides suffered heavy casualties. Van Dorn himself was wounded, though he later recovered. It turned out, however, that the Comanches were on their way to a peace conference requested by the U. S. government. The government delegates had failed to notify the Federal troops in the area of this fact and thus were the cause of an unnecessary and bloody encounter between soldiers and Indians.

The camp was closed in 1859 and the troops moved to nearby Camp Cooper.

23. Fort Richardson

After the Civil War, the Federal government began to respond to complaints by frontier settlers about Indian attacks. The government established more forts along the frontier and tried to ensure that Indians stayed on the reservations. One of the forts was Fort Richardson, founded in 1867 near present-day Jacksboro. Arrival of Federal troops in Texas did not stop complaints.

Many Texans thought the officers in charge were more interested in local politics than in being soldiers. In response to the continuing criticisms, General William Tecumseh Sherman decided to personally visit Texas in 1871 to investigate the Indian situation. Sherman traveled northward from San Antonio to Forts Concho, Griffin, and Belknap, reaching Fort Richardson on May 17. Along the way he saw no signs of Indians and was convinced the Texans' complaints were unjustified.

Meanwhile more than one hundred Kiowas, Comanches, Kiowa-Apaches, Arapahos, and Cheyennes from the Fort Sill Reservation crossed the Red River into Texas. Led by Satank (Sitting Bear), Satanta (White Bear), Addo-etta (Big Tree), and Maman-ti (Skywalker), the Indians were less than 20 miles from Fort Richardson. As Sherman traveled to the fort on May 17, Indians were watching him pass their hiding place. On May 18, these Indians then attacked a wagon train and killed the wagon master and six teamsters but allowed five to escape. The Indians lost one man and returned to the reservation.

General Sherman was very embarrassed and traveled to Fort Sill where he personally arrested Satank, Satanta, and Big Tree. He ordered the men returned to Fort Richardson to be tried for murder in the civil courts in nearby Jacksboro. As troops transported the men to Texas, Satank tried to escape in an obvious suicide attempt. He was killed, which he preferred to the dishonor of the trial. The other two men were found guilty in July 1871, and sentenced to hang. Quakers convinced Governor Edmund J. Davis to commute the sentences to life imprisonment, and in October 1873, they were paroled. Sherman was outraged and felt sure the Indians would raid again. Satanta did indeed do as Sherman predicted and was eventually imprisoned again where he committed suicide by diving headfirst from a prison hospital window. Big Tree, however, lived to be eighty, converted to Christianity, and taught a Sunday School class.

Nevertheless, continuing raids from the reservations convinced Federal officials that more drastic measures would have to be taken. Sherman ordered the troops to begin offensive operations against Indians found off the reservation, a policy that started the Red River War of 1874-75. During the 1870s when raids were frequent, Indian and Anglo encounters were mostly hostile. A community to the west called Lost Valley was given the name "Indian death trap" because of the many bloody conflicts there.

In 1870, a 58-man patrol from the fort ran into a band of 100 Kiowas near the Little Wichita River just south of present-day Lake Kickapoo. Soldiers were outnumbered and outgunned as the Indians were in possession of a number of Sharp rifles. The unit tried to retreat but lost so many soldiers they had to abandon their dead on the field. Finally, the Kiowas cut off their attack early in the evening; the cavalry was able to escape across the West Fork of the Trinity River. Thirteen of the soldiers were awarded Medals of Honor for gallantry in action.

The fort is in Fort Richardson State Park where several buildings are reconstructed. It is open daily 8 a.m. to 5 p.m. Every November, actors at the Fort Richardson Day reenactment acquaint visitors with the typical activities of the soldiers that were garrisoned there.

24. Fort Buffalo Springs

Before Fort Richardson was built, the troops were stationed at Fort Buffalo Springs, 30 miles north of Jacksboro, in Clay County. Companies of the Sixth Calvary occupied it in 1867 until inadequate water and a shortage of timber forced its abandonment. It was then that Fort Richardson was built. A sub-camp, Camp Wichita operated in the area from 1858 through 1873.

Stories from the time of the fort serve as reminders of how to survive on the frontier. A devout Quaker man named Goodleck Kooser learned too late how harsh life could be. As he was traveling to settle in Clay County, he and his family met an Indian hunting party led by Chief Whitehorse. Kooser extended his hand in friendship to the Indian. Whitehorse also extended a hand, but with the other hand drew a revolver and shot the Quaker. Kooser's son ran and hid while Kooser's wife and his two daughters were kidnapped by the Indians. Whitehorse later turned the three over to Federal officials at Fort Sill. He escaped any punishment.

A second story shows how clear-headed resourcefulness on the frontier could pay off. Soldiers at Fort Buffalo Springs left their women and children at the fort while they went on a patrol. While they were gone, the Indians that they were looking for surrounded the fort. The women hurriedly dressed themselves and their older children in spare uniforms and marched around the fort like real soldiers. The Indians never attacked and eventually left.

25. Fort Rowland

It is known that Texas Rangers established Fort Rowland in 1861 in northern Montague County. No other history about the fort has been found. The area around the fort and the Red River, however, has a lively and varied history. The Red River was the site of the wars by the same name fought in 1874-75 to end Indian raiding in the area.

There was another battle over territory along the Red River, but it was a battle fought not on the prairie or on the river, it was fought in the courts. Texas claimed a strip of land north of the river, but according to a strict interpretation of the treaty made in 1819, the Red River was the boundary of Texas. A Supreme Court ruling, known as the Greer County Case, almost 80 years later found against Texas. The ruling resulted in the loss of more than a million and a half acres of Texas land to Oklahoma.

When oil was discovered 25 years later in the bed of the river, another argument ensued. Militias on both sides of the river engaged in a few outright confrontations along this border, but the United States Supreme Court ruled that the boundary of Texas began on the south bank of the river (instead of in the middle of the river as river boundaries are normally fixed). The boundary dispute was settled, even if it was not to Texans' liking.

26. Spanish Fort

Spanish Fort received that name because later settlers found artifacts of the fort and assumed Spanish had left them. In fact, Spanish Fort was an Indian fortification and the site of one of the most complete victories the Indians ever won over the Spanish forces.

The fort was located on the Red River in what is now Montague County. The Spanish were searching for the fort in order to punish the Indians (mainly Comanches) responsible for a massacre in March 1758 at a Spanish mission, Mission Santa Cruz de la San Saba located near present-day Menard. Imagine the surprise of the 380 Spanish soldiers when they reached the end of their 200-mile journey north and found a fortification spanning both sides of the river, manned by some 6,000 Indians, and flying a French flag. The village was fortified with entrenchments, wooden stockades and a moat. This was a Taovaya village used by allied Indian tribes to meet and exchange goods with French traders.

The Spanish attacked but were turned back in a resounding defeat. They were forced to retreat to their presidio, leaving behind the mules that carried their baggage and two big cannons. Although the Taovaya tribe later was destroyed by a smallpox epidemic, in this battle they beat one of the mightiest military powers in the world at the time.

By early 1870s, a town called Burlington, serving as a watering hole for cattle drivers headed for the Chisholm Trail, developed near the site. When local citizens applied for a post office in 1876, postal authorities rejected the request because another Texas post office had the name. The men then suggested the name "Spanish Fort" after the misnamed ruins.

At its peak, Spanish Fort had many businesses and churches, a Masonic lodge, five physicians, four hotels, and several saloons. In the town, Herman J. Justin founded what was to become internationally known as the Nocona Boot Company. Justin took orders from drivers going north and had their boots ready in time to be picked up on the trip south.

The population reached 300 by 1885, but Spanish Fort had developed a reputation as being a rough town. Outlaws hiding in the Indian Territory would cross the Red River to obtain supplies in the town. Over 40 murders took place during cattle drive days, and one Christmas morning, three men were killed in Spanish Fort before breakfast. Excitement died down when the cattle drives moved west and the railroad bypassed the town. Justin moved his boot factory to Nocona in the 1880s. The population declined to less than 50 by 1952, and during the 1990s, Spanish Fort became a virtual ghost town. Ruins of the Taovaya forts disappeared.

A marker near the Red River on Highway 103 north of Nocona designates the site as being "The Site of the 1759 Taovaya Victory over Spain."

27. Fort Fitzhugh (Also known as Elm Station)

Fort Fitzhugh was established 3 miles south of Gainesville as one in a chain of military outposts established from nearby Preston to the Rio Grande by the Volunteer Texas Rangers for protection of settlers from Indian raids. The Volunteer Texas Rangers were a special force of Texas Rangers led by Captain William F. Fitzhugh after the Mexican War.

The 1845 treaty through which the U. S. annexed Texas provided for the United States to protect the Texas frontier from Indian attacks. The problem was not with the treaty, but with the execution of it. Many Texans thought Zachary Taylor did not like Texas because while he was the President of the United States, he ordered thirty-two companies (in the vicinity of 3,200 troops) to Florida to fight 600-700 Indians. However, he only sent 400-500 soldiers to Texas to protect settlers against Indians estimated to number upward to 15,000. The state was prohibited by the treaty from employing Rangers and only did so when the Federal government paid them.

A few former Rangers, however, answered the need of the frontier and volunteered to defend the frontier thus earning the name "Volunteer Texas Rangers." It was ten years after the annexation before the Texas Rangers again became a legal unit of the Texas government.

In 1847, Captain Fitzhugh led a company patrolling a line across North Texas from Fort Warren on the Red River south to Bird's Fort, now Birdville, and Johnson's station at present-day Arlington. His patrol route included Fort Fitzhugh, which was built that year. It consisted of a small log stockade with a single row of blockhouses and a stable. The fort was closed in 1850.

The fort did contribute to the area being opened to travelers along several trails, including the Mormon Trail, a branch of the Chisholm Trail, and the Butterfield Overland Mail route.

Ruins of the fort, once on private property, have disappeared. A plaque donated in 1948 by the local Boy Scouts unit to mark the spot where the fort once stood has also disappeared.

28. Fort Coffee

Holland Coffee operated a trading post in the area of Preston Bend (which is now under Lake Texoma). He was rumored to have traded guns and whiskey to the Indians, an act that was forbidden by law. In 1837, Coffee was called before the government and "made a satisfactory explanation of his actions." His fort, consisting of a tall fence made of pickets, was said to have been more to prevent the Indians from stealing livestock than protection from raids.

Whatever dealings Coffee had with the Indians, his trading skills came in handy for the family of James Goacher of Bastrop. Coffee traded the Indians beads, blankets, and 400 yards of calico for a daughter of Goacher who had been kidnapped by Indians. Holland Coffee was killed in a knife fight in 1846 when he took offense at a remark that a man made about his wife.

Nearby Coffee's Crossing was a landmark when the Republic of Texas built a Military Road linking Central and North Texas. The fort became a station when the Butterfield Mail stages passed through the area in the late 1850s.

Also nearby was a fort built in the 1840s by Daniel Dugan who was later killed during an Indian raid. That fort has also disappeared without leaving any history, not even a name.

29. Fort Preston

The town of Preston and Fort Preston is now located under Lake Texoma, in Grayson County. When the United States Army Corps of Engineers completed the Texoma Dam in the 1930s, the resulting lake covered both the town and the site of the nearby fort. The community had been a rip-roaring, fast paced town and a destination of Indians seeking liquor. Due to its location on the Red River, the settlement was very active. Fort Preston may have been named for Captain William Gilwater Preston who accompanied the Texas' Military Road expedition of 1840-41 and established a fort at that time.

Captain Randolph B. Marcy and Lieutenant Nathaniel Michler passed through as they returned from El Paso in 1849 after establishing the route for westward bound settlers going to the California gold rush. Then in1852, the depot provided the supply and transport for Captain Marcy's expedition that explored the upper Red River looking for the sites to establish Indian reservations. The supply depot closed during early May 1853 after the army decided to supply Forts Belknap and Phantom Hill from Indianola through Austin. Captain Marcy came through in 1854 with John Pope, and later General Albert Sidney Johnston marched the Second Cavalry by way of Preston in 1855.

Settlement of the area was still in progress in January 1865, when 100 Indians from the Indian Territory raided a nearby community of Rosston, killing nine people and stealing horses.

30. Fort Johnson

Fort Johnson was built on private property in 1840, four miles from the Red River, near a now abandoned town (named Georgetown) in north central Grayson County. This fort had a short life, but from it the Republic of Texas unofficially launched a pirate attack against Mexico, but into United States territory in 1843. It was called the Snively Expedition.

In retaliation for the losses by Texans on the Santa Fe Expedition and for the cruelties suffered by Texans following the Mier expedition, a man named Jacob Snively organized and out-fitted an expedition to intercept and capture property of Mexican traders on the route from Saint Louis to Santa Fe. This expedition was not a government undertaking, although any goods captured were to be divided between the Texas government and the members of the expedition.

About 150 men volunteered for the force designated as the Battalion of Invincibles who marched westward along the old Chihuahua Trail, crossing the Red River two miles below the mouth of the main Wichita. Their course was across present-day Oklahoma, reaching the Arkansas River in the vicinity of present-day Edwards County, Kansas. They took a position to command the Cimarron branch of the Santa Fe Trail.

One volunteer, Charles A. Warfield, with 3 or 4 other Texans followers met a force of 100 Mexican soldiers and took them by surprise. In the ensuing fight, 17 Mexicans were killed and 82 were taken prisoner without any Texans injured. A month later, bored due to a lack of action, the volunteers became restless and released their Mexican prisoners. Texans divided the captured mules, saddles and arms, and dissolved with some men heading home, the others still seeking other adventure and bounty.

One group, with Snively in command, marched towards the Arkansas River, where United States Dragoons, protecting a Mexican caravan, discovered them. Told that he was on United States land and that his men must disarm, Snively protested that he was on Texas territory. The dragoons, however, came across the Arkansas, surrounded the Texan camp, and ordered Snively's men to surrender their guns, which they did. The Texans again divided.

One group finally encountered a large Mexican force but avoided any battle when the troops greatly out-numbered them. They all then returned home. The Snively expedition officially disbanded at Bird's Fort. The Texas government later complained that the dragoons had invaded Texas territory. The U. S. made a settlement for Texans engaged in the expedition.

Fort Johnson's life was short and any possible ruins are now below Lake Texoma

31. Fort Inglish (and Gilbert's Fort)

(See colored picture in the center section)

Bailey Inglish, considered to be the founder of Bonham, had to move his family from Arkansas when the United States made a treaty with the Cherokee Indians giving the Indians the land on which Inglish had settled his family. So in the winter of 1836, Inglish, with five of his children and at least eight other families, moved to Texas. The group arrived in the central part of now Fannin County in March, and Inglish staked claim to land bordering Bois d'Arc Creek.

The following year, Inglish and neighbors built a blockhouse and stockade on Inglish's land. The fort served in the late 1830s as a center for a small frontier village called Fort Inglish. Although families took refuge in the fort, only one raid took place there. Replicas of Fort Inglish and other early settlers' buildings are next to the Sam Rayburn Library in Bonham.

Fannin County's Historical Society has a museum of artifacts in the train depot near downtown Bonham. The fort and museum are open various hours (call 903-583-8042).

Another family fort in Fannin County was Gilbert's Fort established by Mabel Gilbert. It was a compound also built near Bois d'Arc Creek about five miles from Fort Inglish. Gilbert's farm was too far from any fort to seek protection in case of Indian attack, so he made a fort of his home by replacing his doors with heavy timbers that could be locked from within and covering the windows with shutters, which had loop holes large enough to fire rifles through. Each side of the house had a view of the approaches from the surrounding countryside. The fort contained a blockhouse similar to that at Fort Inglish. There are no ruins of that fort.

Settlers in the area made a practice of wearing side arms when working in the fields and were fully armed when they went anywhere. There are stories, however, of massacres occurring in this county. One occurrence happened near Bois d' Arc Creek when two men (William Dority and Andrew Thomas) and Thomas' two sons were searching for lost pigs. Indians surprised them and killed one son then attacked the small cabin where the others were preparing a meal. Surprised by an Indian, who came bursting through the door, Andrew Thomas drew a hot poker from the fire and attacked the Indian, who withdrew.

Several years later, 25 miles south in present-day Collin County, settlers, the Whislers and the Clemmons were clearing land when a band of screaming Indians ran at them. Cut off from their houses, the two men were shot, tomahawked, scalped and their bodies mutilated. Wives of the men watched the entire slaughter, but when they started for help the Indians' gunfire caused them to run inside the house. When it became dark, Mrs. Whisler went to find help while Mrs. Clemmons and her two children waited; listening to the howl of wolves and the sounds of a mountain lion nearby, till help arrived the next morning.

Also in the area was a Camp Jordan, established in 1842 by Captain M. B. Houghton who recruited men from nearby Timber Creek where they were working on the Military Road. The camp was near the site of modern Randolph in Fannin County. There are no ruins.

32. Fort Warren

Fort Warren was located on the Red River south of where it joins with Choctaw Slough on the present-day Fannin and Grayson county line. Wooden walls surrounded the structure built by Abel Warren. Two-story towers were on every corner to watch for Indian raids.

Abel Warren was an early trader who set out from Massachusetts for adventure in the American southwest at age 21. In 1835, hearing stories of the potentially lucrative Indian trade with hunters and trappers, he decided to establish a trading post on the upper Red River. The following year, accompanied by adventurers and Indian guides, Warren ventured into Texas and constructed a post on the south bank of the Red River. Warren's party erected a stockade and storehouse and began to bargain for hides and furs with the Indians who ventured to the post.

The operation met with little success, however, as the majority of the Indians with whom Warren hoped to deal were too far west to visit the post with regularity. The arrival of Anglo settlers reduced the possibility of the Indians coming, and he abandoned the fort. Other settlers started operating the fort. Then when Fannin County was established from Red River County in 1837, Fort Warren became the county seat of an area that included present-day Grayson County. A courthouse and a two-story cabin were built in Fort Warren, and in 1838 a new stockade was built around the fort. Then on January 16, 1843, the Texas Legislature changed the county seat to Bonham.

The old courthouse remained in Fort Warren until the 1920s, when it was dismantled and moved to Bonham to be a landmark. However, it was never rebuilt and slowly rotted away.

33. Fort Lyday (Also Lyday's Fort or Fort DeKalb, and Fort Jessie Shelton)

Isaac Lyday, in the 1830s, built Fort Lyday for his family north of Lyday's Crossing on the North Sulphur River in present-day southwestern Lamar County. The location, in the Territory of Arkansas at the time, is near the old community of Bledsoe whose cemetery includes Fort Lyday settlers. That cemetery is located south of Honey Grove via FM 824 to Fm 904, then turn east to Fannin County Road 3625 (a dirt road), and then continue to where it becomes a Lamar County road. Headstones may be seen a few yards to the east of the Lamar County road sign on the north side of the road. Weeds and vines are now slowly consuming this cemetery.

A private fort, Lyday's covered a quarter acre, with several 10-by-12-foot storerooms against its north wall and similarly sized living quarters arranged against the other three walls. The fortification was surrounded by a picket stockade and had a large well in the middle of the parade ground. Livestock were penned in a corral located outside the stockade. The fort was constructed for the defense of all of the settlers on nearby Cypress Creek. There were at one time 85 men protecting the fort. They frequently scouted the area for Indian raiding parties, but life and property were only secure within gun shot range of the fort. Each full moon the Indians rode into the area and the settlers stood watch throughout those nights.

A legend has it that the families living within the fort had a pet pig, which spent most of its days simply resting on the porch of one of the houses. One day, the women in the fort heard noises coming from the nearby woods. Although it could have been an Indian trick luring them from the fort, the women grabbed their rifles and went to find the source of the noises. They found their pet pig in the clutches of a black bear. A woman shot the bear, saving the pig.

When the Military Road was built, it passed next to the fort. Records show the Red River County Rangers under command of Captain William B. Stout later garrisoned the fort. Stout's men repaired the fort and brought in 14 families for protection from any marauding Indians. History of the area is quiet as to the need for the repairs and also to the disposition of the Lyday family, though it is noted that the fort population grew to 25 to 30 families.

The fort saw sporadic activity until about 1843. There are some records of the fort that have it in existence until around 1890. It may have become a part of the small community of Bledsoe, which has now disappeared, its cemetery is traveling the same route. An area resident tells of finding a cannon ball in a wooded field south of the road across from the cemetery.

Nearby was Fort Jessie Shelton, a family fort built in the southwest portion of present Lamar County, 15 miles east of Fort Lyday, to protect families and those in nearby Roxton. This was a fort built sturdy with a view in all directions. A fire destroyed it in the early 1900s.

34. Camp Rusk (Also known as Fort Rusk)

This was a Confederate training camp established in 1861 in northwest Delta County near Tread Mill Lake on the south bank of the North Sulphur River. The camp was composed of men from Lamar, Red River, Titus, Grayson, Fannin, and Collins counties. In 1862, an epidemic of measles claiming several lives hit the camp. The camp closed after the troops moved out.

History has forgotten other Confederate camps in the region north and east of Bonham that provided training for enlistees. They were Camp Benjamin (5 miles north of Dodd City), Camp Flourney in Quitman; Camp Jeff Davis (6 miles northeast of Clarksville); a Camp McKnight in Red River County, and Camp Sidney Johnston on Brady Creek near Paris. These camps served their one purpose, training recruits, and then were closed.

Six miles southwest of Petty in Lamar County on U. S. 82 at FM 38 is the historical marker at the site of the "Persimmon Grove and Captain Hill's Military Camp." Methodist lay minister and Mexican War veteran James Hill drilled men there in 1861, before they entered the Confederate Army as the Company E, Ninth Regiment of the Texas Infantry.

35. Fort Saint Louis de Carloretta

The first fort in northeast Texas was probably French. Fort Saint Louis de Carloretta was located more than 300 miles northwest of Natchitoches, Louisiana, near a Caddo Indian village on the Texas side of the Red River in the southeast corner of present-day Lamar County. A dozen soldiers built the 125 by 20-foot fort with a barracks for ten soldiers and installed two cannons. Several French families located in the area and grew corn, tobacco, and vegetables.

Caddo Indians, who are believed to have occupied the Red River valley shortly after A.D. 500, were primarily an agricultural people and only hunted to supplement their food supply. As Europeans began to explore the valley during the 1600s, the Caddoes found themselves between the French and Spanish, both of whom wanted to explore and settle the region. The French had earlier established friendly relations with the Caddoes along the Red River, and maintained an upper hand until 1763, when France ceded the region to Spain after the Seven-Year War.

Fort Saint Louis de Carloretta lasted until 1770, when the territory became Spain's.

36. Le Poste des Cadodaquious

This was a French fort built somewhere in Bowie County, possibly before 1700. As the name implies it was connected with the Caddo Indians with whom the French traded, but there is little other recorded history of the fort. The development of this area was later enhanced by the Red River Expedition undertaken by the United States in 1806.

That expedition was commissioned by President Thomas Jefferson to explore the Red River, while the Lewis and Clark's expedition was exploring the Missouri and Columbia rivers. Jefferson thought the Red River might provide a viable waterway to Santa Fe. He also wanted to test the western border of the Louisiana Purchase, which was being disputed by Spain.

Congress appropriated $5,000 for the Red River expedition in 1805, and by late April 1806, when the expedition left Natchez, expenses had already grown to $11,000. However, the expedition was cut short by the treachery of an American general named James Wilkinson (who had helped negotiate the Neutral Zone on the Texas

and Louisiana border dispute between Spain and the U. S.).
Wilkinson, who allegedly conspired with Aaron Burr to take territory
from Spain for their personal gain, was also, allegedly, a Spanish
informer.   Hoping to start an international confrontation (that could
be used for his own good), Wilkinson told his Spanish friends about
the American expedition. Two Spanish military expeditions marched
to intercept the Americans as they poled their way up the river. The
Red River Expedition was 615 miles up the river on July 28, when
they met. The Spanish force ordered them to turn around at a point
known as Spanish Bluff, in what is now Bowie County.

Though the bloodless confrontation and the expedition's failure
did cause the Jefferson administration some embarrassment it did
not trigger the war that Wilkinson and Burr hoped.

37. Fort Sherman

In southwest Titus County, a Fort Sherman was constructed where
a road from Fort Towson (in Louisiana) going to Nacogdoches crossed
the Cypress Creek south of Gray Rock. The exact time it was built is
unknown. It was a sturdy fort (which was only two-thirds above
ground) made of baked brick with loopholes in each side for shooting.
Nothing else is known.

38. Fort Crawford

This fort (either family or Texas) was built near Hallsville in the
lawless Neutral Zone between Louisiana and Texas in 1839, to protect
settlers from Indians, renegades, and outlaws. The Neutral Zone
was disputed land between Texas and Louisiana. It attracted all sorts
of criminals and bad characters. Even after Texas became a Republic,
the area was still known for it lawlessness

Sketches indicate that the fort may have been a military
encampment with a two-story blockhouse built inside of a tall picket
stockade fence that encircled the entire complex, it may have been a
Texas Ranger encampment, or it may have been a family blockhouse
enlarged by the Rangers. It did serve as a refuge for settlers when
the Cherokee War broke out in 1839, although the supplies inside the
fort were inadequate for the number of people there. This was near
the area Sam Houston had given to the Cherokees earlier, an action

the Texas legislature over-ruled. (See "Camp Ford" in this Region for more information of the Cherokee War.)

At about the same time, another war broke out in this area, this time between the settlers themselves. One group of settlers had formed an organization to deal with the lawlessness in the area. They called themselves the Regulators and dealt with suspected criminals with their own justice, which sometimes included hanging an innocent man. A counter organization formed called the Moderators, which wanted to bring the "out-of-control Regulators" to justice. Pitched battles raged between the peace loving and law-abiding citizens led to ambushes by the members of the two forces with ten law-abiding citizens killed before good sense prevailed.

The number of families living in the fort is unknown but it was large enough for a traveling preacher to have delivered a sermon in Fort Crawford. The minister noted in his diary, "it was difficult to conduct religious services because of the hostilities between the settlers".

The site is on private property, and it is reported that there are no visible ruins of the fort.

39. Fort Le Dout

Reportedly located in what is now Wood County, this fort is one on which there has been little written, and very little known. The French had possibly established it during the 1700s as a post for trading with the Caddo and Wichita Indians. Le Dout may have been located on the Sabine River or possibly on Lake Fork Creek, a fork of the Sabine. A 1989 archeological study suggested that a site, located about 5 miles from the intersection of Lake Fork Creek and the Sabine River, may be the location. If so, Fort Le Dout may be beneath Lake Fork Reservoir.

40. Camp Ford

In July 1863, the Confederacy established Camp Ford near present-day Tyler as the camp for prisoners-of-war then being held in Louisiana. Named for Colonel John S. (Rip) Ford, it was the largest prisoner of war camp west of the Mississippi. It may have been the place where the first baseball was made in Texas. One of the prisoners wound raveling strings from a blanket around a bottle cork then covered his creation with a piece of boot strap leather. Prisoners had little to do, and playing ball may have been a bright spot in a dreary and difficult experience.

Until 1864, morale among the prisoners was passable, and the ranking Union officers maintained a decent sense of order. But the prison population quadrupled when 3,000 prisoners arrived after the defeat of Union forces in Arkansas and Louisiana. The stockade was doubled, but conditions were still deplorable. Quality of the shelters deteriorated. Timber became less plentiful, and shelters had to be constructed quickly. The prisoners improvised all sorts of crude shelters, from brush arbors to blanket tents. Some simply dug holes in the ground for protection from the cold winds. A popular form of shelter called a "shebang" was to burrow into a hill and cover it with an A-shaped framework made of poles, sticks, and clay protecting the entrance.

For the remainder of the war, the Confederates had difficulties in supplying adequate rations for both the prisoners and their own guards as the Union blockaded Texas. Sometimes the standard daily pint of meal and pound of beef per prisoner was down to a quarter pound of each, depending upon the supply that was available to the Confederate commissary.

The clothes that the prisoners were wearing when they were captured saw most prisoners through their captivity. Acute shortages of clothing were due to a lack of cloth milling in the South when the Union blockaded southern cotton shipments. In response to a letter from the Union officer prisoners, two shipments of clothes from the Union government were received.

Smith County's Historical Society has a self-guided, walking tour of restored shelters the soldiers may have built while captive at Camp Ford. The site is near the intersection of Highway 271 and County Road 334, four miles northeast from the center of present-day Tyler.

Near the camp, 23 years earlier in 1839, was the site of the famous Battle of the Neches, the major fight in the Cherokee War. Texans led by T. J. Rusk, Edward Burleson, and Kelsey H. Douglass chased Chief Bowl (Chief Duwali) and his Cherokee Indian warriors through most of East Texas. The first day fighting took place near the Neches River in present-day Henderson County, and the second day fighting

was in Van Zandt County. It was an even battle as Texas troops numbered 500 and the Indians totaled 700 to 800. The Indians were routed and the Battle of the Neches eventually resulted in driving the Cherokee Indians from East Texas. One of the victims of the battle was aged Indian Chief Duwali who remained (until dead) on the field on horseback, wearing a handsome sword and sash given him by his friend, Sam Houston.

41. Fort Houston (Anderson County)

Built in 1835, the fort site is west of present-day Palestine, though no traces remain. It was to here that some of the survivors of the massacre at Fort Parker fled in 1836. Also that same year as General Santa Anna led the Mexican army through Texas, burning and destroying all of the Texans' settlements, General Sam Houston sent a Protestant minister, the Reverend Peter Fullinwider, to Fort Houston to lead the settlers to safety in Nacogdoches. This retreat was part of what became known as the "Runaway Scrape" where settlers buried the belongings that they could not carry and sought protection from Santa Anna. Later the fort was part of a barrier of forts established to protect against raiding Indians. Other forts in the barrier included Little River Fort, Fort Milam and Fort Colorado. These forts were credited with producing a lull in the conflicts between settlers, and the Kiowas and Comanche Indians in 1837–1838.

Later, during the Cherokee War and Nacogdoches uprisings, settlers sought protection at this fort. An old Fort Houston cemetery is located off of the highway loop now circling Palestine.

42. King's Fort (Also known as Kingsborough)

William P. King, a doctor and a land speculator, organized the Southern Land Company in Mississippi in the fall of 1838 and moved its headquarters to San Augustine, Texas, in 1839. By August of that year he had secretly hired Nacogdoches county surveyor Warren Angus Ferris to survey land on the Trinity River. Ferris was to lay out a city site to be called Warwick on a bluff overlooking the river and to survey 114 land grants for development in the area of present-day Dallas, Kaufman, Rockwall, and Hunt counties. By 1840, Ferris had surveyed nearly half-a- million acres. Ferris described the land he surveyed in his diary:

"I saw in this picturesque region thousands of buffalo and wild horses everywhere. Deer and turkeys were always in view and an occasional bear would some times cross our path. The wolves and buzzards become our familiar acquaintances, and in the river we found an abundance of fish, from minnows to eight footers. The prairies are beautiful."

During the summer of 1840, King constructed a fort, called Kingsborough, on the site of present-day Kaufman. Although many of the land grant certificates held by the Southern Land Company proved to be invalid, King obtained clear title to the survey that included Fort King. From 1840 to 1841, King's Fort, which was comprised of four log cabins and a stockade manned by a dozen-man unit, was the only white settlement between Fort Houston and Fort Inglish. The picket fence around the fort was made from poles ten feet long and several inches think. King encouraged settlers to move to Kingsborough, and managed to attract 40 families to the area. It was the first settlement in the area now known as the three forks of the Trinity River.

The history of the fort mentions several Indian raids, which is not surprising since the fort was built within 50 miles of the largest Indian reservation east of the Brazos River. One legend included in the history of the city of Kaufman tells of a raid when only four men were standing guard. Attacking Indians were repulsed when one of their horses was shot in the head. Other Indians then rode off, stealing the horses of the four men, but apparently forgetting the seven ponies they had stolen earlier in a raid in Red River country.

One Indian fight involved a group of surveyors (although it probably did not include Ferris). A surveying party was attacked in what was known as the Battle Creek Fight. Also known as the Surveyors' Fight, it was a fight between surveyors and about 300 Indians on October 8, 1838, just east of Battle Creek, near the site of present-day Dawson. During the 24-hour battle, 30 Indians and 18 surveyors were killed. Three survivors managed to escape and reach a camp of friendly Kickapoos. The surveyors told the Indians that they had been fighting with different Indians (not Kickapoos), and the friendly Indians supplied the survivors with provisions and helped them reach Fort Parker. Later about 50 men from the settlement at Old Franklin later returned to the site to bury their dead.

One-mile west of Dawson on Highway 31 a state commemorative marker is near the site of the Surveyors' Fight battlefield. In Kaufman, there is a commemorative marker for Fort King.

43. Fort Smith (Hill Country)

This was another of a chain of the forts established by the Republic of Texas to protect settlers from Indians. Located at the headwaters of Richland Creek in present-day Hill County, it was commanded by Captain Thomas I. Smith, who oversaw construction of the fort in 1847. He died that same year. J. C. Connor who commanded for another year replaced Smith. In 1848, the company of dragoons abandoned the stockade moving west to a new garrison, Fort Graham.

There was another Fort Smith a hundred miles to the south. This had caused numerous headaches for investigators who use the diaries and journals of settlers to learn more about the area. Settlers writing in their day did not distinguish between the forts because they were either unaware of the fort or didn't realize historian would want more precise descriptions. Of course, those settlers had no reason to even imagine a place that was a five to ten day ride for them would someday be only a couple hours' drive in the future.

The site of this Fort Smith was to become the home of Inversion School. In 1936, the Texas Centennial Commission placed a marker at the site of this, the northern, old Fort Smith. In nearby Hillsboro at Hill Junior College is an interesting museum about the history of Texas.

44. Fort Graham

In 1849, Fort Graham was established as a United States Army post. It was located near the eastern bank of the Brazos River at Little Bear Creek near present-day Lake Whitney. Major Ripley A. Arnold and companies of the Second Dragoons occupied it as one of the important posts on the upper Texas frontier. The post was near a recognized Indian council spot and close to villages and camps of many Indian tribes. It was in a position to serve as a "listening post."

The fort was named either for Colonel James D. Graham of the Engineers Corp or for Lieutenant Colonel William M. Graham who was killed in 1846 at the Battle of Molino del Rey during the Mexican War. Troops built log and clapboard structures including the commissary, officers' quarters, and stable. Civilian laborers built a hospital, a carpenter and a wheel maker's shops, a blacksmith shop, a wagon and mule yard, and also built a quartermaster's storehouse. Construction was hindered by a lack of adequate manpower.

Annexation of Texas, and the other territorial gains made by the United States as a result of the Treaty of Guadalupe Hidalgo, gave the United States the responsibility for frontier defense and communication in the Southwest. Fort Graham was to help anchor the frontier defense line between the Toway Indian village and Fort Washita (in present-day Oklahoma). Major Arnold's orders directed him to provide escorts for supply trains and travelers, to patrol the countryside as far as the forks of the Trinity, to protect the citizens from hostile incursions by Indians, and to attempt to conciliate the local Indians to stop all the fighting.

Major Arnold turned the command at Fort Graham over to Lieutenant Fowler Hamilton in 1849, and moved north with F Company to the West Fork of the Trinity River to establish Camp (later "Fort") Worth. Soon after Arnold's departure, Graham's new commanding officer reported that he had only one officer and forty-six men available for duty. The situation did not improve until early fall, when General George M. Brooke, the new commander of the Eighth Military Department, was able to send two companies of the Eighth United States Infantry under command of Brevet Lieutenant Colonel James V. Bomford to the post. Company H remained at Fort Graham, while the other company proceeded to the Trinity to reinforce Fort Worth.

Fort Graham was located near George Barnard's trading post, which was a target for criticism from other Indian agents and departmental commanders, who accused the traders of selling liquor and firearms to the Indians. Barnard had set up a trading post at a settlement that was given the name of Fort Spunky. It was never an official fort, but the name Spunky was attached to the settlement because of the fights that took place there, assumed to be due to the alcohol sold in Barnard's trading post. The annexation of Texas by the U. S. left a gap in the law, no one had control over the Indian traders, and Barnard took advantage of the situation to do as he pleased. Stories told about Barnard said he often commented he was more fearful of the army than he was of Indians.

The Texas Centennial Commission arranged for the State to buy the site, reconstructed the barracks and placed a marker there in 1936. With the development of Lake Whitney in the 1970s, the site was flooded, and the remains of the post disappeared beneath waters of the lake. Another building has now been reconstructed. It may be seen at the State Park near Whitney. (Legends tell of another fort, also now under Lake Whitney, but no information was located.)

45. Fort Worth (Originally known as Camp Worth)

Over looking the Trinity River (in present-day Fort Worth) this camp was established in 1849, for protecting new settlers. Major

Arnold, commander of Fort Graham, established Camp Worth. The post contained one cannon; officers quarters built of logs, a hospital and enlisted men's barracks also built of logs. All of the buildings had dirt floors. Stables were built near the camp so the soldiers would have mounts available in the event of an attack; but that also brought the horse flies close to camp, a condition that no one in the camp appreciated.

There was a bit of action at the camp in 1851 when Indians, with thoughts of retaliation for a recent defeat by these same soldiers, came looking for trouble. As the Indians prepared an assault on the camp, the soldiers loaded their new cannon and fired one shot. One cannon shot was all that was required. The surprised Indians, not aware of the cannon, quickly rode away.

When the army abandoned the camp in 1853, new settlers found the beginning of a ready-made town. A plaque near downtown Fort Worth commemorates the camp.

46. Bird's Fort

Following the Battle of Village Creek in 1841, Texan General Edward H. Tarrant ordered construction and garrisoning of Bird's Fort, or Fort Bird as some called it. It was built to protect the northwest corner of the frontier. The fort consisted of several buildings and blockhouse enclosed in a picket stockade.

The Battle of Village Creek was a running gunfight along the banks of Village Creek, a tributary of the Trinity River, in eastern Tarrant County. A series of Indian villages situated along the creek housed Indians including Caddos, Cherokees, and Tonkawas, and served as a stronghold against the encroachments of white settlers from the east, and Comanches from the west. As friction increased between settlers and the Indians, the government of the Republic of Texas authorized a number of raids against the Village Creek settlements. Army expeditions of 1838 failed to locate the Indian towns, and the Indians intensified their raids on the settlements.

General Edward H. Tarrant organized a company of 69 volunteers from the Red River counties and captured a lone Indian the next day. The Indian revealed the locations of the Indians' villages, and the following day the volunteers galloped into the southernmost village with little opposition. Scouting detachments riding down the creek toward the Trinity River, as the remainder of the command burned huts, encountered increasingly larger villages and stronger Indian resistance. Near the thickets bordering the Trinity River, Indian musket fire killed one man and wounded several Texans. General Tarrant, learning that the villages were home to over 1,000 warriors, decided to withdraw. The fight on Village Creek had compromised the Indians' position. Tarrant later returned with 400 men but found the Indian villages deserted.

In September 1843, the Treaty of Bird's Fort between the Village Creek tribes and Texas opened new settlements and removed the Indians to a reservation on the Brazos River.

Located along Highway 21 west of Alto is a commemorating marker for a Delaware Indian Village. It states that the Delaware were instrumental in bringing tribes to a treaty council between representatives of the Republic of Texas and 8 additional Indian tribes at Bird's Fort. Later, Bird's Fort lost in an election to Fort Worth to be the county seat of Tarrant County. The fort settlement survived to become present-day Birdsville.

Region Six

The tour of this group of forts starts in Fredericksburg, northwest of San Antonio, and meanders to the Texas Panhandle. There are interesting fortifications and two big unanswered questions in this area. The need for the forts was based largely on the fact that the Comanches had absolute control of the region. Though they called themselves "the people," they acquired the name "Comanche," form their neighbors. The name they were given means "enemy" or literally "someone who wants to fight me all the time."

Comanches were a tribe that had migrated south to the northern plains of Texas. There they acquired horses (from the large wild mustang herds formed from horses the Spanish had brought to Texas) and they found an abundance of buffalo. When the Comanches moved south, they came into conflict with another Indian tribe living in Texas, the Apaches, who dominated the region. Apaches were now forced south by the Comanche onslaught and the tribes became mortal enemies. When the Spanish established a mission for the Apaches on the San Saba River, the Comanches destroyed the mission. It was the last attempt at a Spanish mission in this region.

The Spanish, nor Mexicans, nor the Republic of Texas ever fully defeated the Comanches. Even the United States found itself nearly powerless to defend the frontier from the Comanche raids. A plan formulated after the Civil War to move the Comanche to reservations failed. In fact, after all the other Indian tribes had been wiped out or moved to reservations, the Comanches were still fighting. The last major battle of the Indian wars in Texas was fought at a location on this tour. The last camp in this book is an Indian camp where the battle takes place.

Region Six Map
(Numbers are as the sites are listed in the text for this region)

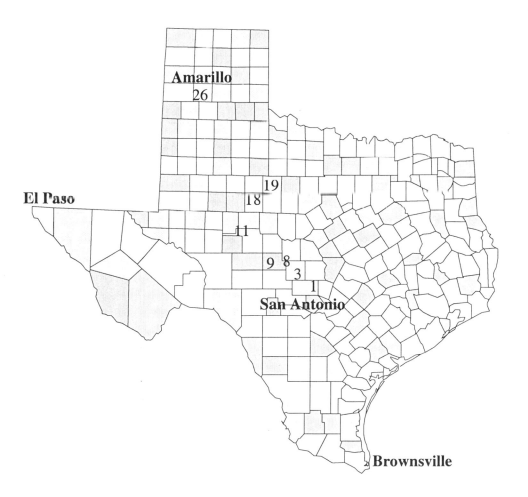

Location   Region Six

1	Fort Martin Scott – in Fredericksburg
2	Camp Davis – in Gillespie County
3	Fort Mason – in Mason
4	Camp Llano – near Mason
5	Camp San Saba – in McCulloch County
6	Bowie's Fort – in McCulloch or Menard County
7	Mission Santa Cruz de San Saba – near Menard
8	Presidio de San Luis de Las Amarillas (San Saba) – near Menard
9	Fort McKavett – in Menard County
10	Mission San Clemente – location remains an unsolved mystery
11	Fort Concho – in San Angelo
12	Camp Joseph E. Johnston – in Tom Green County
13	Camp Charlotte – in Irion County
14	Camp Grierson Spring – in Reagan County
15	Tower Hill – near Sterling City
16	Camp Elizabeth – in Sterling County
17	Camp Johnston – near Robert Lee
18	Fort Chadbourne – near Bronte
19	Fort Phantom Hill – near Abilene
20	Sewell's Camp – in Garza County
21	Camp Resolution – in Motley County
22	Fort Elliott – in Wheeler County
23	Fort Adobe – in Hutchinson County
24	Anderson's Fort – near Spur
25	Camp Roberts – in Crosby County
26	Indian Camp at Palo Duro Canyon – in Tule Canyon

1. Fort Martin Scott
(Originally named Camp Houston)

On December 5, 1848, Captain Seth Eastman, commander of Companies D and H, of the First United States Infantry, built Camp Houston as one of the first army forts in western Texas. Located two miles southeast of Fredericksburg on Barons Creek, a tributary of the Pedernales River, it was built to protect settlers and travelers along the Fredericksburg-San Antonio road from Indian raids. The Eighth Military Department renamed the camp in December 1849 for Major Martin Scott (Fifth United States Infantry), killed at the Battle of Molina del Rey.

Though the early German settlers in Fredericksburg made a treaty with local Comanches in 1847, the arrival of more settlers into the rich valleys nearly led to warfare in 1850, when the Indian tribes met with Indian agent John Rollins. The meeting resulted in the Fort Martin Scott Treaty, which improved the situation enough to prevent open war. As settlers pushed farther to the west, Fort Martin Scott lost any strategic significance. The fort was closed in December 1853, and remained closed until late in 1866, when General Philip H. Sheridan ordered the Fourth U. S. Cavalry to once again defend settlers in the area from Indian attacks.

Twenty miles north of Fredericksburg is a granite dome, called Enchanted Rock that has long been the center of various legends. Spanish explorers believed it was one large chunk of silver or iron. In 1834, an account reported the rock was platinum. Spanish who also sought legendary gold and silver mines nearby and some early Texans believed that the lost "Bowie Mines" were in the area. Some gold was mined in nearby areas, but not enough to be profitable.

Comanche and Tonkawa Indians feared the rock and offered sacrifices at its base. The Indian legends of the haunting of Enchanted Rock were probably bolstered by the way the rock glitters on clear nights and by the creaking noises it often makes.

One Indian legend is that a band of brave warriors, the last of their tribe, unsuccessfully defended themselves on the rock from the attacks of other Indians. Since then their ghosts have haunted Enchanted Rock. Another tale tells of the spirit of a great Indian chief doomed to walk the summit forever as punishment for sacrificing his daughter; indentations on the rock's summit are supposedly from his footprints. There is also a story of a white woman kidnapped by Indians who escaped to live near the top of the rock, and on some nights her screams may be heard.

The scientific theory about the rock is almost as creative as the legends. The glittering being caused by water trapped in pools on the rock's surface or by the moon reflecting off wet feldspar. The creaking noises are caused by contraction of the rock's outer surface as it cools.

Another tale was given official credence when the state commemorated it in 1936 with a plaque near the summit. It tells a heroic story in the life of Captain John Coffee Hays of the Texas Rangers. Cut off from his company by Comanches raiders in the fall of 1841, Hays took refuge on Enchanted Rock. There, single-handedly, he held off Indians in a three-hour battle. It ended when the frustrated Indians fled even more convinced evil spirits possessed the rock.

The Fredericksburg's Heritage Association has started to restore Fort Martin Scott's site as a park on Highway 290 east of town. Several reconstructed buildings are open to the public and a museum is open on Tuesday through Sunday from 10 a.m. to 5 p.m.

2. Camp Davis

Ranger James M. Norris established Camp Davis four miles from the junction of White Oak Creek and the Pedernales River in southwest Gillespie County. It was built in March 1862 as a Ranger station for the Frontier Regiment as one of several such posts set up in central Texas along a generally north-south axis from Camp Cureton on the Trinity River to the Rio Grande. The camp was manned by members of H. T. Davis' company until, due to a shortage of men, the consolidation of all the regiments occurred at Fort Belknap in March of 1864.

3. Fort Mason

Located between the Llano and San Saba rivers in an area that the Apache made their home, Fort Mason was in the vicinity of a great amount of activity. To provide protection for settlers in the area, in 1848, the United States authorized forts from the Rio Grande to the Red River. Fort Mason's location on Post Oak Hill was established by Brevet Major Hamilton W. Merrill and Companies A and B of the Second Dragoons on July 6, 1851.

The fort was named for a Lieutenant George T. Mason, killed at

Brownsville during the Mexican War, or for General Richard Barnes Mason, who died only a year before the fort was established. During the next few years up to the beginning of the Civil War, the fort played an important role in the settlement of the area.

At first settlers stayed close to the fort, but as the military protection increased, they began to locate farther from the post. But, during the Civil War, when the fort was abandoned by the Union troops, Indian raids were worse than they had ever been. Killings,

thefts, and raids terrorized settlers in the area. Texas Rangers and minutemen were unable to handle all of the problems the Indians created. In 1865, fourteen years old Alice Todd was kidnapped in Mason County and never heard from again. Near the town of Paint Rock, there are pictographs of two crossed lances and two long hair scalps that may be the record of the killing of Alice's mother and a slave woman. Near this pictograph is a picture of a woman drawn horizontally, a typical display of captivity. These scenes record the Todd raid and kidnapping. (The pictographs are on private land, but tours may be arranged in Paint Rock.) There is another story that two children kidnapped near Mason were rescued in Santa Fe by the scout and Indian fighter Kit Carson.

After the Civil War, the United States Army reoccupied the fort on December 24, 1866. General John Porter Hatch was the commanding officer. The lawlessness of Reconstruction apparently affected personnel, as a number of desertions and court-martials were recorded.

During 1870, the State organized several companies of Frontier Forces. Fort Mason was reopened as headquarters for Companies A and B. Captain James M. Hunter, later county judge of Mason County, was in command for most of that year. In 1871, the troops were disbanded, and for the last time the fort was closed. Local citizens gradually dismantled its rock buildings and many early homes in the town of Mason still contained materials from the fort.

In 1975, a group of citizens began reconstructing one of the officers' quarters at the site. The Mason County Historical Society has opened the site to the public. Taped messages tell of officers stationed at Fort Mason before the Civil War who later become generals with twelve fighting for the Confederacy and eight fighting for the Union

4. Camp Llano

Located in Mason County at the junction of Rock Creek and the Llano River, Camp Llano was formed as a camp for the Texas Frontier Regiment. Captain H. T. Davis established the camp around 1862 to protect settlers. For the Frontier Regiment no camp was to be more than a day's ride to the next. Camp Llano was established 9 miles from Fort Mason as a place for Rangers to tie their horses and pitch a tent, or sleep under the stars. The Frontier Regiment was constantly in the saddle patrolling for Indians, as this had been a pasture for the Comanches. The surrounding area, which the Rangers scouted, was the scene of several Indians raids.

In 1862, in Llano County along the river, a band of fifteen Comanche Indians raided a ranch near Legion Valley where eight women and their children were gathering while the men were away. Indians killed many of the women and took others captive. One child was recovered months later. One boy who was taken captive was recovered four years later. In 1873, twenty-one Apaches raided ranches around the Pack Mountain area. The settlers then followed the Indians for 25 miles and killed three of them.

5. Camp San Saba

A unit of the Mounted Volunteers of the Frontier Regiment under Captain W.G. O'Brien founded this camp around 1862 to protect the frontier from Indian raids. In 1864, the unit became the 46th Texas Cavalry in the Confederate Army. This camp was located east of Highway 87 in McCulloch County. A 1936 Texas commemorative marker is at the site.

In 1870, a company of Texas Rangers under Captain Rufus Perry heard that Indians were raiding to the south near Dripping Spring and went in search of the raiding party. Near Shovel Mountain, the Rangers found 128 Indians chasing one man. Armed with repeating Winchesters, the 28 Rangers defeated the Comanches who had only muzzle-loaded rifles, bows and lances. The chief's war bonnet and headdress were taken to Austin, and given as a gift to the governor.

6. Bowie's Fort (Bowie's Silver Mine, Lost San Saba Mine)

There is not a complete adventure story of Texas that does not mention the legend of the mine associated with the Alamo hero, Jim Bowie, also of "Bowie knife" fame. The fact that a fortification is named for Bowie is not common knowledge, so it is not surprising the location of the fort is also controversial. Some reports are that it was located in McCulloch County; others say Menard County. Now on private land, both sites are not provable, as any ruins would consist of no more than rocks, which cannot speak.

If the fort was in McCulloch County, the site was along Calf Creek 25 miles east of Presidio San Saba. If it was in Menard County, then the site was only six or seven miles east of Presidio San Saba along Jackson's Creek. The latter site is preferable for adventurers, as there is a cave nearby, which might be the cave associated with many of the Bowie legends. No matter which location is picked for the fort, the reason for its existence is the same.

Bowie was running from unfriendly Indians of the Caddo, Waco, and Tehuacana tribes. Out-numbered by 15 to 1, Jim Bowie and his followers sought the protection of a hastily built structure of rocks.

Fifty Indians were killed and another thirty-five wounded. In Bowie's force, three were wounded, one killed, and most of their horses and mules were killed or crippled. Bowie was not injured. This was probably a few years before Bowie would die in the Alamo.

Could the Seven Cities of Gold which the Spaniards searched so hard to locate have been cities of silver reflecting a bright golden sun? If so, the search would not have been in vain, for throughout Texas there are stories of silver mines of unimaginable wealth. From the area around El Paso east to the vicinity of Nacogdoches and Fort Teran legends tell of the discovery of silver.

One of the legends concerning supposedly fantastically rich silver mines was a discovery by Don Bernardo de Miranda along the Llano River. He sent Miranda y Flores with twenty-three soldiers and citizens on February 17, 1756 to investigate his discovery. After locating the area now known as the Riley Mountains, not far from Honey Creek in Llano County, Miranda's men found a deposit of ore so large that Miranda guaranteed "a mine to each of the inhabitants of the Province of Texas." This mine became known as the Los Almagres Mine, and source of the silver the mission smelted near Menard. Was "Los Almagres" Bowie's mine?

7. Mission Santa Cruz de San Saba

Mission Santa Cruz de San Saba was established in 1757 to Christianize the Apache Indians at their request. The site is on the San Saba River about three miles east of the present-day town of Menard and four miles from the ruins of the Presidio San Luis de Las Amarillas. The Spanish had additional incentives for establishing this mission: there were the prospects of minerals and a Spanish mine owner, Don Bernardo de Miranda, offered to underwrite the cost.

Friars built a temporary church and quarters for themselves. A new presidio was built by the troops for the friar's protection. It was downstream from the mission as the friars hoped the distance between the presidio and mission would reduce the possibility of troops harassing the Indian women. They failed to realize that this distance made the mission vulnerable to attack.

On February 25, 1758, Indians raided the mission's pasture and ran off the horses. Soldiers sent out in pursuit found the countryside crawling with Indians. The captain of the presidio then urged the three missionaries and others at the mission to take refuge at the presidio. By the time the missionaries agreed, it was too late; the air was filled with the war cries of 2,000 Indians as they surrounded the mission. Although the attack was by Comanches and Kiowas, it sent a message to the Apaches that neither their presence nor the Spaniards' was wanted in this area. This mission was never rebuilt, and Spain's attempts to establish missions diminished, then stopped. The loss of this mission was a severe blow to the Spanish hopes of taming the Apaches. Ruins were found in 1993.

Northwest of the town of Paint Rock is one of the premier rock art sites in Texas. There, drawings of horses, a devil, and a mission possibly recall the Spanish presence at Santa Cruz de San Saba. A mission is depicted as a long rectangular building with two crosses above twin towers. (As Mission Santa Cruz only had one tower, some interpreters of the pictographs believe the mission is Concepcion, in San Antonio.) Clouds of black smoke are drawn near the mission, depicting the fire. The rock art pictographs may be viewed for a very reasonable fee.

8. Presidio de San Luis de Las Amarillas (Known also as Presidio San Saba)

(See colored pictures in the center section)

Fore! Your drive has to split two mesquite trees lining a narrow fairway on the ninth hole of the Country Club off Highway 190 on the western edge of Menard. Across the cart path are the ruins of Presidio San Saba.

The Spanish had established friendly relations with the Lipan Apaches in the early 1750s, much to the displeasure of the other Indians who fought the Lipans in competition for hunting grounds. In the eyes of the Comanches and their allies, the Spanish were seen as protectors of the Lipans, for whom Mission Santa Cruz de San Saba was built. Spanish officials believed the San Saba mission would be a buffer between the Comanches and the town of San Antonio, and perhaps begin a chain of settlements between San Antonio and Santa Fe. They did not realize that the mission would also become an attractive target for enemies of the Apaches.

Firing their French muskets into the air, 2,000 Indian braves surrounded the mission in March of 1758. This force, a mixture of Comanches, Wichitas, Tonkawas, Caddos, and their allies told the Spanish soldiers not to fear them, they only wished to attack Apaches who had been raiding their villages. At day's end there were 35 Apaches and Spaniards dead. Indian warriors looted and burned the mission. The presidio's force, numbering fewer than 60, had no choice but to remain barricaded, away from the attack. Destruction of the mission was a severe blow to the Spanish and to their dream of developing the area. In fact, this would be a blow to the development of Texas, for now several tribes had united into a force of armed warriors.

Colonel Diego Ortiz Parrilla, commander of Presidio San Saba, organized a retaliatory campaign against the attackers the next year. Leading more than 600 men, he marched to the Red River and launched an unsuccessful attack on a fortification called Spanish Fort. (See "Spanish Fort" in Region Five.) It cost many soldiers their lives, and Colonel Parrilla his career.

9. Fort McKavett (Also known as Camp San Saba (Menard County))

(See colored pictures in the center section)

Twenty-two miles southwest of Menard, the United States established this fort as Camp San Saba (not to be confused with Camp San Saba in McCulloch County) in March 1852. The camp covered about 2,373 acres near the San Saba River. Several infantry companies were stationed there in an effort to protect settlers from Comanche Indians. When the fort opened, the army reported three Indian tribes, all Comanche, living within 60 to 100 miles of the fort.

The post was abandoned in March 1859, but reoccupied in April 1868, as Fort McKavett (named in honor of Captain Henry McKavett, killed in the Battle of Monterey in 1846). When the army reoccupied the fort, it included 4 barracks, 12 officers quarters, a magazine, a hospital, a guardhouse, a bakery, two storehouses, a post office, three stables, a headquarters building, a forage house, and a 30-acre garden. Supplies for the fort were carted in from San Antonio.

The Texas Rangers used the fort as a base from which they sent

patrols to the headwaters of the Guadalupe, Pedernales, Llano, and San Saba rivers. On one patrol, Rangers under Captain Henry McCulloch followed a band of Indians and captured two squaws. Using the women as bait, he gave them instructions to return to their tribe and tell their chiefs that if the Indians returned all of their prisoners to Fort Martin Scott, the army would return the Indians' property and horses that Ranger had recently captured. The Indians accepted, brought in their prisoners and agreed to not raid again in Texas; they would only attack across the river into Mexico.

In 1861, the First Regiment of the Texas Mounted Rifles was stationed here with the responsibility of the vast territory from the San Saba to the Red River, and as far to the west as they dared to adventure. During the Civil War, a few frontiersmen used the abandoned fort as a base for gathering wild horses and cattle, otherwise the buildings turned to ruins.

On July 28, 1866, President Andrew Johnson signed legislation for the foundation of the post-Civil War army. That act recognized services given to the Union by its African-American troops, and provided for six regiments of African-American regulars: four of infantry and two of cavalry. One regiment was the Ninth Cavalry, which became known as the Buffalo Soldiers. In the spring of 1867, the Ninth Cavalry was ordered to Texas to protect a vast region of Texas along the Rio Grande and reopened the fort to keep the San Antonio-El Paso road safe for travel, and protected settlers from Indian raiders, cattle thieves, and bandits.

Fort McKavett State Historical Park opened in 1968, and many buildings have now been restored. Restoration continues, offering a combination of both stone and wooden structures, and an interesting museum, only open Wednesday through Sunday from 8 a.m. to 5 p.m.

10. Mission San Clemente

Where was the location of this two story (a fortress above a chapel) mission? Mission San Clemente was built in 1684 by the Spanish explorer Juan Dominguez de Mendoza. It served as a temporary camp where Indians who had follow his expedition converted to Christianity. Reports were that more than 4,000 buffaloes were killed to feed the gathering Indians before the Apache raids caused Mendoza to close the Mission San Clemente and return to the Rio Grande.

A 1936 commemorative marker located on Highway 83 just north of Paint Rock places the mission 17 miles southeast of Ballinger where the Concho and Colorado rivers meet, while another historian has placed the location just west of Ballinger along the Colorado River. In 1968, the exciting discovery of a large stone ruin on private property along the San Saba River northeast of Fort McKavett was thought to be that of Mission San Clemente, but an excavation found no artifacts that could link the ruins with this mission, or to that expedition.

A fourth theory places Mission San Clemente on the South Llano River near the present-day community of Telegraph. The postmistress and general store proprietor in Telegraph say they have never heard any stories of ruins in that vicinity. The surrounding areas are still as rugged as it must have been in the 1680s, and still a beautiful location to visit.

Wherever the mission was built it had an active life for a short three months existence.

11. Fort Concho (Originally named Camp Hatch; then Camp Kelly)

(See colored pictures in the center section)

Chosen to find a new fort site for the garrison at Fort Chadbourne, Major John Porter Hatch of the Fourth U. S. Cavalry ordered the Chadbourne post commander, Captain George C. Huntt, to move his unit to the juncture of the Main and North Concho rivers in November 1867. Huntt named the site in honor of Major Hatch, who was awarded the Medal of Honor for leading an attack under enemy fire during the battle of South Mountain, Maryland, in 1862. At Hatch's request, the camp was renamed Camp Kelly in 1868, in honor of Captain Michael J. Kelly, who had died of typhoid fever in 1867.

Camp Hatch, in San Angelo, was one of the U. S. military posts built in 1867 to establish law and order as settlers moved in after the Civil War. It was to replace Fort Chadbourne, which lacked an adequate water supply. In March 1868, the post was renamed again to Fort Concho after the Middle and North Concho rivers, which converge in San Angelo to form the Concho. Concho's commissary storehouse (today the oldest building in San Angelo) and its twin, the quartermaster storehouse, were constructed in 1868. On the south side of the parade grounds were officers' quarters; on the north were the barracks; on the east side the commissary and quartermaster's buildings. Stonemasons and carpenters from Fredericksburg were used in early construction. The fort was not stockaded. Stonewalls were built to surround the hospital and the backyards of the officers' quarters. An open gallery on the hospital afforded a fine distant view.

Soldiers from Fort Concho scouted and mapped large areas; built roads and telegraph lines; escorted stagecoaches, cattle drives, and railroad surveying parties; and served as police. In the early years of the fort's existence, its soldiers skirmished with numerous small parties of Indians. Fort Concho also furnished personnel and supplies for three major Indian campaigns: Mackenzie's 1872 campaign, the 1874 Red River War, and the Victorio campaign of 1879-80.

An Indian-Anglo battle known as the Dove Creek Massacre

occurred near the fort on January 8, 1865. This time the massacre victims were Kickapoo Indians and the perpetrators were Rangers and volunteer Confederate troops led by a local rancher and Ranger, Richard Tankersley. Three years before, a conflict in the area with Kickapoos had cost 16 Texans their lives. It had also turned out that Mexicans were giving the Kickapoos land so that would raid the settlers in Texas, which the Kickapoos did, costing more settlers lives and property. So when Tankersley now found Kickapoos camped near this home, he attacked, killing many Indians.

The army abandoned Fort Concho in 1889. In 1935, San Angelo began a program of land acquisition and building restoration by rebuilding two barracks and two mess halls. Concho was designated a National Historic Landmark in 1961. Now, besides museum exhibits and other building restorations, Fort Concho hosts community activities, and it is a "must-to-see." It is open (except holidays) on Tuesday through Saturday (10 a.m. – 5 p.m.) and Sunday afternoon.

12. Camp Joseph E. Johnston

Camp Joseph E. Johnston was a temporary Federal outpost on the south side of the North Concho River in northwestern Tom Green County. It was named for a man who commanded a topographic party surveying the road between San Antonio and El Paso. This exploration camp was in existence from March through November of 1852. General J. Garland was in command. Its occupants were composed of 284 people including families and servants.

13. Camp Charlotte (And Centralia (Central Station))

Camp Charlotte was a Civil War-era military installation located on the Middle Concho River below where its joins with Kiowa Creek in northwestern Irion County. It was established in April 1868, forty-five miles west of San Angelo at the intersection of the Butterfield Overland and El Paso mail routes. The purpose of the camp was the usual protection against Indian raids, especially those against the mail.

This fort was closer to present-day concepts of what a western fort should look like. It had a large stockade measuring 115 by 190 feet encompassing a mess hall, stables, quarters and kitchens for cooking. There were buildings for a tailor, blacksmith, and saddle maker. All of the corners contained guardhouses, and the main gate was very large.

On October 6, 1872, a fight occurred a half mile south of the camp when Comanches were seen attacking eight cowboys driving a herd of cattle. The Indians attacked a ramuda of the horses that were leading the drive. The horses, frightened by the Indians gunfire, stamped to the hills chased by the Indians. Soldiers followed and attacked the Indians killing two and wounding several others. They also recovered other horses and supplies the Indians had recently received from the Indian agents.

Stealing horses was a frequent problem with Indians in the area. One place not too far from the camp was named Horsehead Crossing. It was located on the Pecos River, and received its name because the Indians would drive their captured ponies towards the river over 60 miles of dry country. When the horses smelled the water from the river, they would often stampede. Many ran over the steep banks of the river to their deaths. It was the large number of horse skulls found on the banks of the river that gave the area its name, Horsehead Crossing.

During the days of the cattle drives, it was estimated that 150,000 head of cattle passed by this fort in herds that contained as many as 1,000 to 3,000 head. Troops at the fort did not have fresh supplies very often so they started taxing the herds, one cow for each herd.

By the middle 1870s, the post had only infantry troops, who found it difficult to police the area, while only walking, against Indian raids. The site of the camp is in an isolated area of northwest Irion County west of State Highway 163, and little of the camp remains.

A subpost was established near the head of the Concho River around 1875. Named Centralia, or Central Station, it was a stagecoach way station and protected by a picket stockade.

14. Camp Grierson's Spring

This camp was located in Reagan County at the head of a branch of Live Oak Creek 30-miles east of the Pecos River and 8-miles southwest of Best. Lieutenant Mason Maxon of the Tenth Cavalry built the camp during 1877-78. It was named for Colonel Benjamin H. Grierson, commander of Fort Concho, who became a hero in the battle against the Apache Chief, Victoria.

The spring that the camp is named for was discovered in 1684 by the Mendoza expedition. Because water of any type was scarce in this country, this became a stop on the Butterfield Overland stage route, on a direct line midway between Forts Concho and Stockton. In May and June of 1878, a military wagon road between the two posts was opened via Grierson's Spring, and another road was extended to Horsehead Crossing on the Pecos. Military telegraph lines from San Antonio and Fort Concho routed to forts through Grierson's Spring.

From Grierson's Spring detachments of the Sixteenth, Twenty-fourth, and Twenty-fifth Infantry and the Tenth Cavalry explored and scouted the surrounding country guarding freight trains and travelers. In 1879, while soldiers on patrol from the camp were watering their horses, a group of Indians attacked the troops and killed several soldiers. After the close of the Victorio campaign in the summer of 1880, the subpost at Grierson's Spring was irregularly manned.

Stone buildings included a corral and stable, a guardhouse, officers' quarters, quarters for one company of infantry, a grain storehouse, a kitchen and mess room, and a telegraph office. The camp was abandoned in September 1882. The camp ruins remain, on private land.

15. Tower Hill

An early day mystery that continues into modern time is a fortification on a hill south of Sterling City. First discovered by a surveyor in 1858, this is a place obviously for defense. The steep slope on the east side of the hill makes the location not easily accessible from that direction, so whoever was fighting from the hill only had the other side to defend. There are pockmarks of gunshots in the walls and loopholes cut in rocks from which to shoot showing that it was used as a fortification. So when, and by whom, was this fortress built?

A clue was found in 1920, when an explorer found a skeleton, supposedly of an Indian chief buried in a small cave on the steep east side of the hill. The skull had been placed in a beaded mantel, the cap piece of which was a silver cup with an inscription. Also found among the remains were a totem in the form of a crouching bear (identified as Comanche), a nose ring of six carat gold, four brass finger rings, four brass ankle rings, numerous loose beads and a silver ornament made from a Spanish dollar. A bullet taken from the chief's skull identifies the death weapon as a Colt "Navy six" revolver, which fired a cap-and-ball type bullet. A dozen old gun barrels, also of the cap-and-ball type, were found in the fortification. Without question, a battle took place and at least one Indian was killed. Since the Texas Rangers and army soldiers seldom buried Indians, one may assume that the Indians won the battle, but who lost it.

As there have been no reports of Texas Rangers missing in action, (though many of the Rangers' records have been lost to fires), and no reports of troops annihilated, was it their fight?

Bullets and gun barrels give us an idea of a time frame. A patent for the Colt revolver used to kill the Indian was issued in 1836 so the death had to take place between 1836 and 1852. That does not rule out that the fortress could have been built at an earlier date. Records show that Coronado camped on Mulberry Creek, maybe ten miles to the south and also the early-day trail blazer, Captain Randolph B. Marcy, passed through the area returning from El Paso, but neither party reported the need for such a fortification nor of a battle fought nearby. There are reports that Comancheros, who conducted trade with the Indian tribes, also camped on Mulberry Creek. They might have been frequent visitors to this area and built a fortification in anticipation of a trade going bad. The Comancheros probably had an opportunity to obtain a Colt revolver in trade with the Indian, or with outlaw renegades, but did they build Tower Hill?

Its location would lead one to think that Tower Hill was built in anticipation of an attack. The early settlers coming from the Gulf on their way to Santa Fe, or to Colorado, often used the North Concho

River, which is near Tower Hill, as a trail. Did an enterprising trail boss build a fortification just in case of an Indian attack? Or did travelers heading for the California goldrush coincidentally find this place while they ran from attacking Indians? Was this the site of an unrecorded battle between Texas Rangers and Indians? It was built too early to be used by most cattle drives, however, Comancheros were in the area as early as the 1700s.

Tower Hill is located on private property and closed gates are locked to keep visitors out. Historians may want to research this mystery in the archives. Coordination of any effort with the Sterling County Historical Society could save time, money, and headaches.

16. Camp Elizabeth (Once known as the Camp at the Head of North Concho)

The archaeological ruins of Camp Elizabeth are located nine and a half miles northwest of Sterling City on Highway 87. It was first established as a camp for Texas Rangers around 1853. Around 1869, when Fort Concho started building subposts, the camp was taken over and used as an outpost hospital.

Camp Elizabeth (it was not until the 1930s that the name Elizabeth replaced "Camp at the Head of North Concho" as the name) was one of several subposts to Fort Concho. The other subposts, Johnson's Station, Lone Tree camp, Kickapoo Springs, Concho Mail Station, and Bismark, have all now vanished, except for their mention in the 1870s records of Fort Concho.

The camp had officers' quarters, a hospital, a blacksmith shop, and rock corrals. The soldiers slept in tents near the officers' quarters. Water was obtained from a nearby spring on the North Concho River. Troops at the camp were from the Tenth and Sixteenth Calvary, including many of the legendary Buffalo Soldiers. Activities assigned to men at Camp Elizabeth included patrolling, escorting travelers and wagon trains, and surveying and constructing roads.

Camp Elizabeth was active from 1867 to 1874, when an unusual large number of Indian hostilities were taking place in West Texas. The site was then abandoned, intact, in 1886.

When the Texas Highway Department later widened Highway 87, archaeological investigations were conducted before the actual road improvement work could commence. Discovering intact artifacts, the work was temporarily halted until further study was completed. That excavation discovered the remains of the blacksmith shop and the location of the tent campground and campfires. The archaeological site is on private property adjacent to the expanded highway. However, at Fort Concho, there is an interesting museum with displays of armory, clothing from the same time period, and an era medical hospital museum and setting.

A state commemorative monument was later erected at its site for Camp Elizabeth.

17. Camp Johnston (Coke County)

Station 1858 of the Butterfield Stage was Camp Johnston, located on the Colorado River about six miles southeast from the present-day town of Robert Lee. The camp was built on the Goodnight-Loving Trail of 1867, which opened the area to the southwest for cattle raising.

The Butterfield Overland Mail Company built its stagecoach stations every 20 miles along the route and drilled water wells where needed to ensure an adequate supply. The soldiers stationed here lived in huts and slept on the ground in less than ideal conditions. Relief mules were kept at the stations, but they were often stolen or driven off by frequently raiding Indians.

18. Fort Chadbourne

Companies A and K of the Eighth United States Infantry established Fort Chadbourne on October 28, 1852, for frontier protection. It was named for Second Lieutenant Theodore Lincoln Chadbourne, who was killed at the Battle of Resaca de la Palma during the Mexican War. The fort was built on Oak Creek near U. S. Highway 277, eleven miles northeast of Bronte in Coke County. The fort was built of stones crafted by stonecutters and masons from San Antonio. One of the rooms in the main building measured 28 x 18 feet with a large fireplace for cooking.

Indian battles occurred in the area started during the 1850s when the settlers started moving west. There were estimated to be 20,000 Indians in the area and the government was pursuing a nonaggressive policy towards them at the time. One skirmish actually occurred inside the fort in 1856, when a visiting brave demonstrating arrogance towards the soldiers, rode across the parade ground with a lance. Hanging from his lance were scalps of long brown and blonde hair, obviously of white victims. The ensuing fight was short; no one was killed.

In 1854, the fort experienced a hailstorm so severe that hailstones piled six to eight feet deep in the creek. Soldiers gathered the hail and used it for ice, storing 20 wagons full. In October, the grasshoppers were so thick their arrival blackened the sky.

The fort provided a defense for a station on the Butterfield Overland Mail route from 1858 to 1861. It was surrendered to Confederate Colonel Henry E. McCulloch in 1861, then Chadbourne was occupied briefly by United States troops after the Civil War, but lack of water, wood, and adequate facilities forced its abandonment in 1868. Fort Concho took its place.

A large sign on U. S. Highway 277 designates the site. The ruins are on private land but the public is welcome (if you remain in your automobiles). The owners have gone to very great lengths to try to retain the historic site for others to see. They have been quoted as saying: "In no other country would monuments of such historic value as the chain of old frontier posts and the first mail stations, suffer such callous neglect and destruction." I am in complete agreement.

The flag in the photograph is show flying at half-mast in memorial to the students killed in the Thanksgiving bon fire at Texas A&M University in 1999.

19. Fort Phantom Hill

(See colored pictures in the center section)

In 1849, the Federal government sent Captain Randolph B. Marcy to explore and mark the best route through the Comancheria, a vast region to the north and west of Austin which was inhabited by the warlike Comanche Indians. The route was meant to provide a safe passage to immigrants headed for the California gold fields. A series of forts, including Fort Phantom Hill, was established as a result of Marcy's recommendations. Located 12-miles north of present-day Abilene, this fort was short lived but later served as a station for the Butterfield Overland Stage.

The fort was located hundreds of miles from any settlement. It was directly on the trail of the Comanches as they traveled into Texas on their marauding expeditions. Although there is a large lake nearby today, at that time water was scarce. The scarcity of local building timbers added greatly to the hardships of the garrison. Lieutenant Clinton W. Lear wrote to his wife at Fort Washita that, "the area was never intended for a white man to occupy such a barren waste." Nevertheless, the troops dutifully began work on the fort. A suitable stone quarry was finally located on Elm Creek about two miles to the south. Blackjack oak logs for the officers' quarters and hospital were carted in by ox wagon from as far away as 40 miles. The company quarters and other buildings in the fort were poorly constructed. All of the buildings had stone chimneys, but only the magazine, guardhouse, and commissary storehouse were built entirely of stone.

There are more tales about the destruction of the fort than of its operations. One tale was to cause the commanding officer, Brevet Second Lieutenant Newton Givens to be subjected to a court martial. When the fort was abandoned in 1854, soldiers set fire to the buildings. During Given's court martial they testified they thought they heard the officer remark that he "wished that nobody would ever have to serve in that hell-hole again." They interpreted this as orders to burn the buildings. A court martial acquitted Givens, finding that he had not given orders.

Fort Phantom Hill was never officially named and military records refer to it as the "Post on the Clear Fork of the Brazos." A legend tells of the origin of the name "Phantom Hill." It says the name derived from the fact that, from a distance, the hill on which it is built seems to rise sharply from the plains, but as it is approached, the hill levels out and vanish like a phantom.

In 1858, the remaining structures of the fort were repaired and utilized as Way-Station Number 54 by the Butterfield Southern Overland Mail. A man named Burlington and his wife managed the station. Most travelers agreed with the New York Herald correspondent Waterman L. Ormsby that Phantom Hill was "the cheapest and best new station on the route." During the Civil War, when only companies of Texas Rangers (and Indians) patrolled the frontier, Ranger Colonel James B. (Buck) Barry used Fort Phantom Hill as a base of field operations.

Fort Phantom Hill is on private land. The owners restored parts of the ruins and make it available to the public. Three stone buildings and more than a dozen chimneys and foundations remain. To get to the fort, take Highway 600 north 12-miles from Abilene, the ruins may be seen on the east side of the highway. There is a road to enter the grounds. Seeing these ruins is worth the drive. As you walk around the ruins among the prickly pear, looking at the chimneys and a cannon ready to be fired, it is difficult to imagine that it was considered a "hell-hole."

20. Sewell's Camp

In the early winter of 1876, a buffalo hunter named Marshall Sewell established a camp below the Caprock near the head of the Salt Fork of the Brazos River in western Garza County. He was unaware that a group of Quahadi Comanches led by Black Horse had obtained a permit to hunt for game (not men) in Texas. Black Horse was angry because of the destruction of the buffalo herds. He planned to camp in Yellow House Canyon and attack buffalo hunters.

On the morning of February 1, 1877, Sewell spotted a buffalo herd, left camp, and set up a firing station. Using a Sharp's rifle, he killed animals until he ran out of ammunition. Black Horse watched the slaughter, then surrounded Sewell, murdered and scalped him. From a ravine a mile away, Sewell's three skinners and a hunter named Billy Devons witnessed the killing. They hurried to Rath City, the largest supply base in the area, to report the killing. Forty men swiftly rode to the camp, buried Sewell, and tried to follow the Indians' trail.

In the meantime, Black Horse and some 170 warriors continued to raid camps until the skin hunters demanded the army return the Indians to their reservation. When their demands were not met by March 4, 1877, a group of 46 men left Rath City to find the renegades. The group picked up the Indian trail from Sewell's camp. After scouts sighted the Indian camp in Hidden Canyon, the group left their wagons, provisions, and teams at the spring and started riding. They found Black Horse's camp in Hidden Canyon (now the site of Lubbock Lake). It was late in the day, but the buffalo hunters decided to go ahead and attack. They divided into three groups; mounted men rode on the high side of the canyon, while the other men dismounted and moved along the creek on foot. When they were within rifle range, the hunters charged.

The Comanches, momentarily frightened, started for their horses. However, when they discovered the attackers were a small force, the Indians turned, ready to fight. Indian women ran toward the charging hunters firing pistols, while the warriors took a defensive position on a slope northwest of their camp. Surprised by the spirited defense, the outnumbered hunters withdrew, and the Indians set the grass afire. The hunters built a bonfire to decoy the Indians, drove their wagons out of the canyon under the cover of darkness, and set fires to obscure their tracks.

When news of the fight reached Fort Griffin, Captain P. L. Lee took 72 troopers of the Tenth Cavalry to bring in the Comanches.

Lee overtook the Indians at Quemado (Silver) Lake in Cochran County on May 4. In a brief skirmish, the soldiers killed a brave, Red Young Man, and his wife. The Indians surrendered and accompanied the soldiers to Fort Griffin, from there they went back to the reservation.

The Battle of Yellow House Canyon, which occurred on March 18, 1877, ended a brief Indian uprising known as the Staked Plains or Hunters', War. It also was the last fight with Indians on the High Plains of Texas. There are no ruins of Sewell's campsite.

21. Camp Resolution

Four camps were given the name Camp Resolution. They were temporarily occupied in August through September 1841 by the Santa Fe Expedition. The first camp was near where Quitaque and Los Lingos creeks meet in northwest Motley County. The second camp was on the south side of Quitaque Creek about where Ranch Road 1065 now crosses the creek in northeast Floyd County. Camp number three was a half-mile above camp number two, and camp number four was only three-quarters of a mile above camp number three. No ruins remain.

It was the hardship of the expedition that prompted one of the participants to title his journal "Through hell to Prison". The expedition was captured near Santa Fe and marched all the way to Mexico City where they were imprisoned, under terrible living conditions.

22. Fort Elliott

Fort Elliott was the only United States Army outpost in the eastern Texas Panhandle from 1875 to 1890. Its troops patrolled the borders of Indian Territory, policed cattle drives headed to Kansas railway depots, and in other ways protected and encouraged settlements of that region.

In 1874, the army had undertaken the offensive to clear the Indians out of the Panhandle after Cheyennes attacked a camp of white buffalo hunters at Adobe Walls. A permanent post for surveillance of the western boundary of the Indian Territory was built above Sweetwater Creek with 263 men of the Fourth United States

Cavalry and Nineteenth Infantry occupying the site. At first it was known as Cantonment on the Sweetwater, then renamed Fort Elliott the following February, in honor of Major Joel A. Elliott, who had died at the Battle of the Washita.

Construction of permanent facilities began in July 1875. Stables, storehouses, and guardhouse were built with cottonwood posts, adobe, and thatch which was available locally. The commander's residence, officers' quarters, five company barracks, a 12-bed hospital, the post headquarters, and a combined chapel and school were built on stone foundations. For substantial buildings, lumber had to be brought in by wagon from Dodge City, 196-miles to the north.

Troops from Fort Elliott patrolled the Texas Panhandle and western Indian Territory to stop the hunting parties of Indians from entering the Panhandle, but on several occasions during the late 1870s, troops pursued bands seeking to escape the reservation. Under protection of the fort, numerous large ranches were quickly established, and by 1880 nearly 300,000 cattle grazed the Panhandle. Attention later shifted to policing the cattle range, keeping any stolen Panhandle stock from being taken to the Indians reservation, and supervising southern Texas herds being driven north through the Indian lands.

On January 29, 1891, years after the Indians had been confined to reservations, settlers near the site of present-day Wellington became convinced hostile Indians were returning to their old lands. Mrs. Will Johnson brought her two children to Henry Stall's farm, where her husband and W. L. Huddleston were visiting. She told them that she had heard "bloodthirsty yells" and had seen smoke in the distance. Huddleston rode to Salisbury, where the depot agent wired for help, and the townspeople barricaded themselves wherever they could. Area ranchers sent runners with news of possible Indian raids, and panic spread as far west as Amarillo and as far south as Plainview. At the Mill Iron Ranch, families without firearms gathered at John Gist's dugout and stored piles of rocks to throw at the Indians. In Clarendon, Henry W. Taylor's hardware store sold out of all of its guns and ammunition. A Ranger company commanded by Captain William J. McDonald traveled by rail to defend Collingsworth County.

Once there, they discovered the cause of the yelling and smoke that Mrs. Johnson had reported. Apparently the foreman of the Rocking Chair Ranch, S. H. Vaughn, had ordered his men to kill a steer for supper. They had fired several shots and accidentally burnt a carcass. Indians were no nearer than the reservations. It took three days for the panic to subside. Some settlers blamed ranchers for spreading the scare in an effort to discourage further settlement.

In 1890, the army decided to close the fort, an outbreak of typhoid that summer speeded its abandonment. On October 2, most of the garrison departed and on October 20 the fort was closed. A commemorative marker is at the site on the north side of Highway 152 a few miles west of Mobeetie in Wheeler County.

23. Fort Adobe (Also known as Bent's Fort)

Adobe Walls was the name of a ranching community located 17 miles northeast of Stinnett along the Canadian River in Hutchinson County. A trading post was established in early 1843, by the trading firm of Bent, St. Vrain, and Company, for trading with the Comanches and Kiowas. It was located on a stream that became known as Bent Creek. Company traders were working from teepees and log structures, as a real fort had not yet been built. Then in 1846, the partners brought Mexican adobe makers to replace the earlier fortification with Fort Adobe, a structure 80-feet square, with 9-foot high walls and only a single entrance, being built.

Occupation of Fort Adobe was sporadic, and by 1848 Indian hostility had resulted in its closure. Following a temporary peace, Bent sought to reopen the post by sending Kit Carson and other employees. Resistance from Apaches forced Carson's group to hide the trade goods they had acquired then return to Colorado. Soon after, Comanches persuaded Bent to make another try at resuming trade at Fort Adobe. A 13-man party, led by R. W. (Dick) Wootton, met the Comanches at the fort and traded through a window cut in the wall, but after Indians killed some of the cattle and the interior of the fort was blown up, the trade was abandoned to Comancheros.

Ruins at Adobe Walls became a familiar landmark to Indians and Comancheros, and to white men daring to venture into the heart of Comancheria. Comancheros, part Mexican and part Indian were traders from New Mexico who started encouraging Indian raids in

Texas by providing the Indians a market for stolen cattle, horses, and kidnapped hostages. Adobe Walls became known as a land of Comanchero-sponsored raids.

In November 1864, Kit Carson used the safety of Fort Adobe to rest his men after attacking a Kiowa village during a campaign against the tribes of the southern Plains. Carson withstood several Indian attacks at the fort. In March 1874, Kansas merchants followed buffalo hunters south to the Texas Panhandle and established the Myers and Leonard Store about a mile north of the Fort Adobe ruins. This business, which included a corral and restaurant, was joined in April of 1874 by a second store operated by Charles Rath and Company. James N. Hanrahan and Rath also opened a saloon and Tom O'Keefe started a blacksmith shop. By summer, 200 to 300 buffalo hunters roamed the area, and trade boomed.

The second Battle of Adobe Walls occurred on June 27, 1874, when a buffalo hunters' camp was attacked from all sides by a party of 700 Indians, mostly Cheyennes, Comanches, and Kiowas, under the leadership of Quanah Parker and Isa-tai. Hunters at the camp were already awake repairing a broken ridgepole when the Indians charged at dawn. The defenders, 28 men and a single woman, gathered in Myers and Leonard's Store, Hanrahan's Saloon, and Rath and Wright's Stores and fought off the charge with a loss of only 2 men. One other man was lost in a later charge, and a fourth man was accidentally killed by the discharge of his own gun.

On the second day, a group of Cheyennes appeared on a mesa overlooking the post. This appearance led to the famous gunshot of Billy Dixon, when Dixon, from inside a stockade, shot an Indian off his horse seven-eighths of a mile away. Other hunters in the vicinity were notified of the attack on Adobe Walls, and by the end of the fifth day there were more than 100 men ready to fight, but the rescue party arrived after the Indians had given up the fight. The fight began the Red River War of 1874-75, resulting in the relocation of Indians to reservations. But, after the second battle at Adobe Walls, merchants and hunters abandoned the site.

During the 1920s, several local and state projects were launched to mark the battle site at Adobe Walls and make it more accessible. In 1978, the complex was added to the National Register of Historic

Places and it is recognized as a Texas State Archeological Landmark. The site is 16 miles east off of Highway 207 south of Spearman. The last eight miles are on unpaved road which, when wet, may become very slick. The road ends at a no trespassing sign.

Commemorative markers are set behind a fence. On a quiet day one can imagine the sound of war cries and rifles being fired in the fields surrounding the markers. A bluff in the distance may be where the Indian rode when Billy Dixon made his famous shot. The public library in Spearman has a photograph of the commemorative markers located at the site.

24. Anderson's Fort (Originally named Camp Swan)

Fortified and manned by Major General Thomas M. Anderson of the Tenth U. S. Infantry, Anderson's Fort was a supply depot that became a fortress. In anticipation of Indian attacks in 1874, Anderson gave instructions for boxes, barrels and logs, any thing that might stop an arrow or bullet, be placed in a rectangle around the depot to protect the troops. The site was originally named Camp Swan and was also referred to as Soldier's Mound by area settlers when the great buffalo slaughter began in 1874, and Indians took up arms to retaliate; raiding buffalo hunters' camps, ranches and small settlements.

Anderson's diary recalled the great battle that took place in Palo Duro Canyon. "I lost a man named Gregg, who we buried at the southwest slope of the butt near the mouth of Canyon Blanco where Quanah Parker shot him out of the saddle. The Chief used Gregg as a shield or else I would have shot Quanah myself, as he was only 30-40 yards away. All of our action took place at or near Blanco, Tule or Palo Duro Canyon and the Red River near McClellan Creek at its mouth. In 1872, we captured 1,300 squaws and children, and 800 ponies. The Indians recovered their horses; we shot the next Indian ponies we captured — 2,200 head."

There is a contradiction between General Anderson's year for fighting Quanah Parker, and the destruction of the Indian's horses following the Battle of Palo Duro Canyon, and dates (1871 and 1874 respectively) mentioned in other journals, otherwise his story of the battle and its results are similar. In his maturity, Anderson must have combined the fights in his mind.

A state 1936 commemorative marker with a golden reef is north of Spur at the site of Anderson's Fort. Present-day families wait there for the school bus to bring their young home.

25. Camp Roberts

Texas Rangers from Camp Roberts in 1880 set off to find the mysterious Lost Lakes which, if found, could open travel through the desert separating Texas and New Mexico. One of the Rangers wrote: "We knew the reputation of this desolate region for bewildering the brain, choking the throat, parching the lips and swelling the tongue of both man and beast."

Following the needle of their compass, the Rangers rode until they found the first of the lakes, and then following directions left by a band of Indians, they found the second lake where they camped. They started the return to Camp Roberts in a blizzard and after running out of food, nearly froze. They did make it back, however, after a trip of 40 days in which they had ridden 820 miles. They had found the Lost Lakes, but in New Mexico, not in Texas as expected.

26. Indian Camp at Palo Duro Canyon

In late September 1874, warring Indians were camped in the protection of Palo Duro Canyon when Colonel Ranald S. Mackenzie led his Fourth United States Cavalry in a plan to trap the Indians in their refuge. At sunrise on the 29th, Mackenzie's troops, with their Tonkawa scouts leading the way down the steep and narrow trail to the canyon, attacked the Indian camp.

An event maybe as important to Texas as any that took place within a Texas fort was the Battle of Palo Duro Canyon for this ended in the return of the Indians (the Comanches, Kiowas, Apaches, Cheyenne, and Arapahos) to the reservations in Indian Territory. Leadership of the Indians was under Cheyenne Chief Iron Shirt, Comanche leader Poor Buffalo, and the Kiowa Chief Lone Wolf. Because their camps were scattered over a large area in the canyon, the Indians were caught off-guard, unable to make a united defense.

The soldiers fought skirmishes against small war parties that lacked the individual strength to defeat them. (A maneuver that the Indians had often practiced by separating troops and settlers into small units to defeat them).

Troops initially destroyed the village of Red Warbonnet, spreading panic among other Indian villages in the canyon. Many of Indians abandoned their belongings and even their horses, fleeing the canyon for the open plains. Some of the warriors fought back, sniping at soldiers from behind rocks, but the Indians' resistance was weak. By nightfall Mackenzie's forces had captured or destroyed the Indians' villages. Indian losses amounted to three dead.

Mackenzie's troops captured more than 1,400 Indian ponies and gave 300 to the Tonkawa scouts. Soldiers shot the remaining ponies; reports vary from 1,200 to 2,200 horses. Another reports say the ponies were stampeded over the deep canyon cliffs to their death. Without the food that was destroyed by the troops, and without the ponies that made them such formidable opponents, the defeated Indians then walked back to the reservations. They were defeated.

The site of this Indian camp is on private property but you may see most of the canyon in the Palo Duro Canyon State Park, see the museum and amphitheater in Canyon.

Ever since the Europeans had first arrived, there was fighting in Texas. Spaniards against French; Spaniards against Mexicans; Mexicans Federalists against Mexicans Centralists; the Texans against Mexicans; U. S. Federal troops against Mexicans, and Texans in blue against Texans in gray. Throughout all these wars another battle was on-going. The battle of the Spanish, the French, the Mexicans, the Texans, and the United States all fighting Indians. After the Battle of Palo Duro Canyon the end was in sight, that fight was almost over.

The Battle of Palo Duro Canyon represented the Indians' last major resistance against the encroaching settlers. In the future, Texas Rangers might establish camps for patrolling and on occasion to fight Indians when they left the reservation to attack settlers and raid Texas towns. But, after this battle, there would not be the need for additional forts to be built in Texas to fight a battle in the State of Texas.

Region   Index and Additional Sources of Information Guide

Region	Index and Additional Sources of Information Guide

Region	Index and Additional Sources of Information Guide

Region   Index and Additional Sources of Information Guide

Region   Index and Additional Sources of Information Guide

Region   Index and Additional Sources of Information Guide

-L-

1	La Navidad en Las Cruces, Mission: See Mission Redonda.
2	Lacy's Fort: *Cherokee County History* (Jacksonville, Texas: Cherokee County Historical Commission, 1986).
5	Le Poste des Cadodaquious: *Adventure on the Red River* (Norman: University of Oklahoma Press, 1937).
2	Little River Fort: Gerald S. Pierce, *Texas Under Arms: The Camps, Posts, Forts, and Military Towns of the Republic of Texas* (Austin: Encino, 1969).
4	Long's Fort: See Fort Las Casas.

-M-

4	Maison Rogue: J. A. Ziegler, *Wave of the Gulf* (San Antonio: Naylor Company, 1938).
1	Mier Expedition: Thomas J. Green, *Journal of the Texian Expedition Against Mier*, (New York Harper 1845).
1	Mission and Presidio San Vicente: See Camp Neville Springs.
1	Mission Apostol Santiago: See Mission Redonda.
4	Mission De Las Cabras: Frederick Charles Chabot, *With the Makers of San Antonio* (Yanaguana Society Publications 4, San Antonio, 1937)
1	Mission El Senor San Jose: See Mission Redonda.
2	Mission Nuestra Senora de Guadalupe de Los Nacogdoches: Robert Bruce Blake, *Location of the Spanish Missions and Presidios in Nacogdoches County* (" South western Historical Quarterly 41" January 1938).
1	Mission Nuestra Senora de Guadalupe de Polacme: See Mission Redonda.
1	Mission Nuestra Senora de la Candelaria del Cannon: Coleman Richards, *The Establishment of the Candelaria and San Lorenzo Missions on the Upper Nueces* (M.A. thesis, University of Texas, 1936)
4	Mission Nuestra Senora de la Luz: Herbert Eugene Bolton, *Texas in the Middle Eighteenth Century: Studies in Spanish Colonial History and Administration* (Berkeley: University of California Press, 1915).
2	Mission Nuestra Senora de Los Dolores de Los Ais: Herbert Eugene Bolton, *Texas in the Middle Eighteenth Century: Studies in Spanish Colonial History and Administration* (Berkeley: University of California Press, 1915).
2	Mission Nuestra Senora de Los Dolores Del Rio de San Xavier: See Mission San Francisco Xavier de Horcasitas.
4	Mission Nuestra Senora del Espiritu Santo de Zuniga: Henry Putney Beers, *Spanish and Mexican Records of the American Southwest: A Bibliographic Guide to Archive and Manuscript Sources* (Tucson: University of Arizona Press, 1979).
2	Mission Nuestra Senora del Pilar de Bucareli: Herbert Eugene Bolton, *Texas in the Middle Eighteenth Century: Studies in Spanish Colonial History and Administration* (Berkeley: University of California Press, 1915).
4	Mission Nuestra Senora del Refugio: William E. Dunn, *The Founding of Nuestra Senora del Refugio, the Last Spanish Mission in Texas,* "Southwestern Historical